SWEDISH ROCK ART RESEARCH SERIES 8

Bronze Age Rock Art in Iberia and Scandinavia

Words, Warriors, and Long-distance Metal Trade

Johan Ling, Marta Díaz-Guardamino,
John Koch, Christian Horn, Zofia Stos-Gale
and Hannes Grahn

OXBOW | books
Oxford & Philadelphia

Published in the United Kingdom in 2024 by
OXBOW BOOKS
81 St Clements, Oxford OX4 1AW

and in the United States by
OXBOW BOOKS
1950 Lawrence Road, Havertown, PA 19083

© Oxbow Books and the individual contributors 2024

Paperback Edition: ISBN 979-8-88857-104-0
Digital Edition: ISBN 979-8-88857-105-7 (ePub)

A CIP record for this book is available from the British Library

Library of Congress Control Number: 2024936680

All rights reserved. No part of this book may be reproduced or transmitted in any form or by any means, electronic or mechanical including photocopying, recording or by any information storage and retrieval system, without permission from the publisher in writing.

Printed in the United Kingdom by Short Run Press
Typeset in India by DiTech Publishing Services

For a complete list of Oxbow titles, please contact:

UNITED KINGDOM	UNITED STATES OF AMERICA
Oxbow Books	Oxbow Books
Telephone (0)1226 734350	Telephone (610) 853-9131, Fax (610) 853-9146
Email: oxbow@oxbowbooks.com	Email: queries@casemateacademic.com
www.oxbowbooks.com	www.casemateacademic.com/oxbow

Oxbow Books is part of the Casemate Group

Front cover: Photograph by John Koch. Interpretation of rock art images from the Olivenza stela (Iberia) and the Hede rock art site in Kville 124:1 (Sweden) by Ellen Meijer, Rich Potter, and Christian Horn from TVT visualizations.
Back cover: Rock art panel from Sweden (Panel in Finntorp (Tanum 89:1)), Bohuslän, labelled with the corresponding Celto-Germanic and Northwest Indo-European vocabulary items. Interpretation based on a visualization from photogrammetry by Christian Horn and Rich Potter.

Contents

List of figures v
List of tables ix

1. Introduction and outline 1

2. Background 5

3. Aspects of social organization, long distance exchange, and
   warriorhood 13

4. Shared copper sources between Bronze Age communities in
   Atlantic Europe 31

5. Iberian and Scandinavian Late Bronze Age rock art:
   Comparing landscape contexts 39

6. Comparing Scandinavian and Iberian warrior iconography 51

7. Linguistic aspects on the warrior iconography in Iberia and
   Scandinavia 83

8. Bronze Age contacts between Scandinavia, Iberia, and the Atlantic
   communities 113

Bibliography 121

Swedish Rock Art Research Series

Bronze Age rock art represents a unique Nordic contribution to world culture, and more than 17,000 localities are known in Sweden alone. They constitute one of the World's most complex and well-preserved prehistoric imageries. Centered in the World Heritage site of Tanum in western Sweden, the Swedish Rock Art Research Archive (Svenskt Hällristnings Forsknings Arkiv – SHFA, www.shfa.se) at the University of Gothenburg was established in 2006 to further documentation and research on this Bronze Age heritage. All original documentation – from large rubbings to photos – are being scanned and made accessible for international research. Based on this material the Swedish Rock Art Research Series will present ongoing research and new documentation in years to come.

Johan Ling & Christian Horn
Series editors

List of figures

Figure 2.1. Some examples of Herzsprung shield images on warrior stelae and their correlates in Europe, and chariot depictions in Iberia and Scandinavia. 7

Figure 2.2. Comparable examples of necklaces and headdresses found in Scandinavia and Iberia. 9

Figure 2.3. Distribution of Late Bronze Age Iberian warrior stelae and locations of confirmed or probable Late Bronze Age/Early Iron Age Baltic amber finds and major mining districts 11

Figure 3.1. Schematic diagram of the interaction between the domestic and the political economies that give rise to the Maritime Mode of Production. 18

Figure 3.2. House K6 at the site of Abildal, Viborg, Jutland. 19

Figure 3.3. Selection of copper and tin ingots from the Salcombe B site. 22

Figure 3.4. Distribution of late 2nd and early 1st millennium BC linear field systems in southern England and northern France. 24

Figure 3.5. Distribution of Bronze Age stelae and statue-menhirs and the distribution of major tin and copper deposits in Iberia. 26

Figure 3.6. Warrior stelae distribution per subtype and connectivity routes. 27

Figure 4.1. Copper and tin resources in the Iberian Peninsula with outline of mining regions and distribution of Late Bronze Age Iberian warrior stelae. 32

Figure 4.2. Lead isotope ratios for some of the Late Bronze Age tin-bronzes found in Scandinavia and the bronzes from Spain. 33

Figure 4.3. Plots of lead isotope ratios to 206Pb of the ores from the Italian Eastern Alps, Sardinia, and Iberia consistent with lead isotope ratios of ores in bronzes from Scandinavia and Spain. 34

Figure 4.4. Comparison of the lead isotope ratios of bronzes found in Scandinavia with the ores from the Guadalquivir valley and Jaén, and bronzes from the site of San Cristóbal, Logrosán, Badajoz, Spain. 35

Figure 4.5. Lead isotope ratios of bronzes found in Sweden consistent with the ores from Jaén, Alcudia Valley, and Los Pedroches (Guadalquivir Valley), Spain. 35

Figure 4.6. Distribution of double-looped palstaves found in the late 1930s with indication of the find from Tåkern. 36

List of figures

Figure 4.7. A comparative plot of three independent lead isotope ratios from Brittany, Britain, Ireland, and Scandinavia with data for copper ores from Southern Spain. 37

Figure 5.1. New visualizations of the stelae of Cabeza del Buey 3 and Cabeza del Buey 5/El Palacio. 41

Figure 5.2. Tumulus A covering urn cremation burials in the necropolis at Setefilla, Lora del Río, Seville, Spain, and the Setefilla warrior stela. 42

Figure 5.3. Location of the Setefilla stela findspot within the necropolis of Setefilla, and its nearby settlement, the Mesa de Setefilla (Seville, Spain). 43

Figure 5.4. Lyre depicted on the stela of Jerez de los Caballeros/El Carbajo. 44

Figure 5.5. Location of Scandinavian rock art close to bodies of water. 46

Figure 5.6. Rock reliefs at Finntorp (RAÄ Tanum 184:1) and Lövåsen (RAÄ Tanum 321:1). 47

Figure 5.7. Funerary cairn overlying the rock art panel of Törnfall 107. 47

Figure 5.8. Shoreline location of the large burial at Kivik with a stone cist constructed of slabs decorated with carvings. 48

Figure 5.9. Location of rock art in Frännarp (RAÄ Gryyt 1:1). 49

Figure 6.1. The site of Penedo do Muro 2 (Ourense, northwest Iberia) with depictions of motifs similar to boats depicted on Period V razors and rock art sites in Scandinavia. 52

Figure 6.2. Early Bronze Age halberds made from arsenical copper from the 'Carrapatas' hoard, and a representation of a halberd on the stela of Longroiva. Mêda, Guarda (Portugal). 54

Figure 6.3. A halberd depicted on the panel in Kville (157:1, Bohuslän) with Early Bronze Age boats and spear fighters. 55

Figure 6.4. Interpretative reconstruction of necropolis 1 at Alfarrobeira (S. Bartolomeu de Messines, south Portugal). 56

Figure 6.5. Findspot and digital visualizations of the stela of Galavís, Alcántara (Cáceres, Spain). 57

Figure 6.6. Stela 2 from Almadén de la Plata and the Palacio III hoard. 57

Figure 6.7. The standing stones at Hagbards Galge with tactile tracings of Asige 17:3 and Asige 17:6. 59

Figure 6.8. Digital visualization and interpretation of Asige 17:3 and Asige 17:6. 60

Figure 6.9. Stela from Kyrkje-Eide (B. 4440). 62

Figure 6.10. Stela of Fuente de Cantos found in El Risco, Badajoz, Spain. 63

Figure 6.11. Panels in Hede (RAÄ Kville 124:1) and Frännarp (RAÄ Gryt 1:1). 64

Figure 6.12. The stela of Valdetorres 1, Badajoz, Spain. 66

Figure 6.13. Stelae of Alamillo and El Viso 3 from the Guadiana valley. 67

Figure 6.14. Stela of Monte Blanco, Olivenza, Badajoz (Spain). 69

Figure 6.15. Chariots on the stelae of Ategua and Zarza Capilla 1/Los Llanos, southern Spain. 70
Figure 6.16. Interpretation of sections of the panels on Brastad (RAÄ 128:1) and Brastad (RAÄ 18:1). 72
Figure 6.17. Comparison between the panel Tossene 926:1, west Sweden and stela 4 from Cabeza del Buey, southern Spain. 74
Figure 6.18. *Bronzetti* from the Uta Abini group in Sardinia. 77
Figure 6.19. Mirrors on Kville (RAÄ 216:1), Tossene (RAÄ 46:1), and Tossene (RAÄ 427:4). 78
Figure 6.20. Finntorp panel relief, in Scandinavia, showing the addition of images of warriors in Period III. 79
Figure 7.1. Drawing of a Scandinavian rock art chariot (panel in Frännarp (Gryt 1:1)), Scania, showing inherited Celto-Germanic and Northwest Indo-European vocabulary for its components as repeatedly depicted in Scandinavian rock art and Iberian stelae. 91
Figure 7.2. Rock art panel from Sweden (panel in Finntorp (Tanum 89:1)), Bohuslän, labelled with the corresponding Celto-Germanic and Northwest Indo-European vocabulary items. 96
Figure 7.3. Drawing of a rock art image of a sizable boat with crew and rigging from Sweden (panel in Järrestad (Järrestad 13:1)), Scania, labelled with inherited Celto-Germanic and Italo-Celtic/Germanic inherited vocabulary items corresponding to items depicted or implied in the image. 101
Figure 7.4. Drawing of detail from a rock art panel from Sweden (panel in Lövåsen (Tanum 321:1)), Bohuslän, labelled with the corresponding Celto-Germanic and northwest Indo-European vocabulary items. 105
Figure 8.1. Selection of strategic landing sites along the Atlantic façade. 116
Figure 8.2. The Isle of Thanet, Richborough, and Cliffs End Farm with the region's ancient place-names. 117

List of tables

Table 2.1. Comparison of main chronological periods in Bronze Age Scandinavia and Atlantic Iberia, with indication of calibrated dates. 10
Table 4.1. Estimation of the flow of metal from Iberia to Scandinavia 34
Table 6.1. Comparison of the number of key motifs between the rock art traditions of Scandinavia and Iberia. 75
Table 6.2. Summary of the comparison of the main defining traits of Scandinavian rock art and Iberian warrior stelae. 81
Table 7.1. Inherited Celto-Germanic and Northwest Indo-European vocabulary for components of the horse and wheeled vehicle package. 92
Table 7.2. Inherited Celto-Germanic and Northwest Indo-European vocabulary for accoutrements of the warrior. 95
Table 7.3. Celto-Germanic inherited vocabulary related to fighting and warfare. 99
Table 7.4. Celto-Germanic inherited vocabulary relating to 'wounding, injury'. 100
Table 7.5. Celto-Germanic and Italo-Celtic/Germanic inherited vocabulary relating to the maritime sphere and watercraft. 102
Table 7.6. Celto-Germanic and Northwest Indo-European inherited vocabulary relating to human beings, gods, and the cosmos 104
Table 7.7. Celto-Germanic and Northwest Indo-European inherited vocabulary relating to social organization. 108

Chapter 1

Introduction and outline

> Let him teach himself to fight by his ferocious deeds, and let him not stand out of range of missiles, since he has a shield, but go close up and fight hand to hand, stabbing with his long spear or his sword, and bring down his foe. Place foot to foot and press shield against shield, thrusting crest to crest, helmet to helmet, and chest to chest, and let him fight his man, holding his sword's handle or his long spear. As for you light armed men, crouch behind the shields and throw large rocks and hurl polished javelins at them in all directions, helping the heavy-armoured troops by standing close to them.
>
> Tyrtaeus, Fragment 11 (Swift 2015, 96)

The passage above, composed by the Spartan poet Tyrtaeus (Τυρταῖος) in the mid-7th century BC, demonstrates how highly the warrior ethos was esteemed by the ancient Greeks, for whom the heroic age was the Bronze Age idealized in the Homeric epics (Chan 2011). What distinguished the Bronze Age warrior in other parts of Europe such as Iberia and Scandinavia, where the evidence of such an early written literature is lacking? Does the warrior iconography depicted on the rocks in Scandinavia or stone slabs in Iberia expand our understanding of this pan-European phenomenon?

The aim of this book is to provide a fuller, critical account and more satisfactory explanation than previously available for the evident similarities of the Late Bronze Age Iberian 'warrior' stelae and Scandinavian rock art, focusing especially on parallels in their warrior iconography and taking into account the socio-economic and linguistic contexts in which they emerged. 3D documentation of rock art has revealed new details of these stones, while other new scientific evidence on the sources of metals, movements of people and contacts between the prehistoric languages also point towards an episode of close connections between Iberia and Scandinavia at this time. As well as this specific aim, this book considers more broadly the concept and place of the Bronze Age warrior. Not so long ago, while a prestigious western civilization continued to be viewed as the main business of the humanities, this figure could be found near that enterprise's foundation, as the leading character of Homer's *Iliad*.

More recently, the non-fiction Bronze Age warrior has become the subject of a wide range of approaches, generating an extensive scholarly literature (Treherne 1995; Earle 1997; Osgood 1998; Kristiansen 1998; Otto *et al.* 2006; Vandkilde 2006; Harding 2007; Molloy 2007; Frieman *et al.* 2017; Ling & Toreld 2018; Horn & Kristiansen 2018; Díaz-Guardamino *et al.* 2022). Surveying this work, a consensus is detectable in recurrent details of activities and socio-cultural domains with which the real and idealized warriors of this era were associated:

- warfare and martial arts
- travel and exchange
- power and politics
- ritual activities
- cosmopolitan and esoteric knowledge
- death, honour, and posthumous fame
- descriptive praise by artisans
- decorative status display
- hunting
- athletics.

It is interesting to note that these listed characteristics – and arguably not much else – are especially pronounced in both the Iberian and Scandinavian warrior iconography, either directly represented in it or implied for the Bronze Age societies that produced it. The focus on this theme is intense and unwavering and, in this respect, it can be likened to a visual counterpart of the *Iliad* as a relentless celebration of the Bronze Age warrior.

Importantly, visual and written imagery and narrative are not direct reflections of reality. Their (re)creation was mediated by social practice and intentionality and their interpretation poses specific challenges. The example of the Homeric epics serves as an important reminder: despite their cultural centrality, they do not provide a balanced picture of Greek society. Part of a well-established genre, they were unhistorical composites (cf. Lord 1960) that took shape to appeal to the values of specific sectors of society (male elites) and to encourage their listeners in battle (Osborne 1996; Swift 2015). But, viewed in the context of a fuller range of evidence, the epics present a paradox, as their fascination with war – like the conquests of Alexander the Great – stand in stark contrast to a pervasive pattern of avoidance of armed conflict in the Greek world (Hornblower 2007).

Equally, warrior imagery within Bronze Age rock art traditions from across Atlantic Europe was created within diverse cultural, political, social and material settings by individuals and groups with distinct agendas and affording rock art varying forms, meanings and agential powers (i.e. powers to act or affect in particular ways), even within societies sharing broad worldviews. Therefore, attention to context in any iconography-driven project or comparative analysis such as the one presented in this book, will be paramount (Díaz-Guardamino 2011; Ling 2014, 165–183). The components that make up this book's investigation are presented in its seven chapters, briefly summarized as follows:

- Chapter 2 lays out background concerning the new technologies and methods that now allow us to pinpoint and document in detail, and potentially to explain, the closely comparable features of the warrior representations in our two coeval study areas. This section highlights also other lines of evidence such as typology of shields, raw materials such as copper and amber and early inscriptions, all of which connect Iberia with the northern fringes of Atlantic Europe.
- Chapter 3 considers in depth key dimensions of the Bronze Age European context of comparative rock art study to give a theorized overview of 'Aspects of social organization, long-distance exchange, and warriorhood'.
- Chapter 4 'Shared copper sources between Bronze Age communities in Atlantic Europe' draws together a range of recent evidence for copper exchange linking far-flung regions of Atlantic Europe, also addressing evidence for the involvement of other metal-producing regions.
- Chapter 5 focuses on the landscape settings of rock art in Iberia and Scandinavia, thus forming prolegomena to contextualized case studies in the following chapter.
- Chapter 6 discusses in greater depth specific comparative examples of warrior iconography, giving special attention to details of the sites, categorization of images, and dating.
- Chapter 7 focuses on linguistic evidence for contacts in later prehistory and its connection to rock art. How can the recurrent motifs be related to the shared inherited vocabulary of Germanic, Celtic, and the other post-Proto-Indo-European languages of northern and western Europe?
- The concluding Chapter 8 begins by returning to and expanding the themes of Chapter 1. This combines a recapitulation of the evidence for connectivity, then extended to concrete examples of where and how exchange and interaction could have taken place in Bronze Age Atlantic Europe.
- The chapters close with a theoretical discussion about the nature of the institutions that conducted long-distance exchange that connected the Scandinavian and Iberian terminus zones of Atlantic Europe.

Acknowledgements

The research behind this book has been made possible through the four-year project 'Rock Art, Words, and Warriors' (2018-01387) financed by the Swedish Scientific Research Council and by the six-year programme 'Maritime Encounters' (M21-0018), funded by the Riksbankens Jubileumsfond of the Swedish Central Bank. Technical support with visualizing 3D files and comparative rock art documentation was provided by the SHFA (Swedish Rock Art Research Archives) and the Riksbankens Jubileumsfond project 'Rock art in three dimensions' (IN18-0557:1). We are indebted to Ellen Meijer, Rich Potter, and Ashely Green, from the SHFA/University of Gothenburg, for their invaluable support throughout the completion of the digital work. We would also like to thank the following individuals, museums, and institutions from Spain, Portugal, and Sweden for greatly facilitating our work digitizing rock art, stelae, and statue-menhirs from their collections: Tanum Rock Art Museum Underslös (Sweden), Guillermo Kurtz and the Archaeological Museum of Badajoz (Spain), Juan Manuel Valadés Sierra, José Miguel González Bornay, and the Museum of Cáceres (Spain), Miguel Ángel Vallecillo and the Ethnographic Museum "González Santana" in Olivenza (Spain), Elena Morán and the Dr. José Formosinho Municipal Museum of Lagos (Portugal), Pedro Salvado, Joana Bizarro, and the Archaeological Museum José Monteiro in Fundão (Portugal), Marcos Osório and the Museum of Sabugal (Portugal), Hermann Scheufler and the Society of Friends of the Museum Francisco Tavares Proença Júnior in Castelo Branco (Portugal), the Parish Council of Baraçal (Portugal), Miguel Serra from the City Council of Serpa (Portugal), João Barreira, Deolinda Tavares, and the Regional Museum of Beja Rainha D. Leonor (Portugal), Antonio Carvalho and the National Museum of Archaeology in Lisbon (Portugal), Ángel de Bodas López, mayor of Aldeanueva de San Bartolomé (Spain), Fernando Luis Fontes Blanco and the Museum of Santa Cruz in Toledo (Spain), Eduardo Galán, Lucía Moragón, and the National Archaeological Museum in Madrid (Spain), Hipólito Collado Giraldo from the Regional Government of Extremadura, Ana Bettencourt (University of Minho, Portugal), Raquel Vilaça and Lara Bacelar Alves (University of Coimbra, Portugal), Beatriz Comendador Rey (University of Vigo, Spain), Ignacio Montero Ruiz (Instituto de Historia, CSIC, Spain), Ben Roberts and Marion Uckelmann (Durham University, UK), and Juan Pereira Sieso (University of Castilla La Mancha, Spain). We are also grateful to all the individuals and institutions who have granted permission to reproduce images. MDG would like to thank her family and her colleagues from the Department of Archaeology at Durham University for their unconditional support throughout the challenging months leading up to the completion of this book. She is grateful to the dedicated and wonderful NHS team who cared for her during treatment. Finally, a huge thanks to Malcolm Nicholson for his impeccable copy-editing work and the final push to bring this book to completion, and Julie Gardiner, Jess Hawxwell, and the Oxbow Books editorial team for their support and patience.

Chapter 2

Background

Recent research has uncovered new evidence of long-distance interactions between Scandinavia and Iberia during the Late Bronze Age. Advances in various lines of inquiry, such as 3D recording of rock art, iconography, metals and amber sourcing, linguistics, and, to some extent, more indirect indications from human remains, as reflected by strontium and aDNA results, have made this possible (McKinley *et al.* 2013; Ling *et al.* 2014; Ling & Koch 2018; Murillo-Barroso *et al.* 2018; Ling *et al.* 2019; Koch 2020; Vandkilde *et al.* 2021; Berger *et al.* 2022; Díaz-Guardamino *et al.* 2022; Patterson *et al.* 2022). The main goal of this book is to cross reference Iberian Late Bronze Age warrior iconography with Scandinavian warrior iconography. However, we will also account for links based on archeometallurgical evidence, linguistics, and other lines of inquiry, such as Baltic amber and metal artefacts. The results have been produced within the framework of the RAW project, financed by the Swedish Research Council. The RAW project is motivated by the discovery of isotopic and chemical evidence for Nordic Bronze Age artefacts made of copper which originated in the Iberian Peninsula (Ling *et al.* 2014). These findings led to the re-examination of two long known, but poorly explained, phenomena: 1) numerous shared motifs and close formal parallels in the rock art of Scandinavia and Iberian 'warrior' stelae and 2) a large body of inherited words shared by the Celtic and Germanic languages but not the other Indo-European branches. An integrated explanation for the three phenomena (Iberian metal in Scandinavia, parallels in Bronze Age rock carvings, and Celto-Germanic vocabulary) could now be formulated as a testable hypothesis: an episode in the Bronze Age when materials and ideas were exchanged over long distances between Scandinavia and the Atlantic West, including the Iberian Peninsula.

Turning to the rock art, the parallelisms between Iberian Late Bronze Age warrior stelae and Scandinavian rock art (the southern tradition) were raised more than five decades ago by researchers such as Martín Almagro Basch (1966, 189–192). He noted formal similarities between some chariot depictions in both traditions, as well as the parallelism between the shields represented on Iberian warrior stelae and those found in other regions, mainly in the eastern Mediterranean and in northwest Europe including Scandinavia (Almagro Basch 1966, 156–170). Two-wheeled vehicles were widely used during the Bronze Age in the Near East and eastern Mediterranean and it is clear that they were known in Iberia and southern Scandinavia in the Late Bronze Age and other parts of temperate Europe (Koch 2013). Noting strong similarities between war-chariot depictions in Scandinavia and Iberia (Fig. 2.1), Koch (2013; Ling & Koch 2018) argues for some sort of direct contact. A recent paper by Vandkilde and colleagues (2021) also favours the similarities in warrior iconography between Iberia and Scandinavia and argues for strong parallelisms with Sardinian iconography.

The origin(s) and routes of circulation of the shields known as Herzsprung-type were hotly debated especially in the 1950s and 1960s (e.g., Hencken 1950; Sprockhoff 1954; Coles 1962; Almagro Basch 1966, 164–165). It should be emphasized that there are two types of Herzsprung shields, V-notched and U-notched, and that the former is the most common in Iberian rock art, while the latter has been found in Scandinavia in the form of real bronze shields, but not depicted on rock art. The U-notched shields are supposed to derive from the V-notched. The combined distribution of the two types is clearly Atlantic, from Iberia via Ireland, then to Scandinavia, where only U-notched shields occur (Uckelmann 2012, 50–62, 127–137, pl. 160). While different hypotheses were proposed for the ultimate origin (Mediterranean v. northwest Europe) and patterns of circulation of these different but related types of shields, most researchers agreed that connections (direct or indirect) between Iberia and Scandinavia, most probably via Ireland, had to be considered to explain the patterns of distribution of such distinctive shield during the time of currency of Iberian warrior stelae, now dated to the Late Bronze Age (*c.* 1250–800 BC; Fig. 2.1; Coles 1962; Díaz-Guardamino 2012; Uckelmann 2014). In support of this argument are, on the one hand, the astonishing similarity between some representations of V-notched shields on Iberian stelae and the Cloonbrin leather shield from Ireland (e.g., the stela of Brozas) and, on the other, the distribution of U-notched shields, with examples in Ireland and one (possibly two) representation(s) on warrior stelae in Iberia, while they are missing in the Mediterranean (Fig. 2.1; Díaz-Guardamino 2010, 328; Uckelmann 2012, 50–62, 127–137, pl. 160; 2014; Díaz-Guardamino *et al.* 2020).

Other figural parallels between Iberian and Scandinavian rock art have recently been noted (Ling & Koch 2018). Bi-horned warriors are a prominent shared theme as well as similar gestures and weapons. In general, the same categories of weapons, shields, bows and arrows, spears and swords have been depicted in Iberian and Scandinavian rock art. In these depictions, however, regional typologies of weapons can clearly be seen in some instances (Brandherm 2013; 2016; Ling & Koch 2018). Even though these horned anthropomorphic depictions were produced at opposite ends of the Atlantic façade, they belong to the same time frame, which bears

2. Background

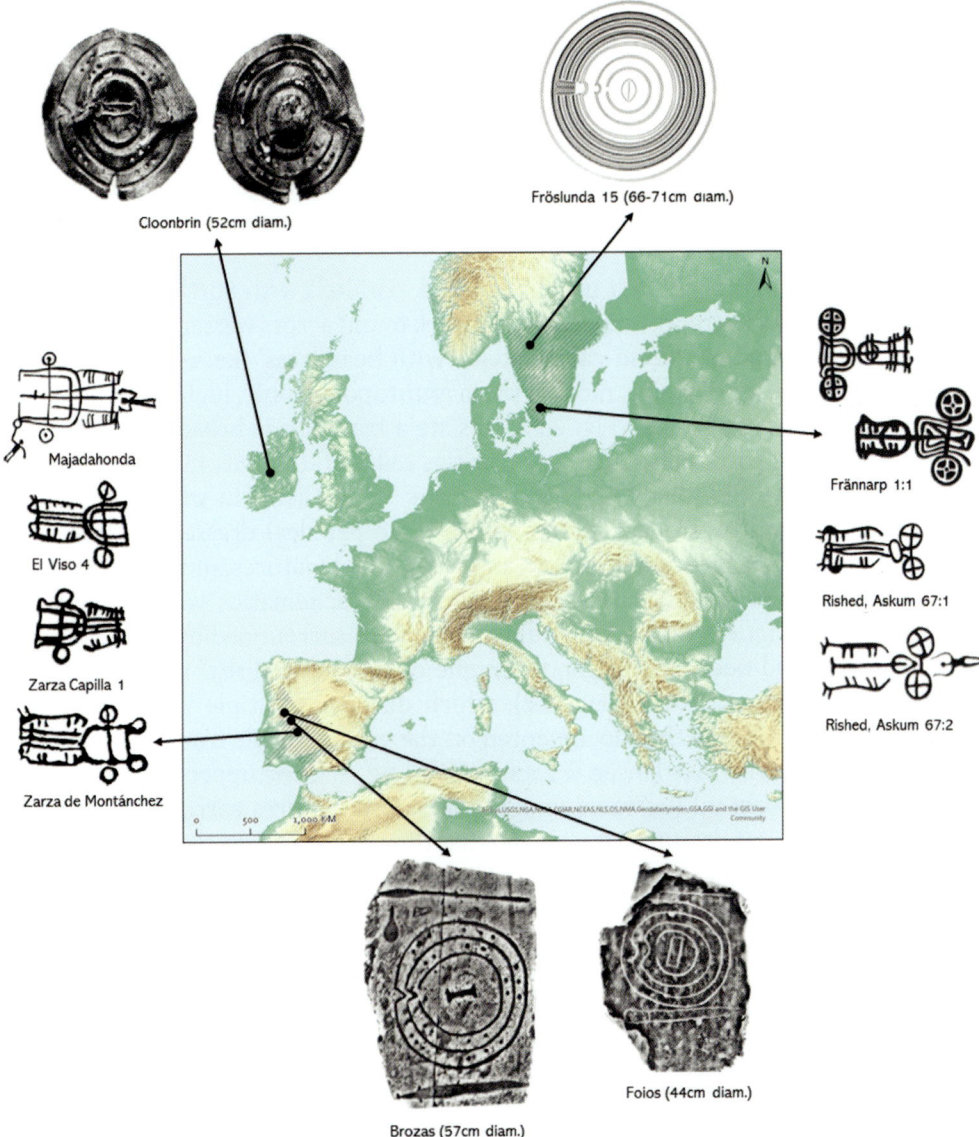

Figure 2.1. Some examples of Herzsprung shield images on warrior stelae (TVT visualizations from laser scans) and their correlates in Europe, and chariot depictions in Iberia (35–45 cm) and Scandinavia (31–75 cm). Image by Marta Díaz-Guardamino.

witness to long range interaction. The images constitute a vivid corpus of a pan-European warrior symbolism, that could be connected with the Urnfield cultures and the eastern Mediterranean (Harrison 2004 168–173; Vandkilde 2013; Ling & Koch 2018; Díaz-Guardamino et al. 2022). Images of mirrors occur in the rock art of both regions, with the 66 in Iberia constituting the largest group in Europe after the latest review (Díaz-Guardamino *et al.* in prep.). Shown in martial contexts, they can be understood as a local interpretation of the warrior ideal (Díaz-Guardamino *et al.* 2022), including physical beauty (Treherne 1995). Similar mirror depictions occur in at least three sites in Bohuslän, western Sweden (Ling & Uhnér 2014; Ling & Koch 2018). Albeit in fewer numbers, these mirror representations in Scandinavia are found in close association with martial motifs such as warriors, bi-horned figures, and war canoes, and they are undoubtedly a local articulation of pan-European warrior symbolism (Ling & Koch 2018).

Other equally significant, but usually ignored, parallels with northern Europe are the Nordic-inspired Sagrajas-Berzocana goldwork found across western Iberia and the headdresses depicted on the so-called 'stelae with headdress' (i.e. *estelas con tocado*, which include a range of stelae, most of them anthropomorphic, including the *estelas guijarro* and *estelas diademadas*; Fig. 2.2). This stela tradition is broadly dated to the Bronze Age (Díaz-Guardamino 2010, 235–250, figs 139–147, 151, 152, 155). Here, human figures are represented following two styles: one 'naturalistic' in which the human body is represented by stone boulders (often large pebbles) dressed with detailed carved arms and hands (sometimes legs and feet), facial features, multiple necklaces and an elaborate headdress; the second style being 'schematic', where bodies are depicted as stick figures with arms and hands and are surrounded by the depictions of headdresses and necklaces. A good example of the 'naturalistic' type is the stela 6 from Hernán Pérez (0.86 m; Fig. 2.2), which displays multiple necklaces and a headdress comparable to that documented on the young female from Skrydstrup in southern Scandinavia (Kristiansen & Larsson 2005, fig. 57). The upper fragment of the stela of Bodonal (0.38 m) (Berrocal Rangel 1987), also features earrings comparable to those found in Skrydstrup. It is possible that the necklaces depicted were inspired by torcs, such as the golden Sagrajas-Berzocana torcs known in western Iberia (Díaz-Guardamino 2010, fig. 155). Two golden decorated torcs (c. 12 cm diam.), originally part of a set of three, were found in the Nossa Senhora da Guia de Baioes hillfort, in north Portugal. This hillfort is close to the Vouga river, which discharges into the Aveiro Lagoon, an important landing area during recent prehistory. Baltic amber, as well as metalwork related mainly to the Atlantic but also the Mediterranean spheres of interaction, were found in the hillfort (Kalb 1995; Senna-Martínez 1998; Murillo-Barroso *et al.* 2018). These torcs have geometric decoration comparable to that found on gold torcs from Brittany and bronze ones from the Nordic area. The stelae 'with headdress' seem to replicate this kind of multiple necklaces.

A Late Bronze Age date for part – if not most (Santos 2009) – of the stelae of this tradition is suggested by the association of the 'schematic' style with images of warriors with Late Bronze Age paraphernalia. They can be found together on the same stela (e.g., Almadén de la Plata 2, Fig. 6.6; García Sanjuán *et al.* 2006; Díaz-Guardamino *et al.* 2015) or depicted on different stelae found at the same site or nearby (e.g., Capilla o Zarza Capilla, Díaz-Guardamino 2010, 262–267). Stelae with headdress are usually small in size (most measuring *c.* 40–100 cm), their facial

2. Background

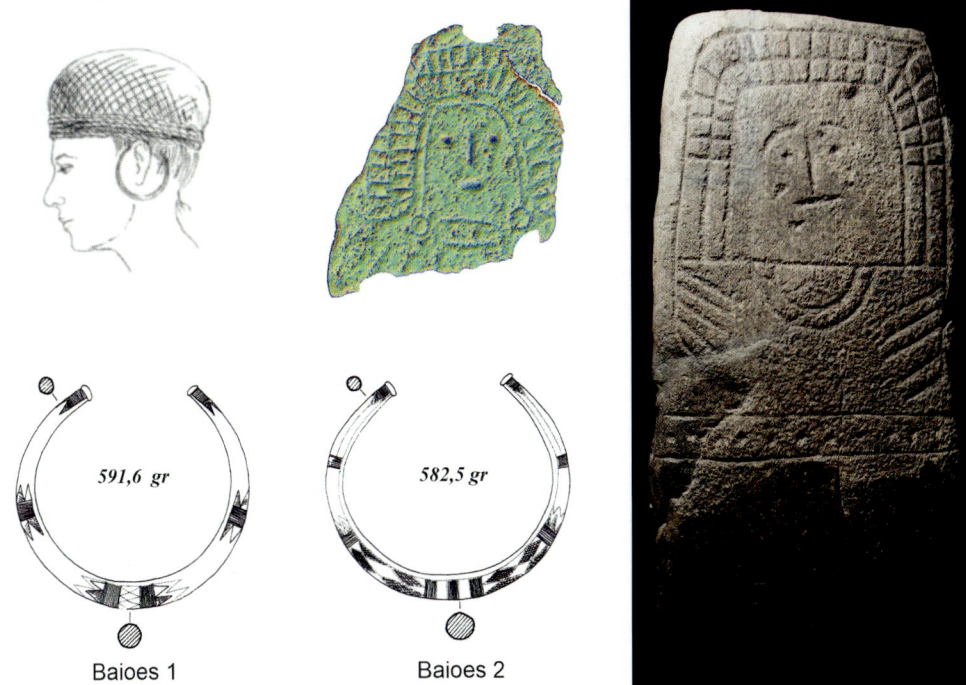

Figure 2.2. Comparable examples of necklaces and headdresses found in Scandinavia and Iberia. From left to right: young female from Skrydstrup (southern Scandinavia), stela of Bodonal (Archaeological Museum of Badajoz, Badajoz, Spain), and stela 6 of Hernán Pérez (southwestern Iberia; National Archaeological Museum, Madrid, Spain). Bottom left: golden torcs from Nossa Senhora da Guia de Baioes hillfort (northwestern Iberia). Images by Kristian Kristiansen and Marta Díaz-Guardamino.

features childlike (in the 'naturalistic' ones) while, in four cases (Salvatierra, Capilla 1, Belalcazar, and Lantejuela), they depict breasts (Díaz-Guardamino 2010, 225–291). These aspects have been used to argue that these stelae could represent young female individuals (Berrocal Rangel 1987; Díaz-Guardamino 2010, 240–250). Overall, it should be noted that the scarcity of clear sexual markers on both stelae traditions (stelae with headdress and warrior stelae) raises questions about the direct association between the roles portrayed and the gender identities they represent (Díaz-Guardamino 2014). Importantly, the spatial distribution of both stelae traditions complements each other and partly coincides with areas where gold and tin ores are very abundant.

All these formal connections gain huge significance when considered within the broader context of long-distance connections newly revealed by the results of recent projects. The first has demonstrated that amber from the Baltic reached Iberia during the Late Bronze Age (Murillo-Barroso & Martinón Torres 2012; Murillo-Barroso et al. 2018). The second (Ling et al. 2014; 2019), which focused on the lead isotope and chemical analysis of samples of bronze metalwork from southern Scandinavia,

Table 2.1. Comparison of main chronological periods in Bronze Age Scandinavia and Atlantic Iberia with indication of calibrated dates

	Scandinavia		Atlantic Iberia		
	Period	Dates BC	Dates BC	Phase	
	I				
Rock art panels with war-related scenes	II	1500–1300	1700–1400/1250	Bronce Pleno	Middle Bronze Age
	III	1300–1100	1260–1200	Bronce Final IC	Late Bronze Age
			1200–1130	Bronce Final IIA/IIB	
			1130–1050	Bronce Final IIC	
	IV	1100–900	1050–930	Bronce Final IIIA	
Rock art panels with war-related scenes	V	900–700	930–850	Bronce Final IIIB/Hierro I	Iron Age
			850–750	Orientalizante I	
	VI	700–500			

indicates that copper with an isotopic signature matching southern Iberian ores from Los Pedroches (within the Ossa Morena Zone), the Alcudia valley (within the Central Iberia Zone) and the upper Guadalquivir valley (Linares; Fig. 2.3) was used to manufacture artefacts in southern Scandinavia from around 1400 BC (Period II, 1500–1300 BC), but specially in Periods IV (1100–900) including samples from swords, and V (900–700 BC) with samples from two Herzsprung shields (Fig. 2.1; Ling et al. 2014, 121–129; Table 2.1.). These important results become even more relevant when we consider that the different traditions of Iberian Bronze Age stelae and statue-menhirs unfolded precisely in regions that are particularly rich in copper, tin and gold; in areas that frequently show evidence for late prehistoric mining activities within communities that played key roles in the circulation of metal within Iberia but also connecting metal producing areas in the Iberian hinterland with the coast (the connection between stelae and statue-menhirs and mining was noted by Díaz-Guardamino (2010, 64–74, 427–451), Senna-Martínez and Luis (2016), Rodríguez-Corral and Rodríguez-Rellán (2023) and, among others, by Almagro-Gorbea (1977, 200–201 for stelae with headdress and warrior stelae), and Harrison (2004, 27 for warrior stelae)). This is particularly significant for Late Bronze Age warrior stelae, as recent findings from lead isotope analysis reveal that a significant part of the copper used to cast swords from the Ría de Huelva hoard and palstaves from hoards in northwest Iberia originated from the mining districts of Alcudia valley or Linares (as shown in Fig. 2.3) (Montero-Ruiz et al. 2007; 2014; Montero-Ruiz 2017; Armada et al. 2023). This suggests that warrior-stelae-making communities likely played a significant role in redistributing this copper between these mining districts and the northwest and southwest of Iberia during the Late Bronze Age.

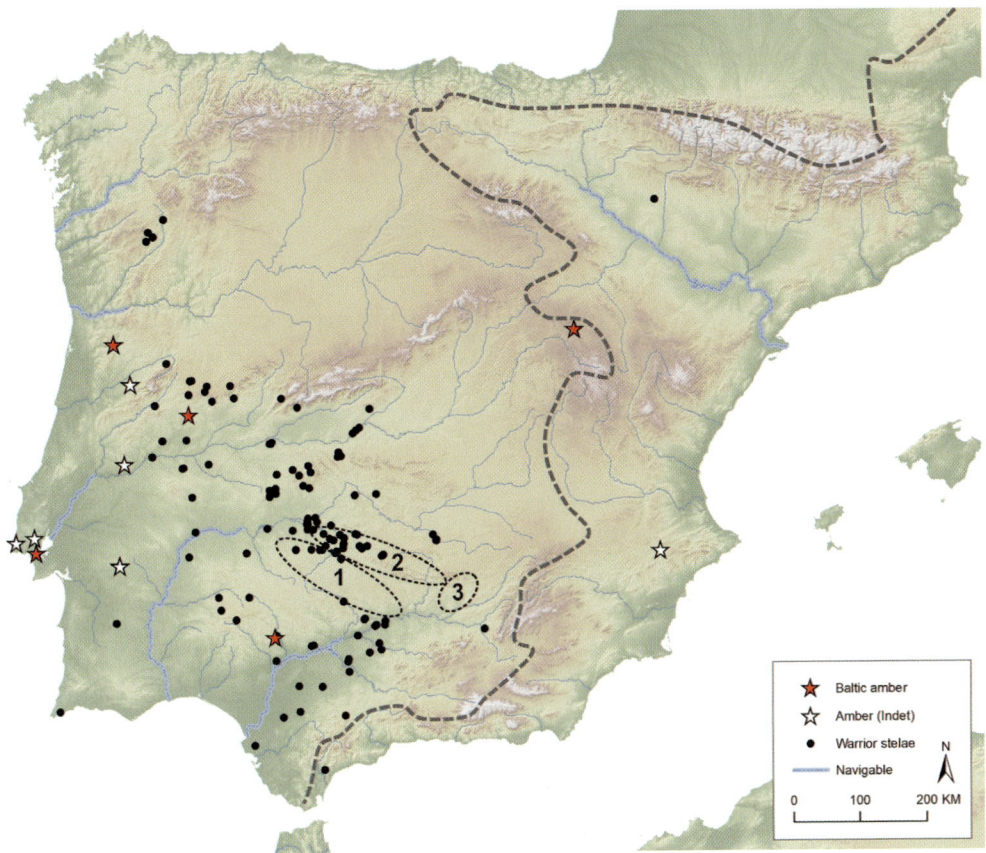

Figure 2.3. Distribution of Late Bronze Age Iberian warrior stelae and locations of confirmed or probable Late Bronze Age/Early Iron Age Baltic amber finds and major mining districts: (1) Los Pedroches (within the Ossa Morena Zone); (2) the Alcudia valley (within the Central Iberia Zone); (3) the upper Guadalquivir valley (Linares). The discontinuous line defines the limits between Atlantic and Mediterranean Iberia. Map by Marta Díaz-Guardamino.

Furthermore, advances in linguistics allow rock-art iconography to be linked to word meanings in Proto-Indo-European, Proto-Celtic, and Proto-Germanic. Recent advances in archaeogenetics have shed new light on processes that have been seen as bringing early Indo-European languages to northern and western Europe in the 3rd millennium BC (Allentoft *et al.* 2015; Haak *et al.* 2015; Olalde *et al.* 2018; 2019; Valdiosera *et al.* 2018; Lazaridis *et al.* 2022). On the other hand, the rapid expansion of this new field against a background of tragic political misuse in the 20th century means that caution must be applied in following the implications of archaeogenetics and critical responses seriously weighed (e.g., Heyd 2017; Klejn *et al.* 2018; Frieman & Hofmann 2019; Furholt 2019; Hakenbeck 2019). Advancing cautiously in the light of these new data sets, we may usefully hypothesize rock art iconography to be linked to word meanings in Proto-Indo-European,

Proto-Celtic, and Proto-Germanic. The shared cultural codes in rock art iconography in Scandinavia and Iberia during this phase point to a *lingua franca* used by polyglot traders/warriors who moved raw materials between these terminus zones (Ling & Koch 2018; Koch 2019b; 2020; see also Harrison 2004, 74–80, 170–178; Vandkilde *et al.* 2021; Ling *et al.* 2022a).

Chapter 3

Aspects of social organization, long distance exchange, and warriorhood

How did the involved Atlantic societies organize long distance exchange of metals? Who were the primary agents in the system? What was the role of rock art, as both cause and effect, in the formation of possibly warrior-led maritime trading systems? And how might this have been reflected in the form of both shared iconography and a corresponding shared linguistic vocabulary? To what extent can the parallels in the warrior iconography in Iberia and Scandinavia be explained with the hypothesis of a warrior-led exchange system between these remote regions in the Bronze Age?

In seeking answers to these questions, new theoretical models have emerged that focus on social organization, institutions and agents, possible structures of political confederacy as well as types of political economy that governed a dependable and stable long-distance exchange in Bronze Age societies (Kristiansen 2018a; Ling et al. 2022b). Theoretical models have the power to highlight key parallels, but also differences, in terms of social evolution, social complexity, and modes of production. In terms of social organization, several authors have stated that Scandinavian societies were ranked and chiefdom-like, although highly decentralized social settings with a high degree of social inequality (Kristiansen 1998; 2010; Earle 2002; Ling et al. 2018; Austvoll 2021; Kristiansen & Earle 2022). On the other hand, regarding Atlantic Iberia, most authors have proposed tribal, Big Men systems and, in some regions, simple chiefdoms with variable but generally low degrees of inequality (Barceló 1992; Harrison 2004, 67–68; García-Sanjuán 2006; Armada 2013, 283–284; Senna-Martínez & Luis 2016, 123–125). There is more agreement between models for both regions on the existence of elites that sustained their positions by controlling long-distance trade. In the case of Scandinavia, these elites controlled metal trade by stimulating the interaction between the political and the domestic economy, converting agro-pastoral and other surpluses into political power. Their power base rested on organising, equipping, and leading warrior retinues that executed their demands (Kristiansen 2002; Kristiansen & Earle 2014; Ling et al. 2018). This system required an adherence to an ideology focused on a warrior ideal on the part of elites and probably commoners as well (Vandkilde 2006; Horn 2023). In Atlantic Iberia, it is thought that the circulation of goods was in the hands of elites aspiring to the warrior ideal and living up to it when possible and practical (Ruiz-Galvez 1998; Harrison & Mederos 2000; Harrison 2004; García-Sanjuán 2006; Senna-Martínez & Luis 2016; Vilaça 2020; but see Araque 2023). These circulating goods were mainly metals in the form of ores, ingots, or scrap, finished metallic artefacts being relatively scarce in the record (as noted by Delgado Hervás 2013), and perishables.

It is crucial to emphasize that research on so-called 'chiefdoms' reveals a variety of political formations (Earle 1997; 2002; Drennan & Peterson 2012; Neitzel & Earle 2014). However, there are some common features for such political structures in that most relied on three basic elemental powers, in varying degrees: an economy capable of producing surpluses beyond subsistence, the coercive might of warriors, and a religious ideology (Earle 1997). Many of these features are implicit in the Iberian and Scandinavian rock art. However, none of these properties was easy to control; therefore, non-complex decentralized chiefdoms were highly unstable social formations so that power retention in these societies was extremely challenging and fragile. Nonetheless, successful political leaders manipulated, mixed, and matched all possible sources of power realized by the resources channeled through the political economy and their investment-controlled mechanisms such as boats and warriors (Earle 1997; 2002).

In any case, the evidence for social organization in Atlantic Iberia and Scandinavia demonstrates highly decentralized social settings. These were defensible hilltop sites in most of Atlantic Iberia (Díaz-Guardamino 2010, 373–389; Bettencourt 2013) and also dispersed agglomerations of long houses and 'pit sites' located on fertile plains in some regions of northwest, central, and southwest Iberia (Blanco-González 2011; Soares 2013; Vilaça 2014; Parcero-Oubiña et al. 2020; Soares et al. 2021), whereas, in Scandinavia, settlements were more widely distributed throughout the landscape with occasional agglomerations in small hamlets, even a few on the scale of villages (Artursson 2009). In both regions, the principal social unit was the autonomous household or farmstead located in an area with favourable conditions for agropastoral production and with access to metal resources or in landscapes that provided opportunities to engage in exchange (for Atlantic Iberia see Díaz-Guardamino 2010, 373–389; Delgado Hervás 2013; Senna-Martínez 2013; Blanco-González 2018; Parcero-Oubiña et al. 2020; for Scandinavia see Ling et al. 2018; Austvoll 2021; Horn et al. 2024).

In Atlantic Iberia during the Late Bronze Age there is evidence of a low – but increasing – degree of social inequality and no clear evidence of specialized production. Access to metal resources (tin and copper) was generalized in the hinterland, across the northwest, western and southern margins of the Iberian Central Meseta, but more limited around the coastal periphery. In comparison with other

European regions, particularly Scandinavia but also other areas including Ireland, the amount of metalwork in circulation in Atlantic Iberia was small (Díaz-Guardamino et al. 2022, 330–331). However, more numerous finds are concentrated in the late phase of the Iberian Late Bronze Age, LBA III, 10th–9th century BC (Comendador Rey 1999; Harrison & Mederos 2000). Evidence of mortuary activity, where inequality might be seen negotiated, is very scarce (Torres Ortíz 1999; García-Sanjuán 2006; Bettencourt 2013; Díaz-Guardamino 2014; Vilaça & Cardoso 2017; Díaz-Guardamino et al. 2019; Soares et al. 2021). Furthermore, evidence of metallurgical activity is mostly restricted to the domestic sphere, more rarely documented in communal spaces, underscoring the non-specialist character of metallurgical, and possibly mining, activities in those regions during the Late Bronze Age (Díaz-Guardamino 2010, 373–389; Armada 2013; Senna-Martínez & Luis 2016; Vilaça 2020).

In Scandinavia the social context is somewhat different, as social complexity increased during the Early Bronze Age (c. 1700 BC) perhaps based on developments already at work in the Neolithic (Horn 2021), but then elevated further by institutions that fostered trade and exchange of metals (Ling et al. 2022b). Of course, a comparable situation cannot be ruled out for some key regions within Atlantic Iberia from the Late Bronze Age (c. 1250 BC), where specific agents may have controlled access to the manufacturing of specialized weapons, e.g., workshops. This could be the case in the Iberian Southwest, where the technological analysis of swords from the Ría de Huelva hoard reveals great homogeneity in their composition indicating that they were manufactured following the same technological tradition, probably within the same region (Ruiz-Gálvez 1995, 59–62; see appendix by S. Rovira in Brandherm 2007, 156–158). The circulation of the ores throughout the hinterland, and especially between the metal producing areas (e.g. Linares and Alcudia districts) and the Iberian northwest throughout the western periphery of the Iberian Central Meseta, and between the hinterland and the coastal periphery of Atlantic Iberia is evidenced by some nodal sites where there are hoards including special artefacts. A good example of this is Senhora da Guia de Baiões, where imports and/or bronzes related to feasting and commensality were found (Ruiz-Gálvez 1998, 285–286; Needham & Bowman 2005; Armada 2013; Senna-Martínez 2013).

3.1. Warrior iconography and modes of production

We hold that the warrior stelae in Iberia and the warrior iconography on the Scandinavian outcrops manifest both similarities and differences between the social organizations in these regions. The Iberian warrior stelae reflect a more terrestrial mode of production, expressed through the warrior and the chariot, whereas the Scandinavian rock art embodies a maritime mode of production expressed by the warrior and the boats. Warriors and warrior ideals can be seen as the apex of the value systems in both regions. In Scandinavia, warriors were needed for collecting tribute as well as for controlling the domestic economy, the agricultural sector and the political economy by regulating exchange through transportation, satisfying the demand for unfree labour and enlarging territories through warfare or by forming territorial alliances, joint ventures for trade and economic expansion. In Atlantic Iberia, there were segmentary systems and simple chiefdoms, political units that are thought to have been relatively autonomous and heterarchical (Ehrenreich et al. 1995; Senna-Martínez 2013). Elite individuals from these communities, e.g., chiefs, Big Men or 'agents of metal circulation', are thought to have been the agents who gained control over access to long-distance exchange networks and the circulation of metal (Vilaça 1998a; 1998b; Armada 2013; Senna-Martínez & Luis 2016). There is a further possible disparity between Bronze Age Scandinavia and Bronze Age Iberia to be considered. Although in both cases it can be shown that the rock art imagery of warriors and other evidence pointing to the rise of warrior institutions and ideals emerge or proliferate in tandem from the mid-2nd millennium, in Iberia it is less clear that a warrior-centred society was already in place at the time when the idealized warrior's panoply makes its appearance on the stelae c. 1450/1250 BC, even when warrior-related imagery is known in northwest Iberia since the Early/Middle Bronze Age on rock art and statue-menhirs. It is possible that a more abundant Iberian armament in earlier times has simply not been found; perhaps many weapons were intentionally deposited in rivers or in the sea as at Huelva, if that was not a shipwreck. But on the other hand, there is the interesting possibility that the concept of the warrior reached the metal-producing terminus of the Bronze system before the actual institution of the warrior had so deeply affected Iberian society. In any case, there was indeed a warrior ideology in Iberia – the result of the appropriation, mixing and re-interpretation of ideals related to the idea of the warrior (and eventually the hero) – that was instrumental in underpinning the status and power of the elite (Harrison 2004, 73–80; Díaz-Guardamino et al. 2022).

The prominence of the figure of the warrior in the visual cultures of Iberia and Scandinavia bears witness to its significance beyond the economic sphere, as a figure of heroic power and ideological, even perhaps religious, significance (Horn 2019; 2022). We will account for this in greater detail later but, first, some of the theory driving these principles must be discussed.

3.2. Traditional approaches: Germanic mode of production (GMP)

Marxist inspired ideas of social organization have been applied to the Bronze Age of both Iberia and Scandinavia. The fundamentals of these societies have been explained using Marx's and Engels' (Marx 1953; Engels 1972; Ling et al. 2017) fairly vague notion of a Germanic mode of production (GMP), which is applicable to southern Scandinavia (Kristiansen 1998) and Argaric Iberia (Gilman 1995) and to some extent to Atlantic Iberia. There is no doubt that Middle Bronze Age (1800–1250 BC) and Late Bronze Age (1250–850 BC) societies in Atlantic Iberia were more decentralized than those of the El Argar culture, which unfolded in Southeast Iberia during the Early/Middle Bronze Age (*c.* 2200–1550 BC). However, this does not mean that they were not complex or that they did not play a strategic role in the development of Atlantic Bronze Age exchange networks (Díaz-Guardamino 2010, 373–389; Armada 2013, 286, n.8; Parcero-Oubiña *et al.* 2020).

In accordance with the idea of the GMP, the political economy is here considered to be highly decentralized, based on free farmers organized fitfully by chieftains and warriors for expansion, defence, and for dispute settlements (Gilman 1995). For example, Gilman used the GMP to explain how Argaric societies in southeast Iberia were organized in the Early and Middle Bronze Age. He argued that they consisted of autonomous agro-pastoral households forming independent production units and that they had organized coalitions of households into tribal assemblies that in turn were connected to hereditary leadership based on warrior might, political and legal activities. Several scholars have seen the Scandinavian longhouse tradition from the Bronze Age in line with this model (Artursson 2009; Kristiansen & Earle 2022). Late Bronze Age longhouses documented in recent years in the centre and northwest of Iberia could also fit this model but they appear in interior regions where no other elements traditionally attributed to the GMP are found (Parcero-Oubiña *et al.* 2020). Otherwise, across most of Atlantic Iberia there are autonomous social/production units (on hilltops or farmsteads in fertile valleys), some of which have stone enclosures and large storage facilities, but the scarcity of mortuary evidence (other than the warrior stelae) and the nature of the broader evidence (especially the amount of metalwork and deposition patterns) indicate that, probably, there was no hereditary leadership based on warrior might in Atlantic Iberia (see above).

3.3. New approaches: maritime mode of production (MMP)

The notion of GMP has been replaced lately with the maritime mode of production (MMP) (Ling *et al.* 2018; Kristiansen & Earle 2022, Horn *et al.* forthcoming). The MMP builds in turn on the concept of Decentralized Complexity, which existed with prestige goods economies (Kristiansen 2010) and had elements discussed as anarchistic (Angelbeck & Grier 2012). The MMP model stresses that the emerging maritime economy in Bronze Age Scandinavia had strong roots in agricultural production but with new maritime, warrior, and trading dynamics that generated a more expansive political economy. In this model, maritime trading and raiding are considered important components that were tied to low-density agricultural communities where farmstead self-sufficiency was the norm. Chiefly farmsteads, however, were able to control larger areas and intensify production with additional labour to generate surpluses that chieftains used to control a political economy based on wealth finance derived from distant maritime expeditions, raids, and the accumulation of metal wealth. The Scandinavian social order consisted of chieftains, warriors, and free farmers at the top segment of society followed by commoners and then captives at the bottom.

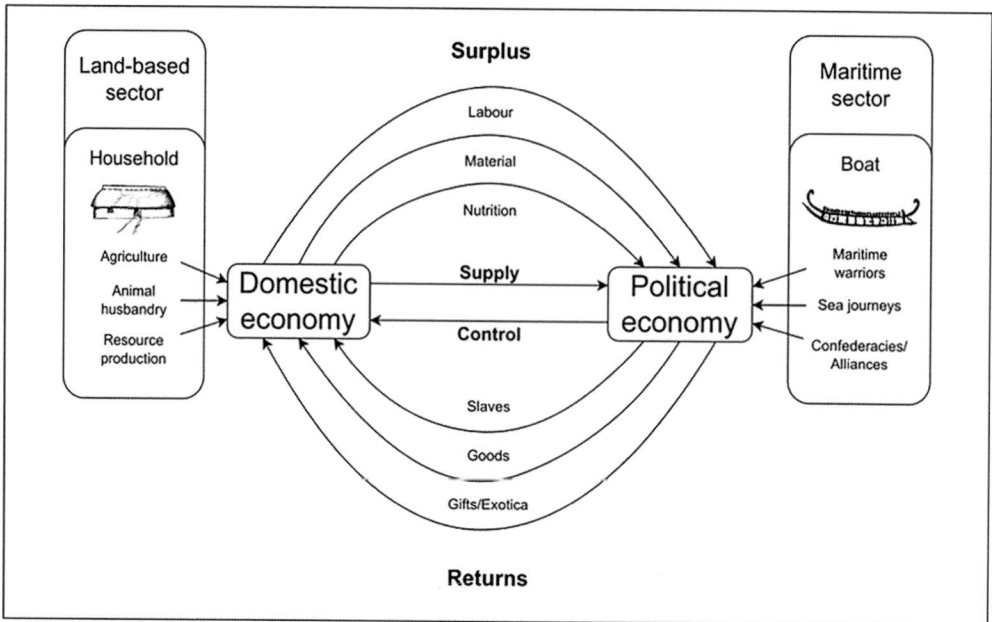

Figure 3.1. Schematic diagram of the interaction between the domestic and the political economies that give rise to the maritime mode of production. Image by Christian Horn.

Evidence for this model of social organization is seen in patterns of differentiation in graves and settlements. The MMP operated through a variety of strategies, including political control of agro-pastoral production, maritime trade, regional alliances, and violence. Characteristics of the MMP arise from the interaction between the domestic and the political economy (Fig. 3.1). This is exemplified by the presence of two key sectors, i.e., the land-based agro-pastoral sector connected to individual farmsteads and the sea-based maritime sector, connected to the boat unit. To participate in trade networks and warfare, Scandinavian groups depended on both sectors but, because of social and environmental differences, some regions specialized more in one or the other (Horn 2018). The result was a division of labour and comparative advantages between regions with varied forms of environments and social organizations, spanning from more coercive to cooperative social settings (Feinman 2017; Austvoll 2021). Coercive groups used the wealth generated by their large-scale agro-pastoral activities to invest in long-distance exchange (Austvoll 2021). Cooperative communities were often located inland and in mountainous areas but some also in more sea-based coastal areas where communities were forced to resort to a more diverse economy, which included agro-pastoralism along with hunting, fishing and timber extraction.

3.4. The role of captives in Scandinavia and the Iberian Peninsula

The MMP model helps to understand institutional formation in decentralized chiefdoms with low population densities, mobile warriors, and long-distance trading

3. Aspects of social organization, long distance exchange, and warriorhood

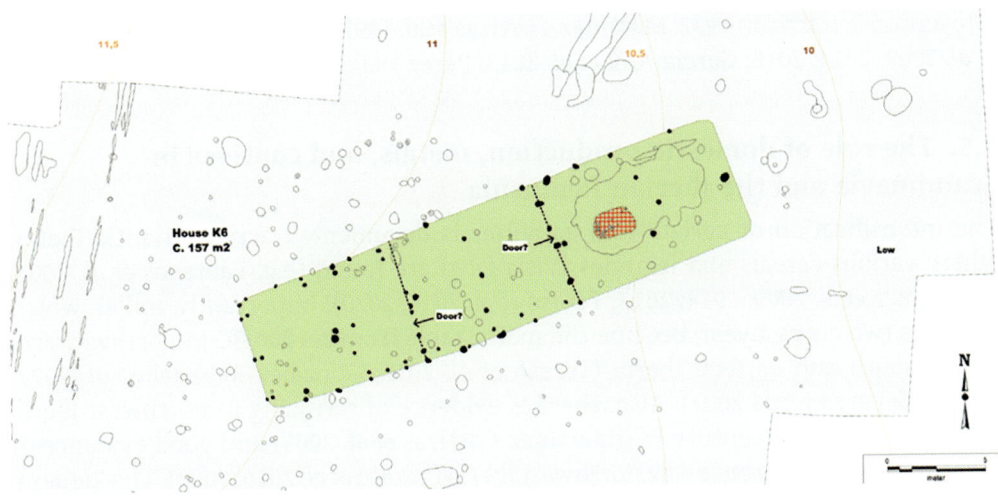

Figure 3.2. House K6 at the site of Abildal, Viborg, Jutland. Image by Martin Mikkelsen.

and raiding in valuables, proliferation of weapons, and the importance of captives to fill gaps in the agriculture sector. In this model, captives are seen as equally important as in the Viking Age, both in terms of supporting the domestic labour force and as a key exchange commodity for trade. The investment in boat crew and warriors for long-distance exchange of metal caused serious labour shortages in the agro-pastoral sector. Some shortages in labour could have been alleviated through alliances but, as in the Viking Age, the main bulk of labour force must have been obtained through captive-taking raids. This is seen as the principal source of workers that filled the labour gaps at the farms due to the investments in boats and crew for long-distance exchange. Evidence of captives has been suggested for the Nordic Bronze Age, including housing arrangements, as in house K6 from Abildal, with a subdivision possibly devoted to hosting unfree people (Mikkelsen 2020; Fig. 3.2); burials in simple, flat inhumation graves (Bergerbrant et al. 2017); the massacre in Sund (Fyllingen 2003); and hostage or slave-images in rock art, e.g. Leirfall (Norway), Ekenberg and Aspeberget (Sweden). Captives themselves may have become a commodity in which some communities specialized, allowing them to engage in local and Europe-wide trade (Ling et al. 2018), moving captives where demand for them was highest. In summary, the MMP model emphasizes the transfer of labour forces from farms to boats, and the resulting gap then supplied by captives.

Captives must also have been an important feature in Iberian societies. For now, clear evidence of captives in Atlantic Iberia is lacking but there is plenty of evidence for economic contexts in which such labour force would have been required (e.g. the intensification of agriculture and/or mining). Palaeo-environmental records from across Atlantic Iberia indicate that from c. 1200 BC human impact on the landscape in the form of deforestation, land erosion, fires, and pollution rose significantly due to the intensification of agricultural activities, livestock raising, and mining activities

(Stevenson & Harrison 1992; Martínez-Cortizas *et al.* 1997; 2002; 2009; 2016; López Sáez *et al.* 2009; 2014; 2018; García Alix *et al.* 2013; Pérez Díaz *et al.* 2016).

3.5. The role of domestic production, metals, and captives in Scandinavia and the Iberian Peninsula

The intensification of agricultural activities is documented across Atlantic Iberia, where various cereals and legumes (*Vicia faba*) are found (e.g. Fábregas *et al.* 2003; López Saez *et al.* 2009; 2014; 2018; Tereso *et al.* 2016; 2020). Importantly, millet, which provides two crops a year, became the main staple from c. 1200 BC in northwestern, north, south and eastern Iberia (Tereso *et al.* 2016; González-Rabanal *et al.* 2022; Alonso & Perez Jordá 2023). Also, there is evidence of terracing in northwest Iberia as early as the 14th century BC (Martínez-Cortizas *et al.* 2009) and good evidence of storage pits in Late Bronze Age northwest Iberia (Tereso *et al.* 2016; 2020). The 'dehesa' agrosilvopastoral system (with grazing land and managed woodland) is documented in combination with increased agricultural activity throughout southwest Iberia and the western Meseta (central Iberia) during the Late Bronze Age (Stevenson & Harrison 1992; López Saez *et al.* 2009). Livestock breeding (ovicaprine, cattle and possibly horse) seems to have become key to the economy of many communities in various regions of Iberia, especially during LBA III (c. 1050–850 BC; Harrison & Mederos 2000). Evidence of the increase in grazing areas in the north points in this direction (Pérez Díaz *et al.* 2016), as well as the new set of material culture related to feasting with meat, which is conspicuous in the northwest (Harrison & Mederos 2000; Armada 2013).

After a period of reforestation during the later part of the Late Neolithic in southern Scandinavia, and especially Jutland (Denmark), the period of massive deforestation with the onset of the Early Bronze Age (from c. 1700 BC) – comparable to what was described earlier for Late Bronze Age Atlantic Iberia – marked a shift to ever-increasing surplus production of the domestic economy (French 2010; Holst *et al.* 2013). Barley (*hordeum vulgare*) and emmer (*triticum dicoccum*) were the stable crops throughout all the southern Scandinavian sphere with the later rising importance of millet (Effenberger 2018). During the Early Bronze Age, these developments occur together with generally increasing house sizes showing an innovation in building techniques, as changes in keeping livestock took effect. During the early phase of the Early Bronze Age the Neolithic tradition of building two-aisled longhouses was abandoned in favour of three-aisled buildings (Artursson 2009), which allowed for the stalling of livestock inside the longhouses. This presumably kept them safer and shows an increased investment in keeping herds, especially of cattle including cattle used as draught animals, and the culling of calves to increase milk production (Nyegaard 2018). While house sizes decreased again with the beginning of the Late Bronze Age, hamlets, small villages, and other settlement structure agglomerations became more frequent (Artursson 2009; 2015).

This increase in domestic product cannot solely be linked to technological innovations because crucial techniques such as manuring only became important at the end of the Late Bronze Age and then into the Scandinavian Iron Age (Dalsgaard & Westergaard Nielsen 2018; Gron *et al.* 2021). Another way of increasing gross domestic product is to employ unfree labour, as cross-cultural studies have demonstrated (Cameron 2016). This fits with evidence of two living quarters in Nordic Bronze Age longhouses, one of which might have housed poorer or lower-class members of the farmstead (Mikkelsen & Kristiansen 2018), and the outbuildings discussed by Mikkelsen (2020) may have been the living quarters of slaves.

In Scandinavia, captive taking and slavery may have been linked to the procurement of metals, though the Scandinavian ores were not mined during the Bronze Age. Evidence for annual raiding and trading expeditions is by now well established in Scandinavia through isotopic studies, the analysis of weaponry and rock art (Horn 2013; 2016; Ling *et al.* 2014; 2019). Such expeditions would have caused a gap in the labour force of any farmstead for weeks and months at a time. This goes along with strong evidence for internal warfare including frequent raids in which defeated enemies perhaps became captives to work on farmsteads to substitute for the missing labour force.

As in Scandinavia, captives must have been important for local agro-pastoral production in Iberia. However, the mining operations had probably a much larger demand for unfree labour. Lead pollution caused by metallurgical activities has been documented in various regions of Atlantic Iberia, including the south, centre and north, from the onset of the Late Bronze Age (Martínez-Cortizas *et al.* 2009; 2016; García Alix *et al.* 2013). In northwest Iberia, 1000 BC has been identified as a critical threshold, when degradation of the environment escalated due to increased forest decline, acidification of soils, and atmosphere pollution, which were caused ultimately by accelerated human activity (Martínez-Cortizas *et al.* 2009). This fits with the distribution of bronze metalwork per period within Iberia because bronze artefacts are most abundant in the later phase of the Late Bronze Age (LBA III, 10th–9th century BC; Comendador Rey 1999; Harrison & Mederos 2000). Having said this, we must consider that the amount of bronze metalwork documented in Iberia until now is much smaller than that documented in other European regions, such as northern Europe (e.g. for swords see Díaz-Guardamino *et al.* 2022). This means that Iberia must have been an important producer and exporter of metal (copper and possibly tin), as the copper ingots documented in various sites within Iberia and beyond prove. Some key examples are the Vila do Touro copper ingot from northern Portugal, whose copper matches the Ossa Morena North Central Belt (NCB) zone in south Iberia (Bottaini *et al.* 2022), the copper ingots recovered from the Rochelongue underwater site, off the coast of southeast France, whose copper also matches the Ossa Morena Zone in south Iberia (Aragón *et al.* 2022), or those found in Salcombe Bay (Fig. 3.3.), southwest England, which match sources in southern Iberia too (Berger *et al.* 2022).

Despite all this, it should be noted that, for now, direct evidence of metallurgical activity in Atlantic Iberia is mostly small scale, related to ore processing and the manufacture of tools, and restricted to settlement sites, which are diverse, and the few mining camps known in the region. Across Atlantic Iberia settlement patterns are diverse and evidence of metallurgical activity can be found across different types

Figure 3.3. Selection of copper and tin ingots from the Salcombe B site.

of sites, from small settlements with enclosures and on top of hills with houses in perishable materials in central-north Portugal to open settlements placed on gentle hillside slopes or the bottom of valleys in northwest Iberia (Bettencourt 1998; 2001; 2013, 162–164; Sampaio & Bettercourt 2011; Armada 2013; Senna-Martínez & Luis 2016; Parcero-Oubiña *et al.* 2020; Vilaça 2020). In the south, metallurgical activity is found in small enclosed or open settlements on the top of hills and small – and insufficiently known – mining camps in the Guadiana and Guadalquivir valleys (Hunt Ortiz 2003, 387–389; Valério *et al.* 2013b; Pavón Soldevila *et al.* 2018; Díaz-Guardamino *et al.* 2019; Hunt Ortiz & Ling 2023) or large enclosed settlements found in landscapes dotted with small farms in southern Portugal (Valério *et al.* 2013a).

As advanced before, there is also increasing evidence of the long-distance circulation of Iberian copper in Europe in the form of ingots, attested through the provenancing of ingots found in various locations across Iberia and off the coasts of southern England and southeast France in the underwater sites of Salcombe Bay and Rochelonge, respectively (Aragón *et al.* 2022; Berger *et al.* 2022; Bottaini *et al.* 2022). Furthermore, there is also considerable new evidence of provenance studies from bronzes from various regions in Atlantic Europe. This includes artefacts found in southern Scandinavia (Ling *et al.* 2014), as well as the western Mediterranean (*bronzetti* from Sardinia, Berger *et al.* 2023). All the previous evidence speaks in favour of a major production of copper in southern Iberia from 1250–850 BC (Hunt Ortiz & Ling 2023).

3.6. Evidence for migration and displaced people

Another line of evidence brings ancient DNA into account and shows a considerable stream of migrants (i.e. 17% migration rate) into southern Britain during the Middle to Late Bronze Age (1300–800 BC), with a quickening pace found in processes of 1000–875 BC (Patterson *et al.* 2022, 590). These genetic data are in accord with evidence for the intensification of connections in the Atlantic Bronze Age, as metals from the south reached the northern Atlantic communities, coinciding with the peak in mining and metallurgical activity documented in Iberia (see above). An important finding of the recent work by Patterson *et al.* is that, while the steppe component was going down (51.8% to 50.4%) and early farmer ancestry (EEF) was on the rise (34.7% to 36.1%) between the Middle and the Late Bronze Age in southern Britain (with an overall rise of 31.0% to 37.9% between a low in the Beaker/Early Bronze Age and levelling off in the Iron Age), the reverse transformation was taking place in Iberia (Steppe 14.9% to 21.4%; EEF 64.5% to 59.4%). Thus, the proportions of the two ancestry types became more alike in the two widely separated regions (Patterson *et al.* 2022, supplementary table 7). The genetic shift in what is now England and South Wales occurred when a major intensification took place in exploitation of the landscape with a new tenure system for agro-pastoral production (Fig. 3.4). This would in turn have increased the demand for people to occupy and work the land. Both metals and people could therefore have been transferred from Iberia – and lands along the way from Iberia – to southern Britain during this phase (Cunliffe 2013, 251–288).

Thus, the re-organization of the Bronze Age landscape in England and Wales created labour gaps. Against the background of a general rise of social complexity during this period, an obvious possibility is that these gaps were filled by individuals at the bottom of the social pyramid, captives traded within the metal networks that linked northern Europe with Iberian elites. If the maritime mode of production theoretical model (see above, section 3.3) is applied, the analogy of the essential role of unfree labour during the Viking Age strongly supports such an explanation. Also consistent with this hypothesis are the oxygen and strontium isotope values of seven of 13 Late Bronze Age individuals from Cliffs End (Kent), which indicate that these were individuals that had migrated into southern England at a young age (Millard 2015): four show signatures compatible with southern Europe (possibly Iberia: two juvenile females who died at the age of 9–10 and 11–14, and two males who died as sub-adult and adult respectively). Added to these southern individuals, whose remains had been redeposited, there were two migrants from Scandinavia whose remains were *in situ* (one adult man and one young (10–14 year old) individual), and one from another region. The Cliffs End funerary contexts are significant, not only because there is an unusual proportion of migrants from Scandinavia and southern Europe but also because most of the individuals buried at the site (migrants and locals) are juvenile sub-adults and female, which mirrors ethnographic, ethnohistoric, historic and archaeological data that consistently show that women and children made up most captives in small-scale societies (Cameron 2016).

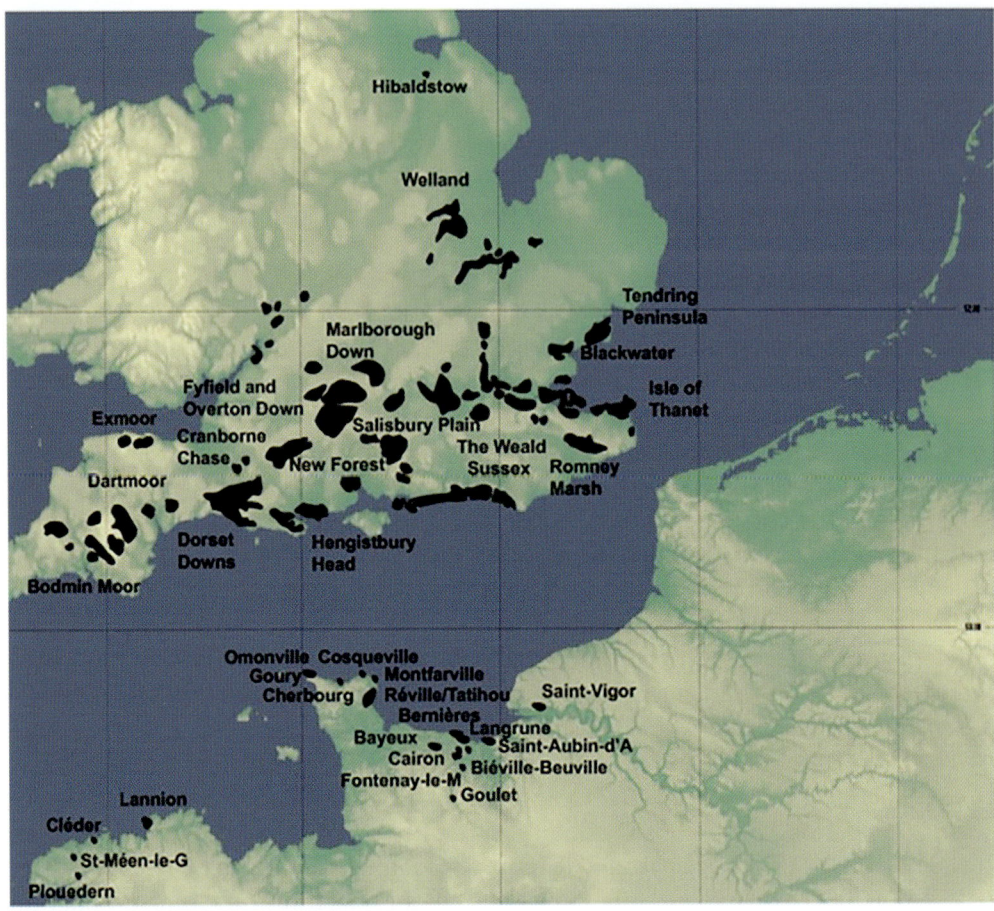

Figure 3.4. Distribution of late 2nd and early 1st millennium BC linear field systems in southern England and northern France. Image by Cyril Marcigny (Marcigny & Peake 2021).

The RAW Project focuses on metal exchange, shared rock art themes, and prehistoric links between Celtic and Germanic proto-languages and thus it is in an excellent position to explore key questions raised by new isotopic and archaeogenetic data through a multi-pronged investigation of archaeological and linguistic evidence. Did long-distance metal trade and cultural contacts drive the large-scale population movements of the later Bronze Age? Or was it more the reverse? Which was the cause and which the effect? Or were they all part of a single complex and integrated process? More specifically, did the rising demand for metal drive the demand for unfree labour? And/or were dependable long-distance trade relationships cemented with high-status marriage alliances and hostage exchanges? Any of these would have obvious linguistic implications – implications differing from those of incoming elites displacing earlier chiefdoms. In other words, a Bronze Age system, in which exogamous marriage prevailed and there was a rising demand for low-status labour, might involve numbers of people moving distances over successive generations. To the extent that foreign brides and/or foreign slaves were numerous as incoming groups, these might have had significant cumulative impact on the genetic make-up of the recipient populations. However, such newcomers are unlikely to have changed the dominant language of the established patrilocal chiefdoms to which they were delivered. A more complex model along these lines might better explain the Middle–Late Bronze Age north–south population exchange suggested by the study by Patterson *et al.* (2022), than a simple 'coming of the Celts' into what is now England from what is now France. While there is no obvious reason to expect speakers of Celtic, an Indo-European language, to be associated with elevated Neolithic farmer and lower steppe ancestry, there are reasons to expect such a genetic profile for low-status farm labour, vulnerable to enslavement and involuntary relocation as commodities. The challenge now is to interpret the explosively expanding evidence for genetic shifts with models that make best sense alongside what else we are discovering about the European Bronze Age, its social history, and the prehistory of its languages.

3.7. Metals and warrior iconography in Iberia and Scandinavia

The appearance of tin-bronze in northwest Iberia is attested in the Early Bronze Age (*c.* 2100 BC, evidence from the island of Guidoiro Areoso), although securely dated contexts first document tin-bronze smelting in the region from around 1850–1700 BC (Comendador Rey & Bettencourt 2011), while tin-bronze appears in El Argar (first also as imports) from 1900–1800 BC (Montero-Ruiz *et al.* 2019; 2022). However, tin-bronzes do not become generalized in Iberia until the end of the Middle Bronze Age and the beginning of the Late Bronze Age (see, for example, Soares *et al.* 2021), probably because of the uneven distribution of tin resources (mostly concentrated in northwest Iberia) and the unavailability of a constant, reliable tin supply across Iberia until those dates. This coincides with the collapse of El Argar in the southeast around 1550 BC due to environmental degradation (Lull *et al.* 2013) and the decentralization of metallurgical production (and generalization of tin-bronze) in the southeast.

Since the appearance of the first tin-bronzes in northwest Iberia in the Early Bronze Age (*c.* 2100 BC) until the generalization of tin-bronze in the southeast (*c.* 1500–1400 BC), there is the development of a series of partially overlapping, standardized traditions of Early and Middle Bronze Age stelae and statue-menhirs (unfolding from the Iberian northwest to the south of the peninsula, along the western periphery of the Meseta) (Fig. 3.5). These monuments were created by communities involved in the procurement and circulation of tin and copper (and possibly gold) (Díaz-Guardamino 2010, 125–423). The first traditions of stelae and statue-menhirs appear in the north, northwest, and southwest of Iberia (Fig. 3.5, B, C; Díaz-Guardamino 2014, fig. 4). Their distribution clearly correlates with some of the richest concentrations of tin and copper in the peninsula (Fig. 3.5; see also Rodríguez-Corral & Rodríguez-Rellán 2023).

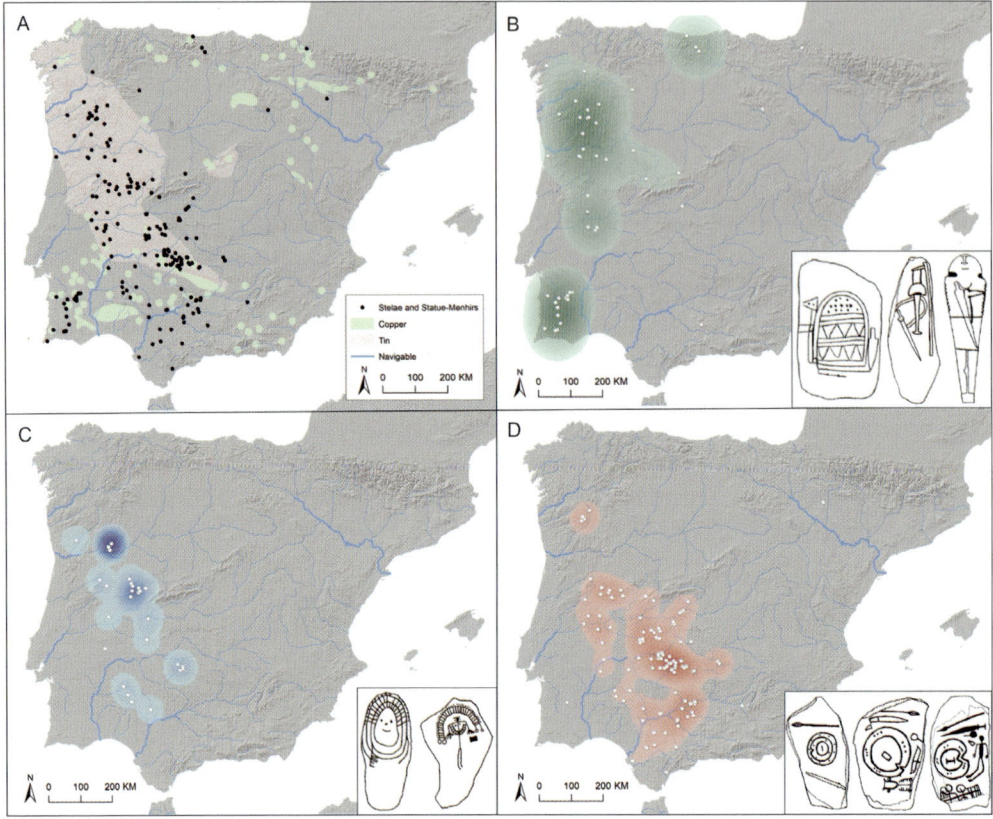

Figure 3.5. (A) Distribution of Early and Middle Bronze Age stelae and statue-menhirs, Late Bronze Age warrior stelae, and the distribution of major tin and copper deposits in Iberia; (B) Early and Middle Bronze Age stelae and statue-menhirs; (C) Bronze Age stelae with headdress and necklace; (D) Late Bronze Age warrior stelae. Maps by Marta Díaz-Guardamino.

And there is important evidence (although still restricted to a few sites) of the exploitation – and circulation in the case of the copper – of these resources in those regions (see Meunier *et al.* 2023 for MBA/LBA evidence of tin mining in north Portugal; Senna-Martínez *et al.* 2011 for evidence of processing in a domestic context; De Blas 2014 and De Blas & Suárez 2022 for EBA and MBA mining in Sierra del Áramo copper mines; and Ling *et al.* 2014 for MBA evidence of long-distance circulation of north Iberian copper).

From around 1450/1250 BC (i.e. end of the Middle and beginning of the Late Bronze Age in Atlantic Iberia; Díaz-Guardamino 2012, table 2), the warrior stelae tradition (focus of the RAW project) emerges along the western periphery of the Meseta, a huge region that spreads from the north of Portugal up to the middle/upper ridges of the Guadalquivir river in the south (Fig. 3.5, D; Díaz-Guardamino 2012, table 2;

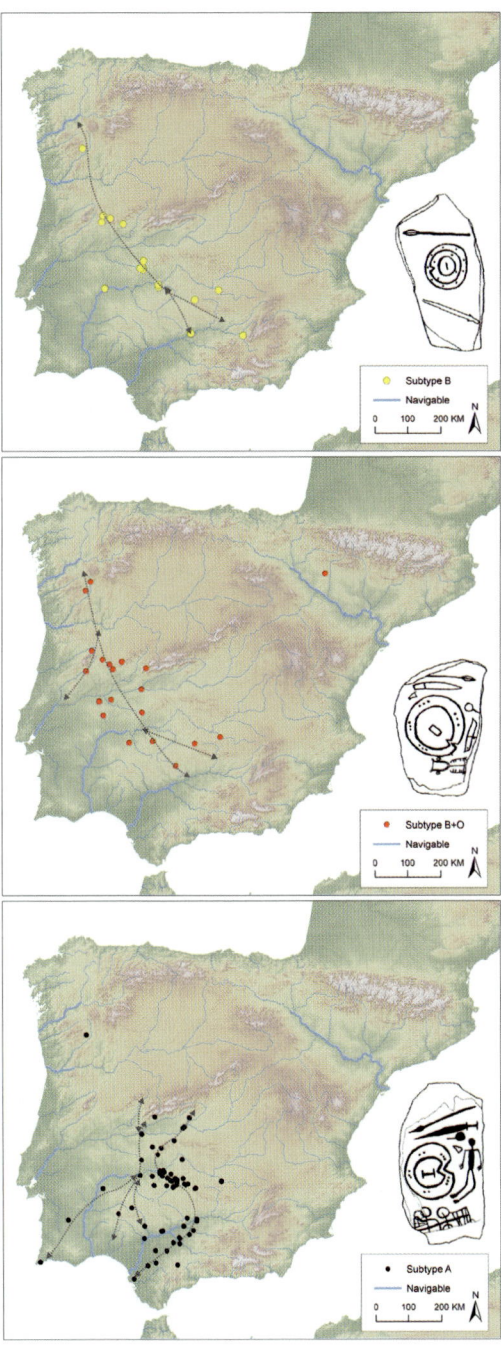

Figure 3.6. Warrior stelae distribution per subtype and connectivity routes. Maps by Marta Díaz-Guardamino.

2014, fig. 6). The earliest iconography of these stelae is very much restricted to warrior paraphernalia that was becoming widespread across Atlantic Europe: shield, sword and spear. This is a region with significant tin resources and, south of the Tagus River, also of copper ores with extensive evidence of prehistoric exploitation in some regions, such as Sierra Morena (Domergue 1987; Merideth 1998; Hunt Ortiz 2003; Arboledas et al. 2015).

We argue that the distribution of the warrior stelae dated to this earliest phase (Subtype B) could be seen as an expansion of interaction networks from northern Iberia towards the ore-bearing copper (and tin) districts (see also Senna-Martínez & Luís 2016; Fig. 3.6). These networks were composed of nodes controlled by local elites who were managing the demand, not only of copper but also of tin. Local elites took control of areas and communities of mining, as well as the trade routes for the circulation of metal. The distribution of warrior stelae, which materialized the appropriation by local elites of warrior ideals that were in circulation (and that had various sources of inspiration), clearly shows how this process unfolded geographically; they are located both in or close to the ore-bearing regions as well as connected to rivers and other inland routes linking these regions and the coast (Figs 3.6 & 4.1; Díaz-Guardamino et al. 2022; Rodríguez-Corral & Rodriguez-Rellán 2023). In a second phase (from c. 1325/1200 BC), stelae (Subtype B+O) incorporate in their iconography new elements from the Atlantic and Mediterranean worlds (e.g. helmets, mirrors, brooches, chariots), which were reaching Atlantic Iberia through the Rias Bajas in the northwest, the lower Duero, the Mondego and Tagus Rivers and inland routes reaching the Iberian southeast. Gradually from 1325/1200 BC, and more broadly from 1150 BC, the iconography and distribution of warrior stelae change as these networks change. Stelae (Subtype A) now also include human figures, some with horned helmets, weights, etc. and are found through the middle Tagus, middle Guadiana and the lower and middle Guadalquivir. In short, the distribution of the warrior stelae indicates the expansion and control of networks connecting to ore-bearing regions.

Turning to Scandinavia, both Bronze Age metal objects and rock art provide evidence for warfare and seafaring warriors, and imply an over-arching demand for tin-bronze. The region has one of Europe's largest concentration of weapons made of tin-bronze and the rock art panels are dominated by images of armed warriors in or near watercraft (Ling 2014; Horn 2018). Most of the rock art panels that include war-related scenes were created during two separate chronological phases during the Bronze Age, periods II (1500–1300 BC) and V (900–700 BC) (Ling & Cornell 2017). Interestingly, these phases correlate with the circulation of the greatest amounts of metals in Scandinavia, indicating that long-distance trade in metal and the depiction of warfare in rock art were supported by the same institutions. Calculations have estimated a yearly consumption of 1–2 tons of copper for southern Scandinavia (Kristiansen 2022). Recent projects based on state-of-the art provenance methods have provided new insights into the networks of metal exchange, leading to new theories about the role of Scandinavians in pan-European metal exchange systems. The interpretations of these datasets suggest a complex picture of various possible connections between Scandinavia and Europe in the Bronze Age (Ling *et al.* 2014; 2019; Melheim *et al.* 2018; Nørgaard *et al.* 2019; 2021). In addition to a steady supply of copper from Alpine, British, and Slovakian ores in the Early and Middle Bronze Age, Iberia seems to have become a major provider of copper to Scandinavia from about 1300 BC onwards. The aforementioned evidence of metals and rock art suggests that northern groups took part actively in the metal trade and that the transportation was mainly waterborne.

Thus, copper and tin came into high demand across Europe. This development in turn gave rise to the increased importance and value of controlling the sources of these metals as well as the routes and trading leading to these sources. The trans-regional barter in metals created radically longer and more complex commodity chains. Production and consumption bottlenecks emerged in the commodity chains that offered opportunities for control by emerging elites, who could dominate mining or transport of metals from the mining regions both on a local and on a trans-local scale. An integrated system of exchange stretched across Europe, which catalysed the comparative advantage of one region over another for 'exotic' products, such as metals and amber (Earle *et al.* 2015; Ling *et al.* 2017). Control of means of production and/or transport of metal for long-distance exchange became a fundamental feature for the development of ranked societies in Bronze Age Europe (Earle *et al.* 2015). With unfree labour working on farms in Scandinavia and possibly mines in Iberia, political leaders could mobilize, train, and support individuals from within the community, clearly warriors in the case of Scandinavia, to participate in long-distance exchange. Recognizing the probable essential factor of slavery or similar implies that these societies had a range of ranked social categories. This is why many researchers see Bronze Age communities as having 'chiefdom' organization. In the case of Atlantic Iberia, only clan-based or 'simple' chiefdoms have been recognized until now (see above) but these are also models in which political leaders can exert a significant degree of control over specific strategic resources, labour, and individuals.

Elites in Iberia and Scandinavia must have established political confederacies and networks between coerced/coercive or cooperative regional polities to develop and sustain the complicated enterprises of long-distance exchange. Confederacies are often considered as hierarchical formations of decentralized complexity (Kradin 2015; Earle 2017) but we argue that they could also include heterarchical formations in the case of Iberia. Such confederacies linked polities with distinct, but complementary, interests and relationships. Thus, it becomes increasingly clear that safe, regular journeys for trade purposes along networks of interlinked trails and spanning several hundred kilometres would have been impossible without the existence of polities and confederacies of polities. These were essential to secure safe passage, host-guest relationships for overnight accommodation or wintering and a range of other necessary services, guaranteed by bonds of reciprocity and mutual obligation (Kristiansen & Suchowska-Ducke 2015; cf. Anthony 2007).

3.8. Secret societies and warrior iconography

Metal production and consumption were central to the Bronze Age, with groups engaging in broad inter-regional communication networks (Earle *et al.* 2015). In this perspective, we have argued for the relevance of warrior institutions and warrior ideals, which can be found in both Scandinavia and Iberia throughout this period. This ideology and its institutions allowed both leaders, individuals and groups to expand their influence and become highly influential. Recently, the role of warriors and warfare in the Bronze Age economy has been re-addressed (Kristiansen & Suchowska-Ducke 2015; Horn 2018; Kristiansen 2018b). This work has recognized that, despite often being portrayed as the result of reciprocal exchange, foreign materials and goods in a region tell us little about how they ended up in the places where archaeologists discover them. In cross-cultural studies the phenomenon of negative reciprocal exchange has been conceptualized already by Marshal Sahlins (1972) as 'taking without giving' or 'acquisition' according to Needham (2000). While these are catch-all terms that contain many different processes, many of them are linked to violence or the threat of violence, such as ransoming captives, tribute extortion and, perhaps the most prevalent, raiding. Raiding warriors can easily turn into traders when they attempt to exchange raided goods for other required resources (Horn & Kristiansen 2018). Where they raided and with whom they traded may have depended on a sliding scale of whom they felt allegiance with (Hedeager 1994). That a boat crew included or consisted of warriors would of course also be important for protection of the cargo and the mariners themselves when they landed, for example, to rest or make repairs. While it is possible that social institutions like guest friendship (*xenia*), the concept known from ancient Greek literature, existed (Kaul 2017; 2022), this again depended on social distance. We cannot assume that a raider-trader party was friends with everyone. Who to trade with and from whom to expect guest friendship may have been regulated by a shared identity of boatsmen and/or warriors between several groups. These could have formed secret societies connected to boatbuilding and guilds that shared esoteric knowledge about boat construction techniques, navigation, sea routes, landing places, networks of allied communities, appropriate rituals, etc. (Ling *et al.* 2022a; cf. Hayden 2018).

We argue that the institutional idea of secret societies (Hayden 2018) is the concept that best connects the warrior ideals shown in rock art in Iberia and Scandinavia and their place in the Bronze Age system. It has recently been proposed that Scandinavian Bronze Age rock art was created by warrior-trader secret societies as part of the ritual practices associated with long-distance exchange activities conducted by initiates of these societies (Chacon *et al.* 2020). Interestingly, these warrior images are often accompanied by depictions of supernatural beings, large ships, the wearing of ritual gear especially with birdlike attributes, bi-horned helmets, masks, and other exotic items characteristic of secret societies. Members of secret societies typically acted to concentrate wealth and power in their own hands and sometimes directly controlled trade in all valuable goods. As such, they also typically dominated or controlled local, regional and trans-regional political organizations, such as confederacies. Thus, secret societies are found in societies that can produce substantial surpluses and wealth, as typified by Scandinavian Bronze Age societies and trans-egalitarian or chiefdom societies in general (Hayden 2018; Ling *et al.* 2021). Secret societies could also take the form of warrior organizations which studies of warfare sometimes refer to as *Gefolgschaft*, *Männerbünde*, or 'brotherhoods' (Raffield *et al.* 2016; Vandkilde 2006; Chacon *et al.* 2020). Such terms are also applicable to networks of leaders of small-scale polities, who had warrior aspirations and control over metal trade, such as in Atlantic Iberia. Secret societies are often found in association with institutions in charge of warfare or with boat guilds that undertake long-distance exchange or slave raiding but also with institutions in control of rituals and ritual activity such as making rock art (Hayden 2018; Chacon *et al.* 2020). We believe that the warriors and elites in Bronze Age Atlantic Iberia and Scandinavia were organized along similar lines and that the evidence of interaction between these regions reflects the presence of a trans-regional political elite network with exclusive access to resources and, advanced knowledge about long-distance exchange, religion, and warfare. In the last section of this book, we will return at greater length to the war-related rock art themes in Bronze Age Iberia and Scandinavia and their connection to the anthropologically recognized institution termed 'secret society'.

Chapter 4

Shared copper sources between Bronze Age communities in Atlantic Europe

The Iberian Peninsula is one of the most important regions of copper, lead, silver, and tin deposits in Europe and these have been exploited nearly continuously for the past 6000 years (Fig. 4.1).[1] The most important mines used in prehistoric times are in the south of the peninsula, in the regions of Badajoz, Huelva, Ciudad Real and Jaen, in the Ossa Morena Zone and the Iberian Massif (Central Iberian Zone) (Santos Zalduegui *et al.* 2004; Saez *et al.* 2021). These mineralizations were mostly formed in the Pre-Cambrian Age (*c.* 600–300 My) (Tornos & Chiarada 2004; Tornos *et al.* 2004; 2005). In the western part of the Iberian Peninsula there are numerous occurrences of tin ores that have been exploited since at least the Middle Bronze Age (Comendador Rey *et al.* 2017; Nessel *et al.* 2018; Meunier *et al.* 2023). Copper was also exploited in the Betic Cordilleras in the south and southeast, where the ores are of a younger age (Murillo-Barroso *et al.* 2019). The abundance of multi-metallic deposits in the Iberian Peninsula and their varied geochronology resulted in a very complicated pattern of lead isotope ratios characteristic of the copper minerals from different mining regions. Therefore, it is of utmost importance to date these mining activities and provide the isotope mapping of the occurrences that can be associated with the Bronze Age mining on archaeometallurgical evidence.

Archaeometallurgical research has been conducted in Spain since the last decades of the 20th century, including many archaeometallurgical surveys and at least a thousand elemental analyses of copper-based prehistoric artefacts (Rovira *et al.* 1997; and many others). The results of the earliest research combining the lead isotope data of ores and artefacts are available on the open access database OXALID (https://oxalid.arch.ox.ac.uk/; Stos-Gale *et al.* 1995; 1999; Stos-Gale 2001; Hunt Ortiz 2003) but, since then, a further several hundred lead isotope data plots of the copper-based artefacts have been published. Lead isotope analyses of the ores from Spain

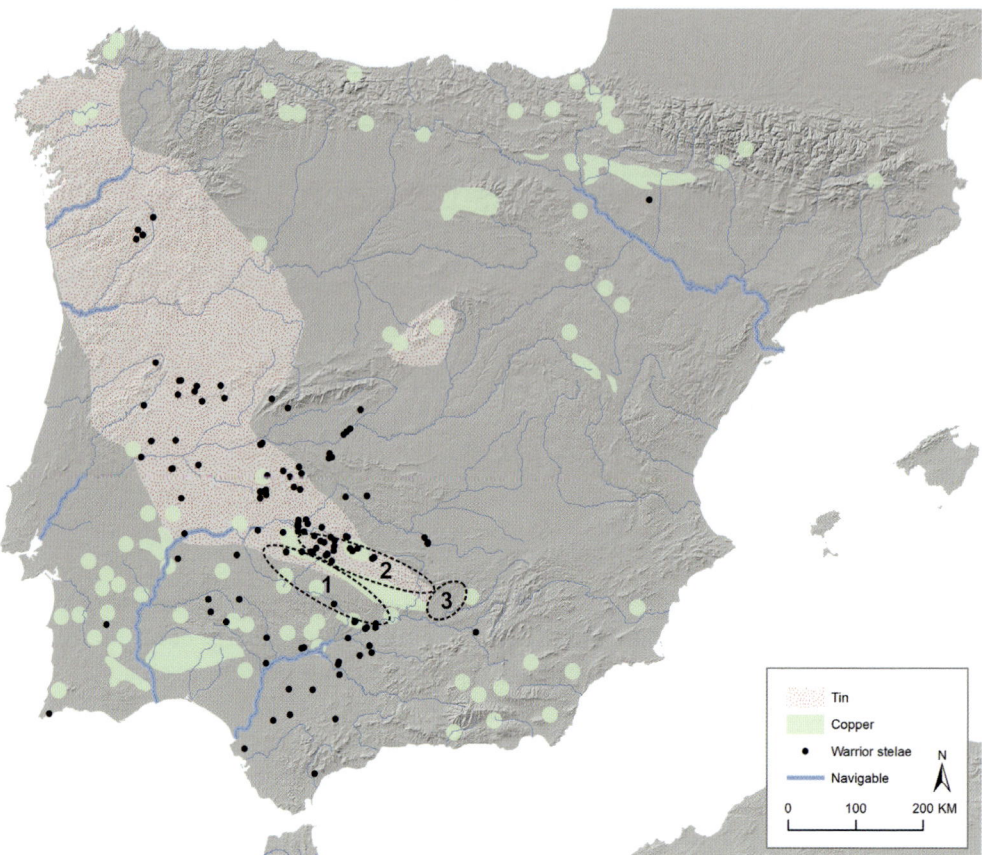

Figure 4.1. Copper and tin resources in the Iberian Peninsula with outline of mining regions mentioned in the text: (1) Los Pedroches; (2) the Alcudia valley; (3) Linares (upper Guadalquivir valley), and distribution of Late Bronze Age Iberian warrior stelae. Map by Marta Díaz-Guardamino.

and Portugal are published in numerous geological and archaeometallurgical papers. Currently a database called IBERLID, containing all published data, is maintained by faculty and researchers from the University of the Basque Country (UPV/EHU) and is available on the Internet (https://www.ehu.eus/ibercron/iberlid; García de Madinabeitia *et al.* 2021).

Post-Argaric Bronze Age copper-based artefacts (the database courtesy of Ignacio Montero-Ruiz) bear striking similarities in their chemical and lead isotope compositions to the bronzes found in Scandinavia dated to 1400/1300–500 BC (NBA II–VI) (Ling *et al.* 2014; 2019, Melheim *et al.* 2018; Fig. 4.2). Among these bronzes from Scandinavia there are many artefacts and casting debris dated to periods II–VI that have lead isotope compositions consistent with the copper ores from southern Iberia. However, the interpretation of these analytical data as evidence that these metals originated from the Iberian Peninsula is limited by the similarity of the range of lead isotope ratios of the copper and lead ores from southern Iberia with some of the ores

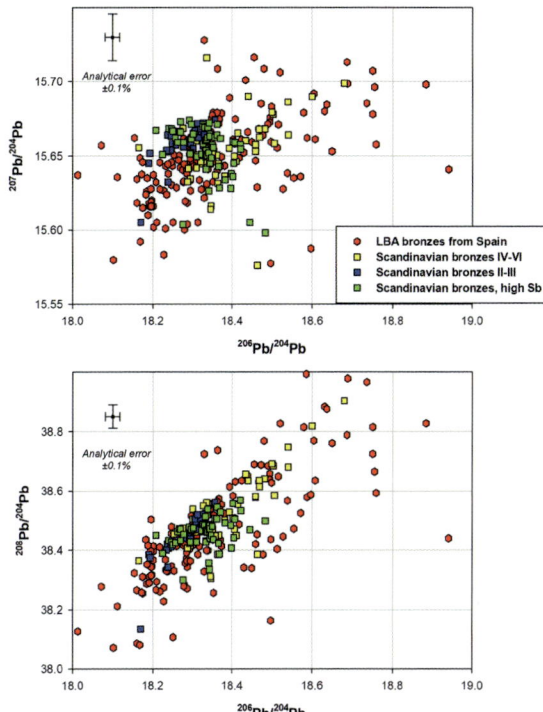

Figure 4.2. Lead isotope ratios for some of the LBA tin bronzes found in Scandinavia and the bronzes from Spain. Image by Zofia Stos-Gale.

from the Italian Alps, that were extensively exploited in the 2nd millennium BC (Artioli et al. 2020) and the ores from Sardinia (Stos-Gale et al. 1995 and the OXALID database). In 2014 we proposed the possibility of an Iberian origin for some of the copper used to manufacture bronzes found in Scandinavia (Ling et al. 2014). Since then, we analysed more bronzes and more data for the Iberian ores became available, and there is now also more archaeometallurgical evidence of the copper and tin smelting for the Middle and Late Bronze Age in Iberia (Comendador Rey et al. 2017; Rodriguez et al. 2019; Saez et al. 2021).

So far, we have analysed about 311 bronzes from Scandinavia dated to periods II–VI (1500–500 BC) (Table 4.1). Practically all of them contain a high percentage of tin (average about 9%) and varied impurities of other metals. Of particular interest is a group of 49 artefacts and casting debris dated to the period 1400/1300–500 BC that have lead isotope ratios consistent with the ores from southern Spain and contain antimony in concentrations of 0.5–3.5%, nickel between 0.5–2% and, in most cases lead, between 0.5–5% (Fig. 4.2). These 32 artefacts from Sweden, Denmark, and Norway and 17 casting debris mainly from casting workshops and scrap hoards in all three countries, all have lead isotope ratios indicating that copper ore was from the mineralizations of Pre-Cambrian origin (about 500 My). Copper mineralizations dated to this period are found in the Alps, on Sardinia, and on the Iberian Peninsula. However, the copper ores on Sardinia and in the Italian Alps used in the Late Bronze Age, are quite pure copper sulphides with no high antimony (Valera et al. 2005; Artioli et al. 2016; 2020). In the Swiss Alps the antimony and silver are associated with copper ores in the mineralization found in the region of le Valais but there is no Late Bronze Age evidence of mining there (Cattin et al. 2011) and their lead isotope characteristics are not similar to these artefacts from Scandinavia. Tetrahedrite ores (Fahlerz) in the Inn Valley in the Austrian Alps (Höppner et al. 2005) and in the Slovak Ore Mountains (Schreiner 2007) are much younger, so their lead isotope ratios are quite different. Spanish copper ores are mostly carbonites, oxides, and sulphides. There are no reports of considerable

Table 4.1. Estimation of the flow of metal from Iberia to Scandinavia (the uncertain chronology of an artefact is counted for the later period, rather than the earlier)

Period	Dates (BC)	Total analysed	Consistent with Iberia	%
II	1500–1300	111	20	18
III	1300–1100	70	24	34
IV	1100–900	48	36	75
V	900–700	48	34	70
VI	700–500	34	10	29
		311	124	Total c. 40%

quantities of copper tetrahedrite minerals with antimony. On the other hand, most copper mineralizations in the Iberian Peninsula are in a multi-metallic context, so copper minerals are often associated with other metals. Antimony sulphides (S_3Sb_2) are found in some quantity, among many other locations in the Alcudia Valley in Ciudad Real, in the batholiths of Los Pedroches in the province of Córdoba, and in Extremadura in the region of Badajoz-Cáceres (Galan Huertos & Mirete Mayo 1979, 204–205). On Figure 4.3 the lead isotope ratios of these high antimony bronzes are plotted together with the new data for the batholiths from the Los Pedroches and other occurrences along the Guadalquivir river valley (Saez et al. 2021). Unfortunately, there are no published combined data for lead isotope and chemical compositions for bronzes from Spain dated to 1500–500 BC with high antimony contents. However, Ignacio Montero shared with us his digital database of about 750 datasets for elemental analyses of the low-lead tin-bronzes dated to this period. In this group there are 130 copper-based artefacts with antimony content above 0.5%, average 1.5%, and average tin content of 13%.

The copper metallurgy in the Guadalquivir valley is well attested from the 3rd millennium BC to about 1800 BC (Nocete et al. 2010). Some 160 km north in the northern limits of the Guadiana river, there is the well-researched tin mining and bronze working site of San Cristobal, Logrosán, dated to the Late Bronze–Early Iron Age (Comendador Rey et al. 2017; Rodríguez et al. 2019). Some chemical and lead isotope data for the metallurgical debris from this site have been recently published

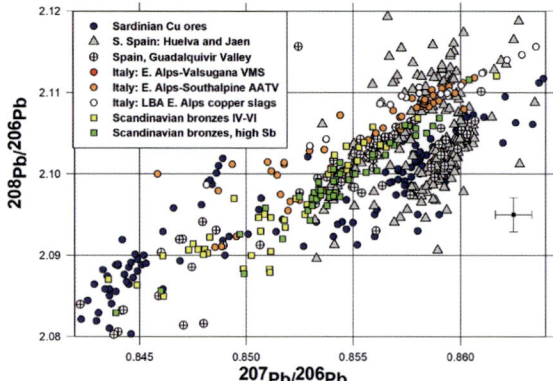

Figure 4.3. Plots of lead isotope ratios to 206Pb of the ores from the Italian Eastern Alps, Sardinia, and Iberia consistent with lead isotope ratios of ores in bronzes from Scandinavia and Spain. Image by Zofia Stos-Gale.

4. Shared copper sources between Bronze Age communities in Atlantic Europe

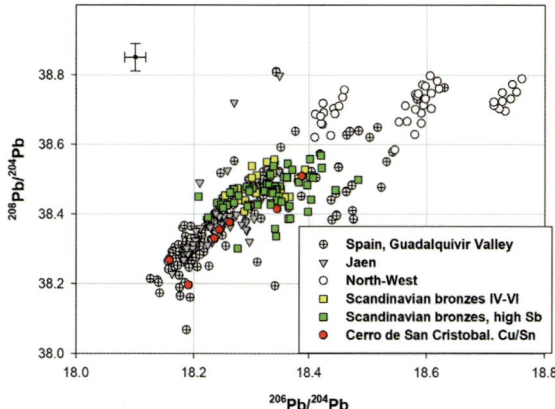

Figure 4.4. Comparison of the lead isotope ratios of bronzes found in Scandinavia with the ores from the Guadalquivir valley (Saez et al. 2021) and Jaén (IBERLID), and bronzes from the site of San Cristóbal, Logrosán, Badajoz, Spain. Image by Zofia Stos-Gale.

and they are consistent with the origin from the local ores (Hunt Ortiz 2019). At present, archaeometallurgical evidence for exploitation of copper and tin and production of bronze in the second half of the 2nd millennium BC from this region is scarce (e.g. Pavón et al. 2018) but new research is ongoing. On geochemical grounds it seems that the group of bronzes found in Scandinavia dated to the periods IV–VI and distinguished from others by a higher antimony content could have been smelted with copper imported from the mining districts of Los Pedroches

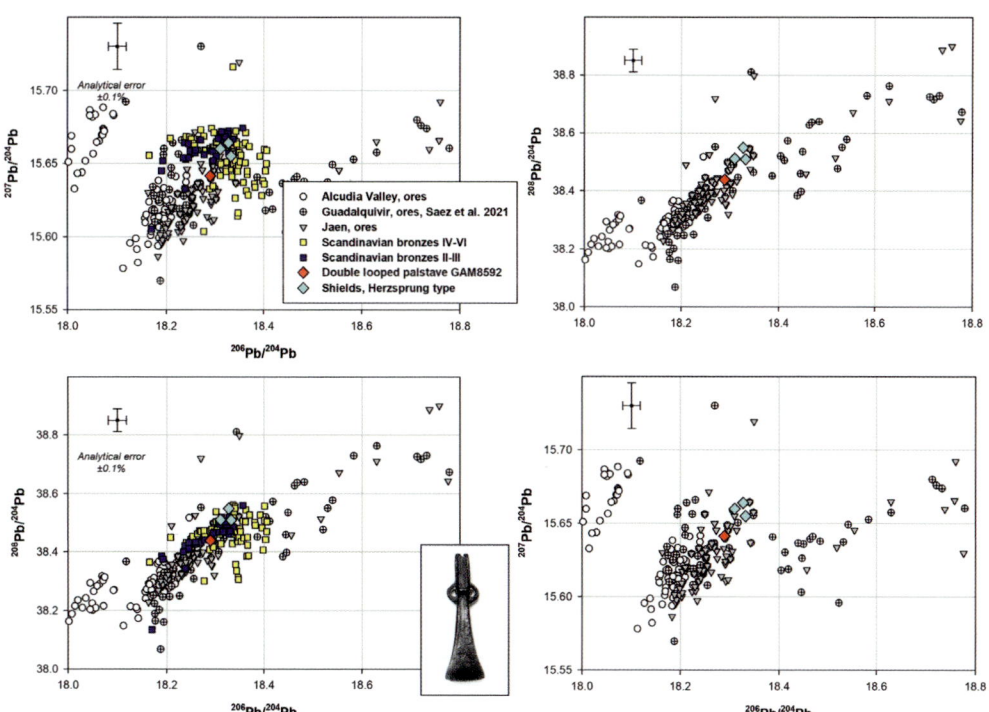

Figure 4.5. Lead isotope ratios of bronzes found in Sweden consistent with the ores from Jaén, Alcudia Valley, and Los Pedroches (Guadalquivir Valley), Spain. Image by Zofia Stos-Gale.

and La Alcudia, in the middle Guadiana, and the upper Guadalquivir (Linares) (Santos Zalduegui *et al.* 2004; Saez *et al.* 2021) and Huelva (OXALID) (Figs 4.4 & 4.5).

A group of bronzes found in Scandinavia dated to periods II–VI, some with lead content mostly around 1% but with contents of all other metals below 0.5% (apart from occasional higher nickel), are also isotopically consistent with the characteristics of the ores in the regions of Jaén, Los Pedroches and Alcudia Valley (Figs 4.1 & 4.5). This circumstance is moreover emphasized by the find of a typical Galician double-looped palstave from Lake Tåkern in Sweden (museum No. GAM 8592) dated to 1300–800 BC (Nordén 1925; cf. Monteagudo 1977, pls 86, 87, & 100) that has lead isotope ratios fully consistent with the copper ores from Jaén and isotopically falls together with this group of bronzes from Scandinavia (Fig. 4.5). The importance of this palstave and the similarities between Scandinavian and Iberian rock art (see Chaps 5 & 6) were already mentioned by Artur Nordén in the 1920s (Nordén 1925). Gordon Childe expressed interest in the palstave and inquired of the curator at the Museum of Gothenburg about the find circumstances, noting that similar examples had been found in southern England, western France, and Sardinia, and that the find from Tåkern (Fig. 4.6) constituted the most northern example of this type (Childe 1939). This particular axe, shows strong consistency in terms of lead isotopes and chemistry with other Iberian bronzes dated to the Late Bronze Age (1300–800 BC) that, in turn, match a group of the Scandinavian bronzes consistent chemically and isotopically with the ores in southern Iberia, in the valleys of the rivers Guadalquivir and Guadiana (see above), where copper was available and definitely smelted in the 3rd, 2nd, and 1st millennia BC, and further northwest where tin ores were exploited in the 2nd millennium (Meredith 2009; Comendador Rey *et al.* 2017). However, one of the most significant findings for this study was that three investigated U-notched shields of the Herzsprung type from Sweden (70: VG 11) had similar lead isotope and chemical fingerprints with copper ores from the Jaén-Linares area as shown on Figure 4.5 (see also Fig. 4.1; Ling *et al.* 2014). Following this hypothesis, it seems possible to estimate the flow of metal from this region to Scandinavia as outlined in Table 4.1.

The hypothesis of imported copper and also tin-copper alloys from western

Figure 4.6. Distribution of double-looped palstaves found in the late 1930s with the find from Tåkern indicated. Map by V. Gordon Childe (Childe 1939, fig. 1).

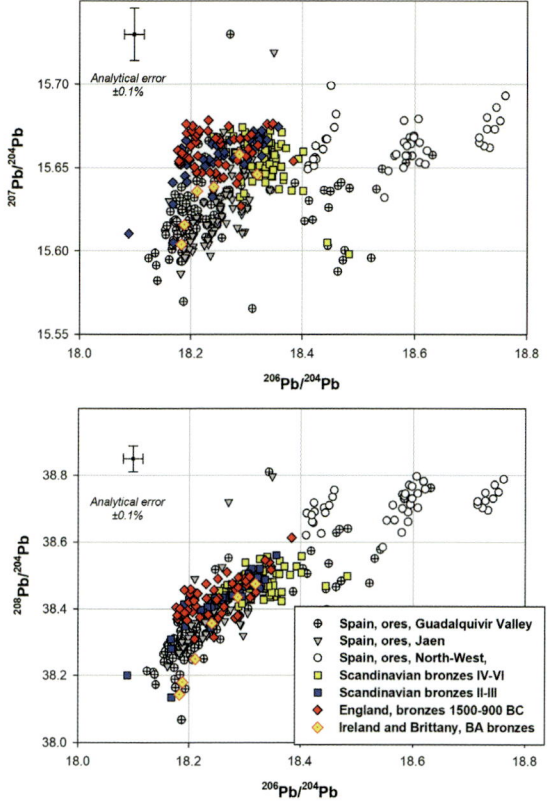

Figure 4.7. A comparative plot of three independent lead isotope ratios from Brittany, Britain, Ireland, and Scandinavia with data for copper ores from southern Spain. The consistency of these data sets indicates that the copper, or tin-bronze, were imported to northwest Europe from Iberia. Image by Zofia Stos-Gale.

Iberia to Scandinavia also gains support from the lead isotope analyses of the Middle–Late Bronze Age copper-based artefacts from England and Ireland (Rohl 1996: Rohl & Needham 1998 and OXALID; Berger et al. 2022). A number of bronzes from England, Wales, and Ireland dated to 1500–900 BC, including the finds from the sea in Salcombe Bay off the southwest coast of Devon (Wang et al. 2016, Berger et al. 2022), as well as some recently analysed bronzes from Ireland (O'Brien 2022) and a bronze spiral from Saint-Brieuc-des-Iffs (Rohl 1996) have lead isotope compositions identical with those discussed above of Scandinavian bronzes and ores from south Iberia (Fig. 4.7). This group includes the Middle Bronze Age palstaves from sites in the mouth of River Thames and Britain's south-east coast: Southall, Thorpe Hall and Langdon Bay. The MBA III (1300–1200 BC) bronzes from the Salcombe Bay hoard analyzed for their lead isotope compositions include two palstaves and two swords of Rosnöen type, and two blades. One of the swords and the blades contain 0.5–1% lead, which rather excludes the possibility of this metal originating from the chalcopyrite exploited in the Italian Alps but is in keeping with the ores from the Alcudia valley in south Iberia. Out of the 12 axes from the Langdon Bay hoard analyzed by Rohl, 10 seem consistent both with the ores from the Italian Alps and Iberia, while two are identical with some of the ores from the region of Jaén, east of Córdoba and south of the upper ridges of the Guadalquivir. Thus, the comparison of these two sets of data seem to prove that they represent a common mode of metal exchange between the Bronze Age communities in Atlantic Europe, from Iberia in the south to Scandinavia in the north.

Five copper-based palstaves dated to the 1400–1000 BC and two socketed axes dated to 900–800 BC from County Cork in Ireland that were analyzed by our project have also given an interesting insight into the Irish trade in metals (O'Brien 2022).

Three of these artefacts, palstaves UCC51 and UCC49, dated to 1400–1000 BC, and a socketed axe dated to 900–800 BC, have identical lead isotope ratios (within the analytical error) to two bronzes found in Scandinavia: a palstave from Thisted in Denmark (11: Ke 5078) dated to period II (1500–1300 BC) and a socketed axe from Gotland, Sweden (SHM96778) dated to period III 1300–1100 BC that have lead isotope ratios consistent with the ores from southern Iberia, indicating the same origin.

Of additional interest is the fragment of a bronze spiral published by Rohl (1996, no. 278 105) from Saint-Brieuc-des-Iffs in northwest France, dated to the end of the 2nd millennium BC. This has lead isotope ratios identical with the main group of all these bronzes consistent with the ores from the Guadalquivir valley (Saez *et al.* 2021).

In summary, it can be said that the artefacts described above, with lead isotope ratios and chemistry consistent with the Iberian ores and bronzes, have been found on sites from Iberia in the south to Ireland, England, and Wales in the west and Scandinavia in the north, strongly confirming that all of these Atlantic communities were involved in metal exchange during the Bronze Age.

Note

1 In this chapter, the denomination "Guadalquivir valley" follows Saez *et al.* (2021), who use it to designate an extensive geographical region covering Sierra Morena, the northern sector of the Guadalquivir River valley, which comprises different geotectonic units, including the South Portuguese Zone, the Ossa Morena Zone, and the Central Iberia Zone. When isotopic results permit, we identify the specific mining districts in southern Iberia that are isotopically consistent with bronzes found in Scandinavia. These are the mining regions of Los Pedroches, the Alcudia valley, and Linares.

Chapter 5

Iberian and Scandinavian Late Bronze Age rock art: Comparing landscape contexts

5.1. The distribution of Iberian stelae in relation to ore data and large rivers

It is commonly noted that Iberian warrior stelae were located nearby, or controlled access to, natural passageways (e.g. mountain passes, river fords) (Galán Domingo 1993). More recently, researchers have also emphasized the spatial association of warrior stelae with resources of economic, social, and (more generally) symbolic 'value', such as fertile land, good summer pastures, water, ores, or even places of special significance because they hold ancestral remains or special depositions (e.g. Celestino Pérez 2001a, 43–77; Enríquez-Navascués 2006; Díaz-Guardamino 2010, 327–450; Díaz-Guardamino et al. 2022). Even if there is general consensus about these patterns, there has been no formalized or systematic analysis of these questions with regard to warrior stelae until recently. There has been, nonetheless, some pioneering work exploring the spatial distribution of warrior stelae (Celestino Pérez & Salgado Carmona 2011; Costa Caramé 2013) or the relationship of Bronze Age statue-menhirs in northwest Iberia with mobility patterns through the landscape (Fábrega-Álvarez et al. 2011).

Recent and current research are addressing these questions from different spatial and archaeological perspectives at different scales of analysis and, while most research looking into macro-, meso-, and micro-scale trends is ongoing (e.g. Díaz-Guardamino et al. 2022; in prep.; Rodríguez-Corral & Rodríguez-Rellán 2023), there are some broad emerging trends that can be highlighted. At the scale of the Iberian Peninsula it is noteworthy that a large proportion (≥85%) of warrior stelae are located in interior regions (≥100 km away from the Late Bronze Age coastline) despite displaying an iconography that is redolent of long-distance connections with the Mediterranean and the Atlantic (Díaz-Guardamino et al. in prep.). It should be noted, however, that the communities making warrior stelae were well situated to access the Atlantic coast via the great Iberian rivers, such as the Duero, Tagus, Guadiana, and Guadalquivir. Importantly, the distribution of warrior stelae describes a broad axis that extends from the upper Támega river in south Galicia (northwest Iberia) through the upper Mondego, middle Tagus and Guadiana river basins down to the middle and lower Guadalquivir river basin, all along the western periphery of the Iberian Meseta, from northwest to south (Fig. 3.6, above). Of special importance is the fact that the Bronze Age communities that made the warrior stelae were distributed through areas that are rich in copper, tin, and gold, that also control passage through the main rivers along the periphery of the Meseta, connecting the Iberian northwest (and ultimately the Atlantic) with the Iberian southwest, south, and southeast (i.e. the Mediterranean; Fig. 3.6, above). This broad distribution is clearly related to connectivity, mobility, and access between/through the northwest and the southwest/south/southeast, as well as the Meseta and its periphery and the coastline, and it is not only seen during the Late Bronze Age (c. 1250–850 BC), as previous periods of the Bronze Age see similar – although more regionally bound – distributions of stelae and statue-menhirs (Díaz-Guardamino et al. in prep.; see for statue-menhirs in the northwest, Fábrega-Álvarez et al. 2011; Rodríguez-Corral & Rodríguez-Rellán 2023; Alentejan stelae in the southwest, Díaz-Guardamino 2010, 293–326). Recently, spatial analysis has confirmed a correlation between statue-menhirs and a subset of warrior stelae (the earlier types B and B+O, see Chapter 6) and tin-rich areas (Figs 3.6 & 4.1), suggesting that the communities related to these statue-menhirs and earlier warrior stelae controlled, to some degree, the access to tin (Rodríguez-Corral & Rodríguez-Rellán 2023) during an extended period of the Bronze Age.

These connectivity networks emerged and then further developed as a response to the stimulus of key resources that were especially abundant in these regions, such as ores (esp. copper, tin, gold but also silver) and fertile land for pasture and cultivation. If we consider the distribution of fertile land, the large majority of warrior stelae were found in areas with the highest values of ecological suitability index for wheat cultivation (8–10/10) (Díaz-Guardamino et al. in prep.). Also, most warrior stelae are found in areas that are particularly rich in tin and this is especially the case with the older types B and B+O (see Chapter 6; Rodríguez-Corral & Rodríguez-Rellán 2023), while approximately half are located in close proximity to areas that are rich in copper, where evidence for late prehistoric exploitation abounds (Figs 3.6. & 4.1; Díaz-Guardamino et al. in prep.).

But the role of warrior stelae communities expanded beyond the procurement of metals. As noted through their iconographies and spatial settings, these were communities closely involved in long-distance connections and their role as (re)distributors of metal resources must have been key. This means that they could have handled and redistributed not only the metals that they procured in their regions but also those originating in neighbouring regions such as Linares in the southeast, for example (Fig. 4.1). The role of these warrior stelae communities as necessary

5. Iberian and Scandinavian Late Bronze Age rock art

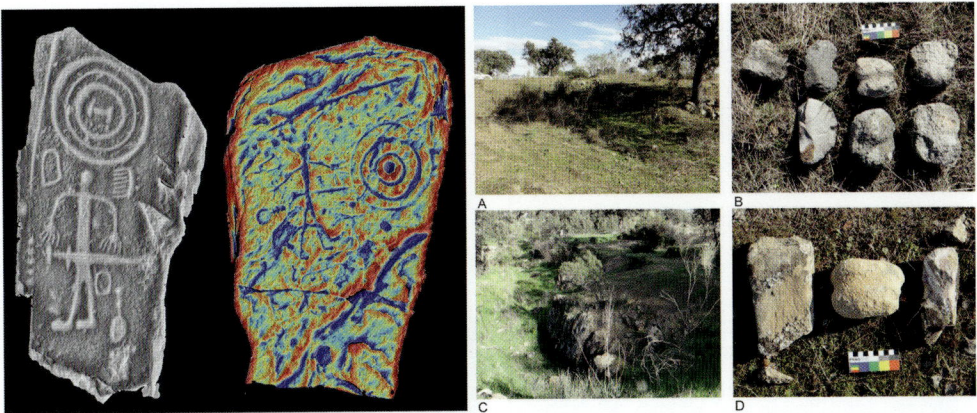

Figure 5.1. New visualizations of the stelae of Cabeza del Buey 3 (carved surface is 0.73 m) and Cabeza del Buey 5/El Palacio (1.15 m) (Archaeological Museum of Badajoz, Spain). Both examples were found in one of the core areas of warrior stelae distribution in La Serena, where the prehistoric mining sites of El Enjambradero (A, B) and Fuente La Zarza (C, D) are also located. Photos by Ignacio Pavón Soldevila. Visualizations created with TVT from laser scans.

intermediaries in the movement of metals between southeast and northwest Iberia, inner and coastal Iberia, and between Iberia and the broader Atlantic seems clear (Fig. 3.6, above).

Here, the analysis of the spatial distribution of the iconographic conventions of warrior stelae shows very clearly the outline of some of the key networks during different phases (Fig. 3.6) (this is work in progress so we will be able to say more very soon, Díaz-Guardamino *et al.* in prep.). Between 1425/1250 and 1150 BC (Fig. 3.6, above and centre) the main and most significant axis seems to have been the Meseta periphery between the upper Mondego and the middle Guadalquivir, with an important focus in the middle Tagus, outlined by the distribution of the earlier, more basic types of warrior stelae (Díaz-Guardamino 2010, 401–411, fig. 253) and whose significance has been demonstrated recently in relation to tin ores (Rodríguez-Corral & Rodríguez-Rellán 2023). These areas would be very well interlinked, also connecting the southeast with the northwest, while they would be closely connected to the coast and the interior. Between 1150 and 850 BC (Fig. 3.6, bottom) the networks change significantly, especially from 1050 BC, when the lower and middle Guadalquivir, the middle Guadiana – and particularly the Zújar region – and the middle/upper Tagus take a prominent role in the circulation of key stylistic traits (with the circulation of goods and people), a network that expands towards the lower Alentejo through inland routes (Díaz-Guardamino 2010, 401–411, fig. 253; Díaz-Guardamino *et al.* in prep.).

The Zújar basin was a corridor of intense cultural and economic activity. It is the locale with the highest density of warrior stelae and also connects metal-rich regions to one another as well as to the wider Atlantic and Mediterranean spheres through the middle–lower Guadalquivir and Guadiana. The prevalence of carved images of chariots,

Figure 5.2. Tumulus A covering urn cremation burials in the necropolis of Setefilla, Lora del Río, Seville, Spain, and the Setefilla warrior stela (1,7 m) (Archaeological Museum of Seville, Spain). Photos by Maria Eugenia Aubet and Marta Díaz-Guardamino. Visualization created with TVT from laser scan.

shields shaped as concentric circles, as well as other motifs reflecting widespread Bronze Age phenomena, is also consistent with a region vitally connected within a system of long-distance contacts (Díaz-Guardamino *et al.* 2022). There are other elements potentially to be seen as inspired, in part at least, by contacts specifically with Northwest Europe, such as the Sagrajaz-Berzocana torcs.

Research developed during the last couple of decades has produced a wealth of knowledge about the landscapes where warrior stelae are found. Nowadays we know that stelae were not placed in a void or in the middle of a landscape with no connection to permanent settlements, as had been proposed in the early 1990s (Ruiz-Gálvez & Galán 1991). Information gathered in the upper Mondego, middle Guadiana, and middle Guadalquivir regions clearly demonstrates that stelae were placed in the proximity (*c.* 0.5–2 km) of contemporary settlements, in some cases including mining sites with prehistoric activity in their surroundings. For example, evidence of prehistoric mining was documented at the sites of El Enjambradero (Fig. 5.1, A, B) and Fuente La Zarza (Fig. 5.1, C, D), located in one of the core areas of warrior stelae distribution, La Serena, Badajoz, Spain (Pavón *et al.* 2018). These mining sites are in the catchment area of various settlements and warrior stelae findspots, including those of the stelae of Cabeza del Buey 3, and Cabeza del Buey

5/El Palacio (Fig. 5.1). Sometimes stelae were placed in a clear attempt to mark the limits of the settlement area or everyday landscape, as it was documented in the cases of Mirasiviene and Setefilla in Lora del Río, Seville (Díaz-Guardamino *et al.* 2019). Furthermore, some recent research (in the Guadalquivir valley and the Huelva mountain range) has been able to demonstrate how some warrior stelae were originally placed within burial grounds, even complex funerary sites such as the one recently discovered at Las Capellanías in Cañaveral de León (Huelva), where three stelae have been found so far, two of them in context (Rivera Jiménez *et al.* 2021; García Sanjuán *et al.* in prep.).

The warrior stela of Setefilla (Lora del Río, Seville, Spain) (Fig. 5.2) (Díaz-Guardamino *et al.* 2015), for example, was found in the eponymous Late Bronze

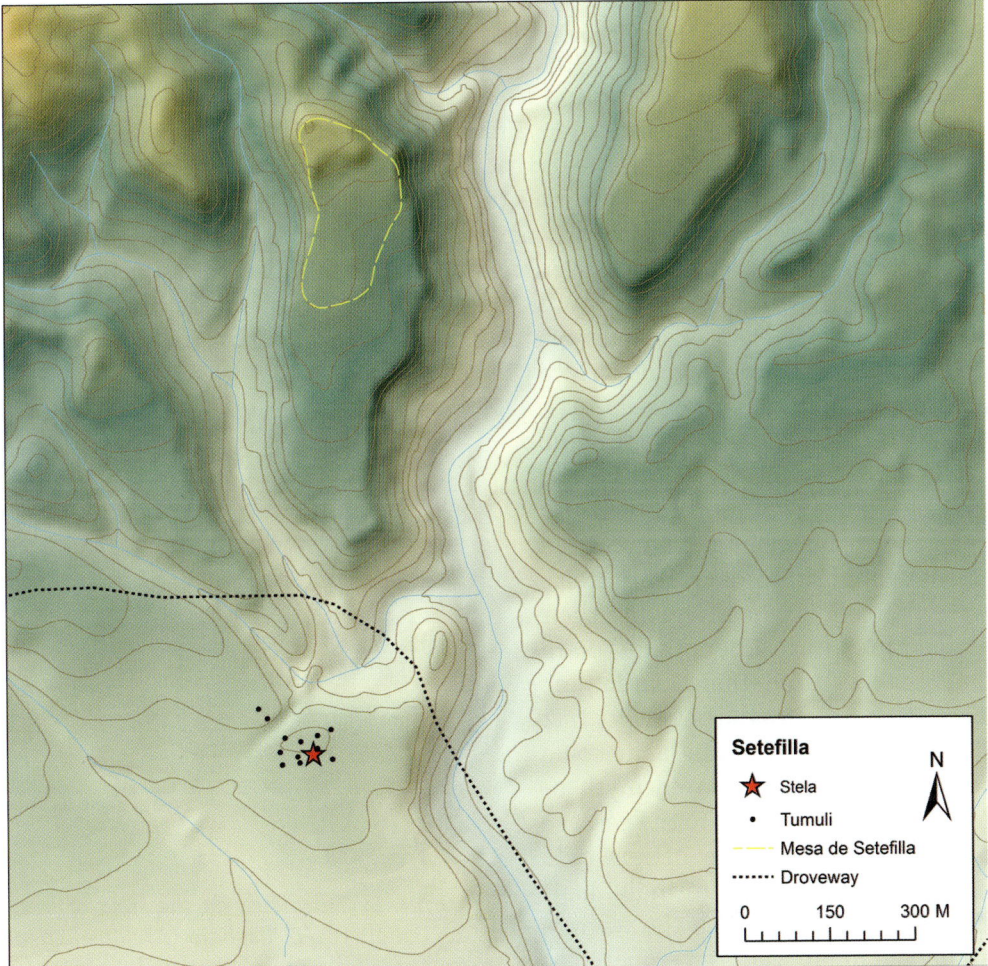

Figure 5.3. Location of the Setefilla stela findspot, within the necropolis of Setefilla, and its nearby settlement, the Mesa de Setefilla (Seville, Spain). Map by Marta Díaz-Guardamino.

Age/Iron Age necropolis, where there are several funerary graves, tumuli, and chambers. Tumulus A contained Late Bronze Age and Iron Age urn cremations and was located *c.* 75 m away from the stela findspot and there is a nearby settlement with metallurgical activity (Figs 5.2 & 5.3; Aubet 1975; 1978; Aubet *et al.* 1983; Díaz-Guardamino *et al.* 2019). These sites occupy relevant locations in the landscape, as they exert visual control over specific resources (e.g. fertile land, water) or articulate movement and connectivity across the landscape. The settlements and stelae findspots of Setefilla or Mirasiviene controlled strategic access routes to the Sierra Morena and its resources, including copper ores (Díaz-Guardamino *et al.* 2019). Another good example is the funerary complex of Las Capellanías in Cañaveral de León, which controls the main communication route between the lower Guadalquivir valley and the middle Guadiana through Sierra Morena (Rivera Jiménez *et al.* 2021; García Sanjuán *et al.* in prep.).

Warrior stelae are relatively small monuments. Most of them are around 80–120 cm in height. To be seen in the landscape they would need to have been placed in areas that were cleared and maintained to be visible and accessible. Recent research, as mentioned above, reveals that at least some stelae were placed on sites of special significance, places that were recurrently visited and maintained. These could be funerary complexes (as in Cañaveral de León and Setefilla) or sacred sites where special rituals and offerings were conducted (as possibly in Mirasiviene). Fresh investigations conducted by the RAW team and others on the manufacture of warrior stelae also reveals that the making of stelae could be, for the most part, improvised and that it most probably took place in loco (Díaz-Guardamino *et al.* 2019; Gutiérrez *et al.* 2020; Díaz-Guardamino 2023; García Sanjuán *et al.* in prep., but see Araque *et al.* 2023). It has also been shown that the techniques used in the manufacture of warrior stelae were pretty idiosyncratic while their iconography was rather standardised and broadly shared (Díaz-Guardamino 2023). This indicates the possibility that this warrior-related iconography could represent a broadly shared myth or heroic narrative related to the passage of the warrior to the otherworld and that prominent elite individuals that were identified with the warrior archetype in life were remembered as ancestral heroic warrior figures within this broadly shared (but at the same

Figure 5.4. Lyre depicted on the stela of Jerez de los Caballeros/El Carbajo (Archaeological Museum of Badajoz, Spain). Photo and visualization created with TVT from laser scans by Marta Díaz-Guardamino.

time idiosyncratic or locally interpreted) mythological framework expressed in a local traditional format (i.e. rock art carved on stone stelae) (Díaz-Guardamino et al. 2022). It is relevant to note that clearly represented (and often large) lyres are one of the motifs present on stelae (albeit in small numbers, i.e. nine of almost 150 warrior stelae registered until now) (Mederos Martín 1996; Santos Cancelas 2015; Berrocal Rangel et al. 2023; Fig. 5.4). This strongly suggests that epic poets were recognized as having a central role in the system of meaning represented in the warrior stelae. It might be interesting at some point to identify how many of the objects represented are mentioned by Homer (see also Harrison 2004, 114–117). Within this context it is relevant to note that warrior stelae-making was, most probably, part of mortuary rituals (including storytelling) and not an activity that took place outside of this realm. This is indicated not only by rock art carving tools that are found in stelae findspots (e.g. Mirasiviene, Cañaveral de León) but also the appearance of many warrior stelae that seem to have been manufactured quite quickly and recarved very soon after initial manufacture (e.g. Díaz-Guardamino 2020; 2023).

5.2. Distribution of Scandinavian rock art in the landscape

Since the Bronze Age, the landscape of Scandinavia has undergone significant shore displacement which affected some rock art regions strongly, like Bohuslän in western Sweden, Uppland close to Stockholm, or Östfold in Norway (Ling 2012; 2014). This means that most of the figurative rock art was placed at or close to the seashore in the Bronze Age, in shallow bays or lagoons and on small islands and isthmuses. This can still be seen in, for example, Högsbyn (RAÄ Tisselskog 15:1; Fig. 5.5, a), which is located inland on small peninsulas and inlets right next to the water of a lake. Being inland, this region's location on the shore was not affected by the land uplift. There are locales within close proximity to the sea in Bohuslän that can still convey the closeness of rock art to fjords, for example, a single cupmark in Skredsvik (RAÄ 492; Fig. 5.5, b) or in Rixö (RAÄ Brastad 123:1; Fig. 5.5, c), which was a tiny island during the Bronze Age. Many other places are seemingly unrelated to the shore like the famous Vitlycke (RAÄ Tanum 1:1; Fig. 5.5, d), where the shoreline during the Early Bronze Age would have reached right up to the modern walkway, and the valley behind was a large bay adjacent to many other important rock art panels.

In contrast to the warrior stelae in Iberia, rock art in Scandinavia was not made in inland regions with the highest ecological compatibility rating for wheat cultivation or in areas with prehistoric mining evidence. Instead, it appears that areas with rock art were connected by a shared proximity to the seascape, in places which would have been considerably more accessible by water during the Bronze Age (Skoglund 2016; Nimura et al. 2020). Thus, it is hardly surprising that water symbolism is a recurrent theme in Scandinavian rock art (Coles 2005; Goldhahn & Ling 2013). This is true also for rock art on higher ground, located close to lakes, bogs, springs, streams, rivers, and creeks. Furthermore, rock art sites located on higher ground are sited close to

Figure 5.5. Location of Scandinavian rock art close to bodies of water: (a) Högsbyn (RAÄ Tisselskog 15:1); (b) Skredsvik (RAÄ 492); (c) Rixö (RAÄ Brastad 123:1); (d) Vitlycke (RAÄ Tanum 1:1), where the shoreline during the Early Bronze Age would have reached right up to the modern walkway. Photos by Catarina Bertilsson (a), Andreas Toreld (b, c), and Lars Noord (d).

old roads, trails or natural passages in the landscape. In this respect, we identify strong links with Iberian stelae that were often found close to water or old roads or pathways in the landscape (Galán Domingo 1993; Díaz-Guardamino 2010; see also Díaz-Guardamino *et al.* 2020; 2022; Rivera Jiménez *et al.* 2021 for specific case studies), in addition to Bronze Age rock art from northern Portugal and Galicia with boat iconography (e.g. the sites of Penedo do Muro and Santo Adrião, studied by Comendador Rey & González Insua (2017) and Santos-Estévez & Bettencourt (2017), respectively) (Fig. 6.1).

Most rock art panels were made on low-lying horizontal rock outcrops forming the ground surface. They were not placed vertically, like the stelae, and would have been almost invisible in the landscape unless the viewer were standing directly

Figure 5.6. Rock reliefs at (a) Finntorp (RAÄ Tanum 184:1) and (b) Lövåsen (RAÄ Tanum 321:1). Photos by Christian Horn.

Figure 5.7. Funerary cairn overlying the rock art panel of Törnfall 107. Image by BOTARK.

upon them (Ling 2014). This indicates that they were meant to be viewed by a local community or people who knew exactly where the sites were located and that their symbolic content was linked to the esoterica known to those visiting the site. In this context, it has been proposed that Scandinavian Bronze Age rock art may have formed part of a maritime warrior's esoteric ritual of warriors associated with boats (Ling *et al.* 2022a). The panels have often been carefully chosen for their quality suitable for carving though some rock art was made on panels with rougher surfaces. Another point of interest is that water runs over the panels and that the carvers deliberately made the rock art on surfaces with regularly flowing water (Fig. 5.6; Horn *et al.* 2022). At various sites of differing sizes, slope angles, and altitudes, ship images were placed right in the waterflow or at its border, giving the impression that they were sailing through fjords or on rivers. The intended outcome was perhaps that the flowing water, which also caused reflections, created the impression that the ship images were in motion (Bradley *et al.* 2002; Nordenborg 2004; Horn *et al.* 2022). A good example is located in Finntorp (RAÄ Tanum 184:1; Fig. 5.6, a), where two boats were carved directly on a channel filled with rainwater transforming it into a miniature landscape scene. In Lövåsen (RAÄ Tanum 321:1; Fig. 5.6, b), water streams over two small boats out of an overflowing puddle. There are also several rock art locations in southern Scandinavia where features on the rock panel, such as cracks and exfoliations, seem to have been deliberately used to accentuate the articulation of the rock art composition (Goldhahn & Ling 2013).

Figure 5.8. Shoreline location of the large burial at Kivik (a) with a stone cist constructed of slabs decorated with carvings (b, c). Photos by Jan Norrman (a) and Catarina Bertilsson (b, c).

Many rock art sites seem implicitly or explicitly to illustrate the landscape or actions connected with the landscape. In general, panels dominated by ship images were made close to the shore. Also, human figures, animals, and ship images in a broad sense appear to have been represented and adjusted after certain landscape concepts and ideals (Ling 2014). For example, the largest human images were often made on higher ground, such as in Bohuslän, Uppland, and Scania, where we find human depictions that are abnormally large relative to the ship depictions on the

Figure 5.9. Location of rock art in Frännarp (RAÄ Gryyt 1:1) (indicated in blue) and a cairn on the hilltop close to the lake (red). Inset: interpretation of the carved chariots acquired from digital TVT visualization by Christian Horn.

same panels. On lower ground, human representations seem more-or-less to have been adjusted proportionally to ship images (Ling 2014).

There is also a significant link between Bronze Age rock art and burials. Grave monuments such as stone settings, barrows, cairns, stelae, or cairns of fire cracked stones dated to the Bronze Age constitute the prehistoric remains with the closest spatial relation to the rock art (Goldhahn 2013; Goldhahn & Ling 2013). In contrast, Bronze Age settlements and settlement finds are generally located at some distance from areas with dense clusters of figurative rock art sites, usually 500–1000 m. In fact, graves are the cultural relics with the closest spatial link to rock art in the landscape, much closer than settlements (Ling 2014). This bears a striking resemblance to the pattern emerging for Iberian warrior stelae. Rock art has been discovered in or beneath graves on several occasions in Sweden and many rock carvings may be seen at or near cemeteries (Fig. 5.7). Moreover, there are quite a few examined graves from the Bronze Age that contain figurative rock carvings; cup marks being especially common. Some of the graves with figurative rock carvings are remarkably extensive and spectacular, such as the cairn in Kivik (Fig. 5.8) or the barrow in Sagaholm (Goldhahn 2013).

The figurative elements from Scandinavia that show the closest similarities with Iberian rock art, such as warriors, chariots, weapons, or mirrors, are also in general connected either to water or graves. For instance, the most prominent site with chariots, located in the inland area in Frännarp Scania (Fig. 5.9), is located close to a small lake that in turn is connected to a system of waterways, leading all the way to the Baltic sea. Chariots are also depicted in the Kivik grave (Fig. 5.8) and on two lose boulders, one from Villfara in Scania and another from Lofta in Småland. Both figurative boulders were most likely associated with a burial (Goldhahn 2013).

Chapter 6

Comparing Scandinavian and Iberian warrior iconography[1]

There has been a renewed interest in studying the similarities in rock art iconography between Scandinavia and Iberia due to several significant developments not only in the dating and 3D documentation of rock art but also in the context of new evidence for long-distance exchange, stressed by the results of recent analyses of copper and amber and advances in the field of linguistics (Koch 2013a; 2020; Ling et al. 2014; Ling & Koch 2018; Murillo-Barroso et al. 2018; Díaz-Guardamino et al. 2022). As a result of these studies, new significant parallels have been observed regarding the rock art iconography in Scandinavia and Iberia relating to motifs, such as chariots, warriors, weapons, mirrors, and style, such as the poses and gestures of human figures (Ling & Koch 2018; Koch 2020; Díaz-Guardamino et al. 2022). Some of these aspects are highlighted in the recent comparative study by Vandkilde et al. (2021). Of special interest is the account of the recent radiocarbon dates of the organic material connected to one of the Viksø helmets which show that the helmets probably date to a late phase of Nordic Bronze Age (NBA) IV or early NBA V transition to period V (MAMS-42233: 2791±21 BP, 1006–857 cal BC (with 95.4% probability) and 976–907 cal BC (with 68.2% probability)) (Vandkilde et al. 2021, 136). This result justifies a somewhat earlier date for the bi-horned warriors on the rocks in Scandinavia that traditionally had been dated to NBA V proper, that is 800 BC (Ling 2014). An important theory put forward in this paper is that the iconographic similarities between the representations of bi-horned warriors in Sardinia, Scandinavia, and Iberia belong to the same phase about 1000–750 BC, and that this indicates direct contact.

> Three possible explanatory scenarios for the horns can be outlined: firstly, that they arose from autonomous local processes; secondly, that they were products of multidirectional culture flows in a phase of globalisation; and thirdly, that they were the product of directional movements of goods and ideas as they were strategically appropriated by local culture and

society. In the first two scenarios, the similarities between the figures are random and not directly connected, while in the third scenario, the interconnections are concrete and the result of planned movements. (Vandkilde *et al.* 2021, 132)

While Vandkilde and her colleagues (2021) published a highly important contribution, some aspects require revision. For instance, there are no depictions of Herzsprung shields currently known and there are *c.* 88 (not 39) bi-horned warriors depicted in Tanum. Furthermore, the warriors are sometimes depicted with clothing and/or armour, similar to the Iberian ones (see Bergerbrandt & Wessman 2018).

Even though there are several figural parallels between rock art in Scandinavia and Iberia from this period (1350–800 BC), there are also many differences that must be highlighted. For instance, most of the Iberian warrior-related iconography appears less dynamic in its presentation compared to the Scandinavian in which action is more vividly conveyed. For example, there are no images of actual conflict represented in Iberian iconography and some of the warriors appear to have been depicted in a funeral situation. There is also a disparity in maritime iconography. Boats, or rather, war canoes are abundant in Scandinavian rock art but absent from the Iberian warrior stelae, although there are northwest Iberian bedrock panels that

Figure 6.1. The site of Penedo do Muro 2 (Ourense, northwest Iberia) (A) with depictions of motifs similar to boats depicted on period V razors (B) and rock art sites in Scandinavia. (A) Photo by Beatriz Comendador Rey. Visualization from laser scan with TVT. (B) Image by Fleming Kaul.

include boat depictions that are very similar to the Scandinavian ones, such as Penedo do Muro 2 in the upper Támega valley (Fig. 6.1; Bettencourt 2017; Comendador Rey & González Insua 2017; Santos-Estévez & Bettencourt 2017). Most warrior iconography in Iberia is known from stelae or free-standing stone slabs while, in Scandinavia, open-air panels predominate. However, it should be noted that warrior iconography on bedrock panels does occur in Iberia (e.g. Díaz-Guardamino et al. 2022). Also, stone slabs with warrior iconography are recorded in Scandinavia, especially in funerary contexts dated to the Bronze Age, at sites such as Kivik, Sagaholm, Hagbard, Sparlösa, and Klinta, of which some have been proposed as parallels for the Iberian stelae. Some of the Scandinavian 'stelae' that are very well known, such as those at Kivik (Goldhahn 2013), show chariots and warriors, as well as many other features. The similarities and differences between Iberian and Scandinavian warrior imagery, as well as new discoveries, will be discussed in the following sections.

6.1. Rock art and warriors: a long tradition

In both Iberia and Scandinavia, the typical Late Bronze Age warrior iconography finds precedents in earlier traditions which show some general similarities. Before swords were introduced, halberds were used in both regions, in Iberia in combination with daggers. Halberds are dagger-like blades that are hafted perpendicular to a long handle and they were the specialized weapons in Europe during the 3rd millennium BC and earlier (Horn 2014). These halberds also occur on stelae and open-air rock art panels in north, northwest, and southwestern Iberia. They were engraved in larger numbers, as individual weapons or in combination with daggers, on the bedrock in northwest Iberia (Brandherm 2003; Díaz-Guardamino 2010, 150–161, fig. 105; Fábregas & Rodríguez-Rellán 2015; Santos-Estévez 2021). Halberds were also carved in combination with other items (added to daggers, other weapons, such as swords or axes, tools, or elements protecting the body) as part of warrior panoplies on anthropomorphic statue-menhirs and stelae dated to the Early and/or Middle Bronze Age (c. 2200–1800/1500–1250 BC) (Fig. 6.2). More than 40 halberd depictions cluster on bedrock panels in northwest Iberia, while there are ten halberd depictions on stelae and statue-menhirs (Díaz-Guardamino 2010, 301–305). The types of halberds depicted on Iberian rock art, statue-menhirs, and stelae reproduce metallic correlates (made in arsenical copper) found in Iberia (usually as part of hoards or in funerary contexts) and which are normally classified as Atlantic (Carrapatas) or Mediterranean (Montejícar) types (Senna-Martínez 1994; Delibes de Castro et al. 1999; Díaz-Guardamino 2010, 159–160, fig. 105).

In Scandinavia the numbers are considerably lower with only three halberd depictions identified so far. There are two potential halberds depicted as individual weapons in Järrestad (Scania), that were later transformed into the stem and prow of a boat (Burenhult 1980). However, these cases are perhaps much older because they

Figure 6.2. Early Bronze Age halberds made from arsenical copper from the 'Carrapatas' hoard and a representation of a halberd on the stela of Longroiva (2.40 m), Mêda, Guarda (Portugal). Both were found in the district of Guarda, north Portugal. Photos by Maria Jesus Sanches (2019, fig. 9, after Silva 2011) and Mario Reis.

resemble stone halberds discovered in Funnel Beaker contexts of the 4th and very early 3rd millennium BC (Horn 2021). A less ambiguous halberd depiction has been discovered on the northern part of Sweden's west coast in Kville (157:1, Bohuslän) on a panel with many Early Bronze Age boats and spear fighters (Fig. 6.3). This halberd has a triangular blade and only the beginning of a handle. It resembles the halberds from the Unetice region which have a metal shaft head either cast on to a blade or the blade and shaft-head are cast as one (Drescher 1958; Rassmann 2010; Horn 2014). These halberds correspond with those found in the hoards from Melz, Bresinchen (both Germany), Prague (Czech Republic), and the grave from Łeki Małe (Poland) dated to the end of the 3rd and the beginning of the 2nd millennium BC (Rassmann & Görsdorf 1993; Müller 1999; Moucha 2005; Horn 2014). In Iberia, the tradition of carving weapons into the bedrock becomes less frequent during the Middle Bronze Age whereas weapons (i.e. later types of halberds, swords, and daggers) continued to be depicted on stelae and statue-menhirs (Díaz-Guardamino 2010, 129–224, 293–325; 2021). In Scandinavia, particularly in Sweden, the tradition of engraving

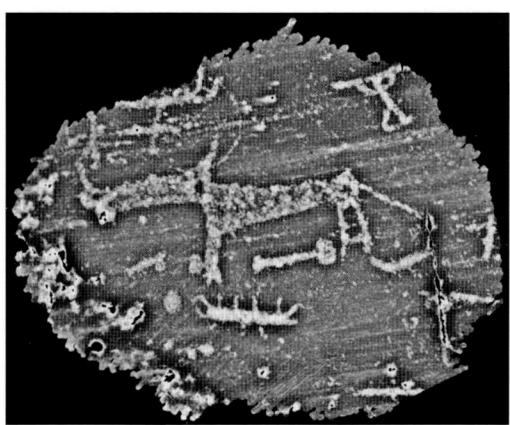

Figure 6.3. A halberd depicted on the panel in Kville (157:1, Bohuslän) with Early Bronze Age boats and spear fighters. Visualization made from laser scans using TVT.

individual weapons like swords, axes, and spears also continues, and even increases in number in some regions, for example in Norrköping, Uppland, Scania, and Tanum. The depiction of individual items of metalwork in both Iberia and Scandinavia is tied into a wider European trend that can also be seen in Britain with axe petroglyphs and the halberd pillar of the cist of the Ri Cruin cairn in Kilmartin, Scotland. The pillar itself has been described as a palimpsest of added engravings (Needham & Cowie 2012) which suggests the possibility that it could have been re-used to mark the entrance to the cist.

The use of stelae on burial sites including later re-use has also been evidenced for the Iberian stelae of the Middle and Late Bronze Age (Díaz-Guardamino 2014; Díaz-Guardamino et al. 2022; García Sanjuán et al. in prep.). For instance, the Middle Bronze Age (from c. 1800 BC) stelae from across southern Portugal (the so-called 'Alentejan' stelae), depicting warrior paraphernalia such as swords, halberds, axes, tools, or elements interpreted as attributes of power (the 'anchorform'), are found repeatedly within the confines of funerary contexts (i.e. cist necropolises). While there is some contextual uncertainty about their specific use within these funerary complexes, as none of them was found *in situ* (and some were found in Iron Age necropolises where they appear to have been re-used as cap stones for cists), a few examples show signs that they were designed to mark specific locations within Bronze Age necropolises. This is the case of Alfarrobeira (Fig. 6.4), where a probable Neolithic menhir was re-used in the Middle Bronze Age when it received carvings of a sword [rapier?], a halberd, and an 'anchorform', and was probably – as indicated by the archaeological evidence unearthed in excavations directed by M.V. Gomes– placed on one end of a small cist located in the periphery of the Middle Bronze Age necropolis (Gomes 1994; Díaz-Guardamino 2010, 293–325; 2014).

Previously, the contextual evidence for other Middle and Late Bronze Age stela traditions in Iberia has been largely circumstantial or based on oral reports. More recent reviews of the evidence have established that some anthropomorphic stelae depicting complex headdresses and necklaces dated to the Bronze Age (perhaps Middle/Late) were found within or nearby cist necropolises, none of which have been excavated (Díaz-Guardamino 2010, 225–292). Fortunately, the recent discovery of the stela of Galavís (Alcántara, Spain) within a mound with no large stone structure (Fig. 6.5), presents a fresh opportunity to shed some new light on these contexts of use.

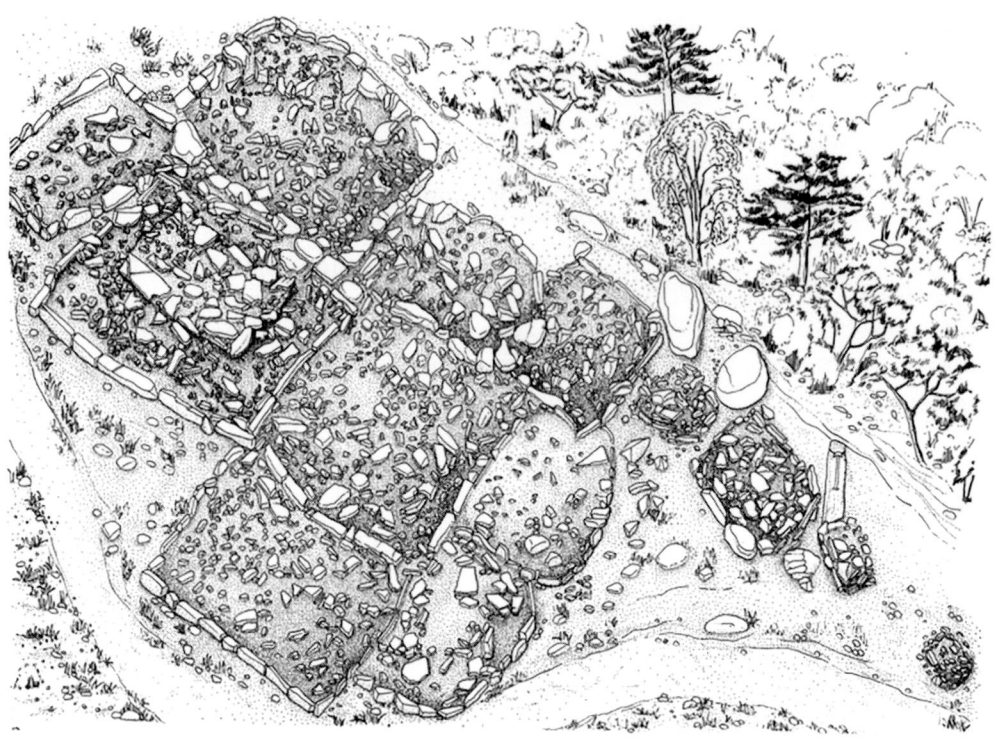

Figure 6.4. Interpretative reconstruction of necropolis 1 at Alfarrobeira (S. Bartolomeu de Messines, south Portugal). Image by Mario Varela Gomes (1994, 68, fig. 48).

These stelae do not typically include images of weapons but their neck ornaments seem to represent multiple torcs or complex necklaces such as the Sagrajas-Berzocana torcs found in the region and which bear Nordic-style decoration (see Fig. 2.2, above). The Galavís stela (Fig. 6.5.) is a typical example of this form, depicting a headdress, earrings, and necklace; the only anatomical details being the eyes, nose, and arms/hands, while the body is represented three-dimensionally by a pebble (González Bornay & Domínguez 2021, 56–57).

Furthermore, images with such headdresses are found on some Late Bronze Age warrior stelae (e.g. Almaden de la Plata 2; Fig. 6.6; Garcia-Sanjuán *et al.* 2006; Díaz-Guardamino *et al.* 2015) or close to them (e.g. Cañaveral de León; García Sanjuán *et al.* in prep.), which indicates that the iconographies of both traditions were complementary and should be considered jointly. In common with the above, the evidence linking Late Bronze Age warrior stelae with funerary practices is scarce and mostly composed of oral accounts reporting the association of the stela with cremated bones or covering significant funerary deposits (i.e. urns with ashes and bones) when found (Díaz-Guardamino 2012; 2014). More secure contextual information confirming the relationship between (at least some) warrior stelae and funerary sites has only been produced recently through the multidisciplinary study

Figure 6.5. Findspot and digital visualizations of the stela of Galavís (0.88 m), Alcántara (Cáceres, Spain). Photo: Archaeological Museum of Cáceres. Visualizations from laser scans created with TVT.

and scientific dating of already known stela findspots (e.g. Setefilla: Brandherm & Krueger 2017; Díaz-Guardamino *et al.* 2019) or new fieldwork conducted at sites where stelae have been recently discovered in context (e.g. Cañaveral de León; García Sanjuán *et al.* in prep.). The newly revealed evidence confirms that warrior stelae were placed by or within funerary contexts (e.g. earthen tumuli covering groups of urn cremations, cairns overlying cists). Finally, both iconographies (warrior and headdress) can be found in the environs of places holding persistent, significant symbolic power. This is the case with the stelae of Almadén de la Plata 1 and 2 (Fig. 6.6; García Sanjuán *et al.* 2006), found barely 2 km from the Palacio III hoard, dated to the Early Iron Age (9th–6th centuries BC), which includes amber beads of Baltic origin (Murillo-Barroso *et al.* 2015), and was found within a Copper Age megalithic tomb.

Figure 6.6. Stela 2 from Almadén de la Plata (0.76 m) and the Palacio III hoard. RTI image by Marta Díaz-Guardamino; photo by Mercedes Murillo Barroso.

While it is impossible to claim direct connection between these two phenomena, the association of stelae with mortuary practices in two regions within Atlantic Europe needs to be considered. In Britain this phenomenon is rare in the case of figurative images. However, there is a clear association between abstract rock art and burial contexts with the re-use of cup-and-ring engraved stones in burial cists (Waddington 1998). Something similar is documented in northwest Iberia, as there are Early Bronze Age cists made with slabs (some cap stones) that bear geometric decoration, albeit in these cases they seem to be primary carvings (Brandherm 2007; Bettencourt 2010). Whether other more-or-less famous examples of rock art in Scandinavia are cases of re-use in burials, as in the case of Mjeltehaugen (Norway) or the cupmarked stones in Ingelstorp (Sweden), is first difficult or perhaps impossible to prove (Strömberg 1982; Linge 2005) and, secondly, there is no clear link to warriors. Therefore, this will not be explored further.

6.2. Nordic Bronze Age rock art stelae

As has been set out in the previous section, Iberia and Scandinavia had long-term, comparable traditions of warrior-related iconographies. The two traditions seem to follow different trajectories when selecting canvasses and specific elements in the repertoires of their motifs. Even if the open-air rock art was the main expression of warrior iconography in Scandinavia and the stelae in Iberia, it should be emphasized however that stelae, stone slabs, or boulders with warrior iconography do occur within various funerary contexts or supposed funerary contexts in Sweden, Norway, Denmark, and northern Germany while, in Iberia, open air rock art panels with warrior iconography are also known (e.g. Goldhahn & Ling 2013; Díaz-Guardamino et al. 2022). Some of the Scandinavian 'stelae' are very well-known. For example, images of warriors, other human figures, chariots, weapons, and animals have been discovered on the stone slabs/stelae associated with the famous cairn of Kivik and in the burial mound of Sagaholm (Glob 1969; Cappelle 1972; Mandt 1991; Goldhahn 2013; 2016; Bertilsson et al. 2017). Other standing stones have a specific iconography depicting stylized hand images. Such images have been discovered, for example, in a so-called cult house in Sandagergård in Denmark and are, in many cases, linked to burials. Furthermore, some standing stones in Bohuslän and metalwork throughout Scandinavia bear similar motifs in general and both these media are associated with Bronze Age burials (Goldhahn 2007).

Most of the Nordic stelae with carvings dating to the Bronze Age tend to have been made on somewhat smaller stones than those in Iberia. However, there is one exception that bears many parallels to the Iberian stelae. We will therefore devote special attention to this site. It is located between Bohuslän and Skåne in western Sweden in the region of Halland which has otherwise surprisingly few figurative rock art sites. The site known as Hagbard's Galge (Gallow) is located in Asige parish (stone B, RAÄ 17:3 and stone A, 17:6). The entire site consists of two stone settings and four stelae

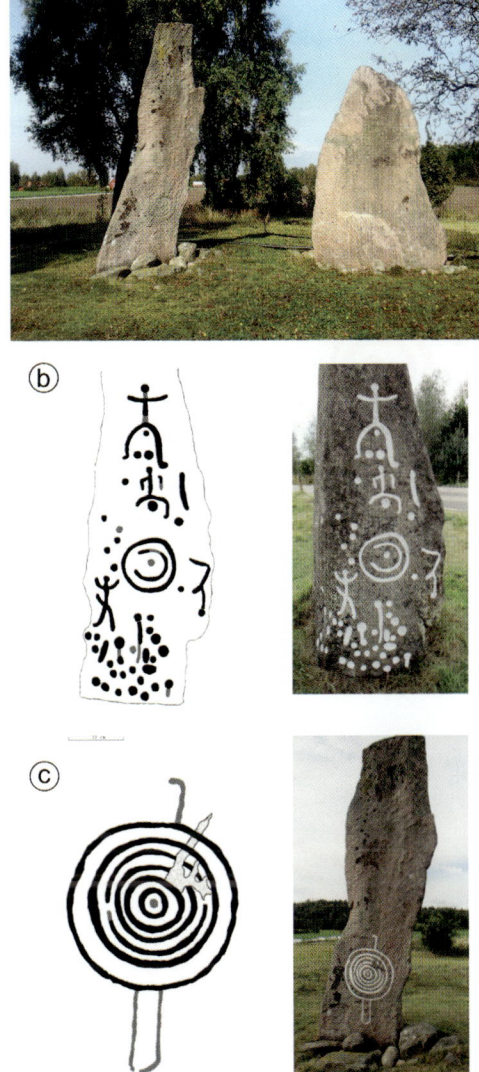

Figure 6.7. The standing stones at Hagbards Galge: (a) with tactile tracings of Asige 17:3 (b); (c) Asige 17:6. Photo by SirAclaus CC BY-SA 3.0. Tactile documentation by Broström and Ihrestam (2017).

measuring about 3.5–4 m in height and 1–2 m in width (Fig. 6.7). The name of the site is linked to a folk tale of the Viking chief Hagbard and his wife Signe who were executed at the site. Some images have been known for a long time but this corpus was extended by new documentation using traditional analogue methods conducted by Sven-Gunnar Broström and Kenneth Ihrestam (2015; Fig. 6.7). They discovered rock art on three of the standing stones (A–C) but here we are concentrating on the two stones with human figures (A & B). In November 2017 a new documentation was conducted using a Handy Scan 700 red light laser scanner. The results largely supported those of Broström and Ihrestam but various new discoveries were also made (Fig. 6.8).

The laser documentation on stone A showed that the six concentric circles with a cupmark at their centre, discovered by Broström and Ihrestam, was in fact a shield carried by a human figure with a relatively long neck that seems to end in a hook (Fig. 6.8, b). This hook could represent an exaggerated nose or beak of a type paralleled by many other Scandinavian rock art figures. Moreover, the two lines below the shield were interpreted as legs with feet and a carved half circle behind the right leg that could indicate the attempt to form an exaggerated calf. The shield itself has only ribs without decorative buckles which is most closely paralleled by the Harlech type that has its main distribution in southeast Britain, without any physical finds in Scandinavia. This shield type also begins in Bronze Age phase D and declines at the beginning of Hallstatt phase A1, around 1200 BC (Uckelmann 2012). Thus, in the main, these shields are somewhat older than the Dreiwulst swords, perhaps dating to period III of the

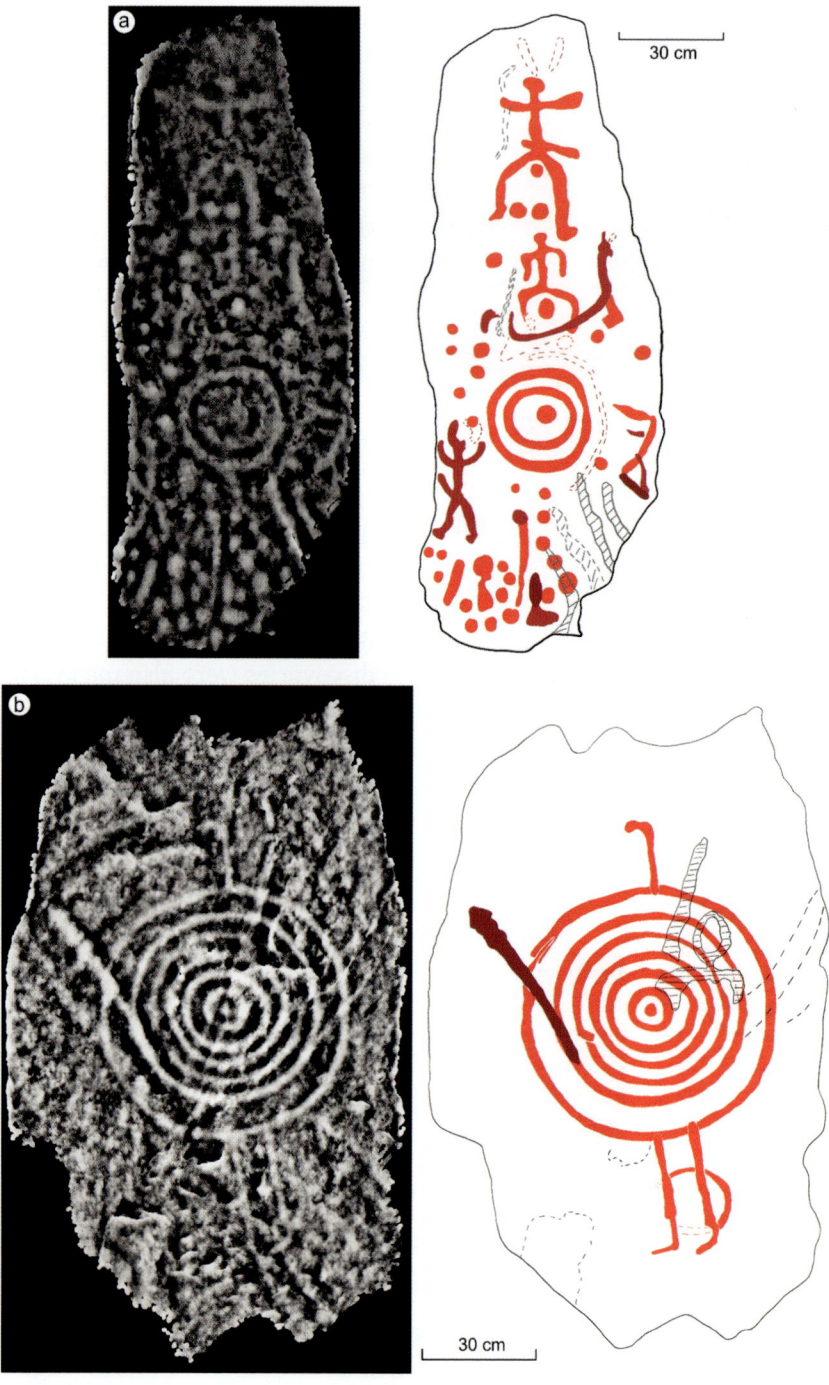

Figure 6.8. Digital visualization and interpretation of Asige 17:3 and Asige 17:6. Visualizations created from laser scans with TVT and interpretation by Christian Horn.

Nordic Bronze Age. This means sword and shield could have been carved at the same time or with a short time passing between two engraving events, presuming each was carved at a time concurrent with their respective correlates. At the top left, the outer two concentric circles are interrupted by a long and relatively deep engraving on the left side. The overall form seems to depict an actual sword, parallel to the so-called Dreiwulstschwert type. These swords begin during the Central European Bronze Age phase D but most of them date to the Ha phase A1 (Sperber 1987). That means this sword could have been engraved 1200–1050 BC. In Scandinavian terms this is the late period III transitioning to period IV, or the transition from the Early to the Late Bronze Age.

On stone B's north side, it was possible to confirm the three human figures, the concentric circles, and other features like the cupmarks discovered by Broström and Ihrestam (2015; Fig. 6.8). We argue that it is possible to interpret the concentric circles at the centre of the stela as a shield. However, the lower number of ribs may indicate a different type of shield then the one on stone A. Regardless of whether there are two or three circles, the closest parallel is the Nipperwiese type which has its densest distribution in Central Europe with a smaller occurrence in southeastern England. The dating for this type begins perhaps as early as the end of period II, about 1300 BC, but is more securely attested during its main phase when it appears simultaneously with the Harlech type shields (Uckelmann 2012). This may indicate that both stelae were initially decorated around the same time.

The newly discovered boat on this slab is difficult to date because of its fragmentary state. The outward turned stem on one side seems to indicate a Late Bronze Age date and the potential horse head on the other may put it early in this phase. This is in line with the observation that the boat was applied over the central human figure and, thus, represents the latest carving phase. Summing up the new observations made on the two stelae at Hagbards Galge, it seems as that both stelae were initially carved around the same time, about 1200–1000 BC.

The stela from Kyrkje-Eide (Sogn and Fjordane, Norway) was discovered in 1885 on the periphery of Bronze Age Europe and provides comparative material to the stelae in Iberia (Fig. 6.9). It is loosely connected to a burial area because bones have been found in the vicinity but it is not directly connected to any burial context. It is a unique find in Scandinavia and has many unusual images. However, some are more familiar. Mandt (1991) interpreted a snake, a dagger, two palstaves, three hook-figures, a comb, a stake figure, two ring figures, and parallel lines. Various objects were identified and dated to different periods of the Nordic Bronze Age from period I to the Late Bronze Age. She dated the entire composition to period II–III (1500–1100 BC). More recent research on the rock art panels (Bengtsson 2004; Bertilsson 2015; Ling & Bertilsson 2015; Milstreu 2017; Horn & Potter 2018), has also made it possible to assume that images might have been added at various stages. While the identification of the palstaves and some of the ornaments, including their dating, seems tenuous, the concentric circles appear to share parallels with examples interpreted as shields in Hagbard's Galge and at other rock art sites. If the central ring represents the boss of the shield, such as the Nipperwiese type on stone B at Hagbard's Galge, then a similar date period III (1300–1100 BC) could be inferred. Curiously, Mandt did not identify the dagger which finds an interesting parallel in the Scandinavian flint daggers. The wide butt of the handle and the relatively elongated blade place this depiction close to the type V of the Scandinavian flint daggers. This type is dated to Late Neolithic II and perhaps the very beginning of period I (1950–1700 BC). If that is the case, then the sickle-shaped figure could in fact be a flint sickle. However, the shape could also indicate a fish rather than a fish-shaped object. Fish depictions occur on the spears of the Valsømagle type and in the rock art in the Bredarör tomb in Kivik. These parallels could date this depiction in period Ib and the beginning of period II (1600–1450 BC). In either case this could indicate that the stela also collected images over time.

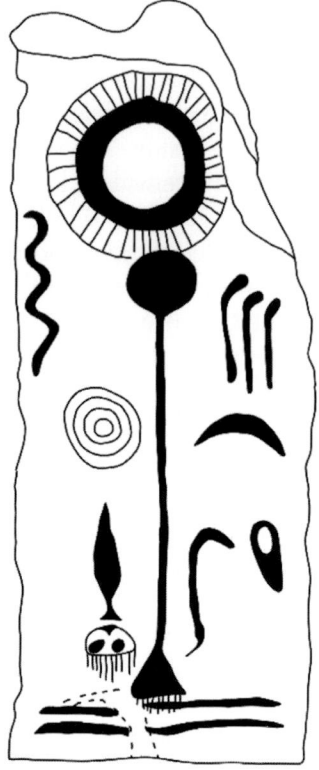

Figure 6.9. Stela from Kyrkje-Eide (B. 4440). Image adapted from Mandt (1991).

The prominent position of the shield on the Asige stela provides an immediate analogy in terms of shared traits and distinctions between Scandinavian and Iberian rock art. Furthermore, the Asige shield is comparable in size to some found in Iberia. For instance, the extraordinary number of rings on the shield from Asige bears resemblance to a five-ringed 'Iberian' example on the stela from Substation (Herault, France), although compared to the one in Asige it lacks the dot at the centre and has v-notches. Other Iberian parallels without notches but with a central dot are known from Cogolludo and Fuente de Cantos (Fig. 6.10; Díaz-Guardamino 2010). Nonetheless, these have only four rings compared to Asige that has seven and are depicted at a smaller scale. On the stela from Asige, the shield is placed on the body of the warrior, whereas in Cogolludo and Fuente de Cantos the warrior and the shield are placed side by side. In the latter case, the warrior has headgear with liriform horns similar to those seen in Scandinavian examples (Ling & Unhér 2014). In terms of the size and position of the shield in Asige, parallels can be drawn also with shields on Iberian stelae found in the Guadiana valley, such as the already mentioned Cogolludo (4 rings, dot in centre), Fuente de Cantos (4 rings, dot at centre), as well as Chillón (4 rings, handle at centre), or Cancho Roano (3), where the shield measures 25–35 cm in diameter and, as noted, in one case appears combined with liriform horns (Fuente de Cantos). Examples in the Guadalquivir valley tend to be depicted at a smaller scale, such as in El Coronil and Écija 5,

Figure 6.10. Stela of Fuente de Cantos (2.35 m) found in El Risco, Badajoz, Spain (National Archaeological Museum, Madrid, Spain). Images by Marta Díaz-Guardamino and Martín Almagro Basch.

with three rings and handle at the centre placed at the sides of warriors wearing headgear with horns. Setefilla, also in the Guadalquivir valley, depicts a shield with four concentric circles and handle at centre albeit at a slightly larger scale with a similarly schematic human figure (see Fig. 5.2) to the one documented in the Nordic stela at Asige.

Another intriguing parallel with the stelae in Asige and the Iberian ones is their connection to some kind of funerary context. This is proven for the stelae of Asige (Janson *et al.* 1989) and has been recently confirmed for a set of Iberian stelae through fieldwork and re-analysis of older evidence (e.g. Setefilla, Cañaveral de León, possibly Mirasiviene; Díaz-Guardamino *et al.* 2019; Rivera *et al.* 2021; García Sanjuán *et al.* in prep.).

6.3. Comparative case study between warrior iconography on Nordic outcrops and Iberian stelae

Bi-horned warriors, shields, weapons, and gestures

In terms of warrior iconography, some sites with rock art made on flat bedrock in northern Bohuslän display interesting parallels with the Iberian warrior iconography. Thus, we will begin this section with a case study in which we compare and contrast the iconography of the open-air site Kville 124:1 in west Sweden (Fig. 6.11, a) with that of the stelae in Valdetorres, Spain (Fig. 6.12), with a focus on bi-horned warriors, shields, weapons, and gestures. At the end of this section we will make a more general comparison of depictions of chariots in Sweden and Iberia.

The site Kville 124:1 is adjacent to a small creek and is well-known for the many depictions of shields and warriors found there, including a scene showing an acrobat, warriors, and an adorant associated with a large war canoe. For the purpose of our comparative study we will be focusing on the shields, the bi-horned warriors, and the adoring figure. As well as paying attention to some of the poses and gestures of the figures, an essential part of the analysis will be an examination of shield types. As we shall see in the comparison with the Iberian warrior iconography, shield typology provides an important set of chronological anchors that in turn offer clues to the collective biographies of the images as a whole.

Recent 3D documentation reveals a fairly fine-grained relative sequence of superimposed motifs. The large war canoe dates to period NBA V (900–700 BC). To the right of this canoe is a bi-horned warrior with very pronounced calves which can be dated more securely to period V by the winged chape on his sword sheath. Interestingly, this warrior superimposes another bi-horned warrior also with a different winged chape and smaller calves. The larger warrior is engraved additionally on top of a number of individual shields. In another scene at the centre of the panel, two warriors, one bi-horned, the other with yet another winged chape, are holding a shield that matches the style of those superimposed by the large warrior. In other words, the warriors holding the shield were engraved after the shield had been engraved. Most of the shields can be compared to the type

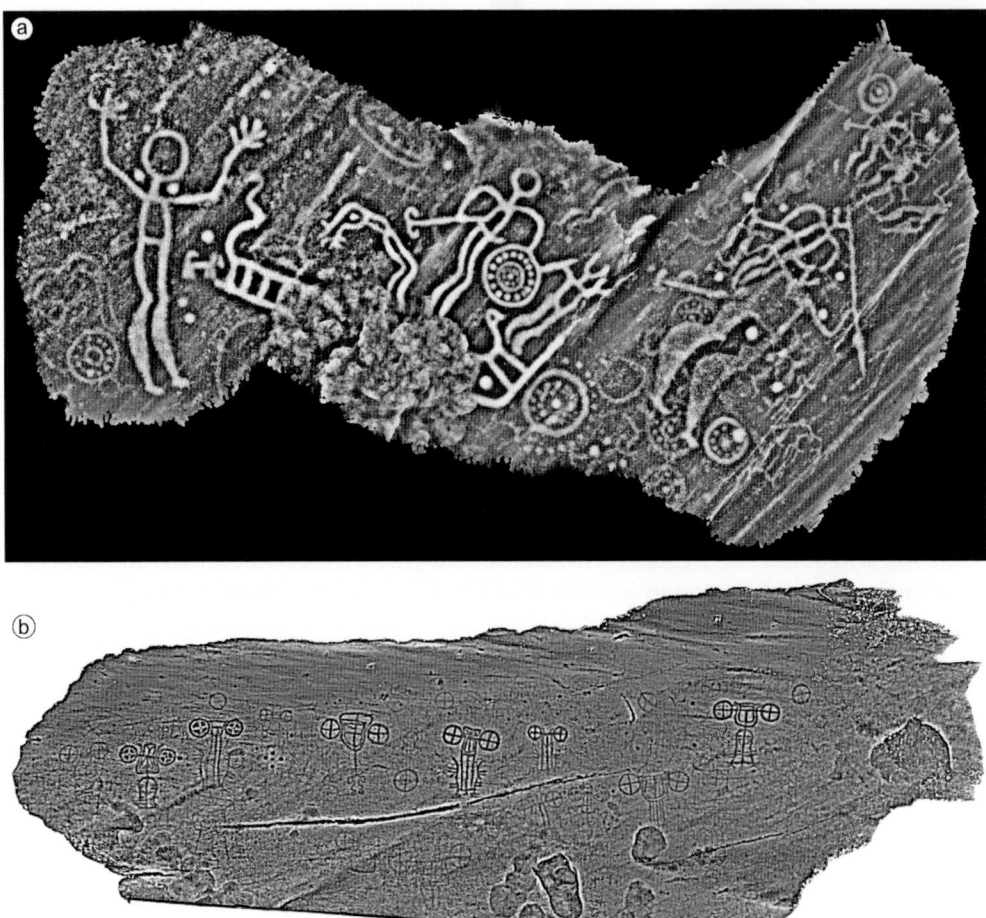

Figure 6.11. Panels in a) Hede (RAÄ Kville 124:1) and b) Frännarp (RAÄ Gryt 1:1). Visualizations created using TVT.

Athenry-Eynsham (originally found in Ireland: Uckelmann 2012, 35, fig. 24) because they have a limited number of rings and bosses within rings. Furthermore, the bosses on this shield type are relatively large. Oscar Montelius (1889) noted this connection already in the 1800s which has been confirmed by later studies (Uckelmann 2012). The Athenry-Eynsham type has a relatively wide dating range from the middle of NBA period III to the middle of period IV, from c. 1200–1000 BC (Montelius 1889; Coles 1962; Uckelmann 2012). That the carving of these shields falls in this period is supported by the three warriors that are superimposed on them and probably belong to period V, 900–700 BC.

As mentioned above, shield typology is useful not only from a dating point of view but also for exploring possible successive carving events in the biography of the images. This, of course, has limitations, as the typology of depicted objects can only be used as a *terminus post quem* reference (i.e. the moment from which an item appeared and was in circulation; Díaz-Guardamino 2012). Some artefacts used as referents for the images depicted on stelae and rock art may have had long biographies that expanded beyond the currency of their types/styles, as it is shown through the composition of some hoards that include artefacts of typologies belonging to different periods (the Ría de Huelva hoard is a case in point, although the event or process that brought about the formation of the assemblage is not well understood). For this reason, superimpositions are key to aiding interpretation of the biographies of stelae.

Back at the site in Kville, one of the shields has an outer circle of dots and on the inside of the only ring are two more dotted circles as well as a central boss. It is of course unclear, how realistic these depictions are, but the lack of a solid outer rim like that on the usually folded metal shields could indicate that an organic shield, made of hide or wood, was depicted on the rock. The outer dotted ring has the updated boat superimposed on it, but one of the dots cuts across a simple circle above the shield. The boat's right-hand stem could be parallel to boats from period IV, which means that this shield may have been engraved earlier during period IV or before that. These shields have a wide dating range between period II to the middle part of period IV. Although this does not narrow it down, it fits with the described relative position. None of the shields seem to have notches, so they cannot be classified as Herzsprung shields (Coles 1962; Uckelmann 2012). At the top left section of the panel, adjacent to a scene with two bi-horned warriors, a shield is depicted with concentric circles that shows parallels with the shield from the stela at Cancho Roano, Iberia and stone B from Asige, Sweden (see above). The closest parallel for all these depicted shields is the Nipperwiese type which regularly have only three ribs and no notch (Uckelmann 2012).

Turning to the scene with the warriors on board the war canoe, on the lower section of this panel, here we find a composition of two warriors, one bi-horned, the other not, both attached to a shield. A comparable scene has been discovered on the stela from Valdetorres 1 (Fig. 6.12.), including two warriors depicted on either

Figure 6.12. The stela of Valdetorres 1 (1 m) (Archaeological Museum of Badajoz, Badajoz, Spain). Photo: Vicente Novillo. Centre and right: visualization of a 3D model using TVT and interpretation of outline and superimposition of motifs by Marta Díaz-Guardamino.

side of a shield, one bi-horned the other not (Domínguez de la Concha *et al.* 2005; Díaz-Guardamino 2020). Even though the composition is less precise than in Kville it is a very close match because, in both scenes, the warriors stand to either side of the shield touching or holding it with their hands. In both cases, the warriors are superimposed on the shield which means that they were later additions and, in both cases, at least one warrior is depicted with pronounced shoulders. It should be noted, however, that in the case of Valdetorres 1 the carving of the human figures followed the same techniques deployed to engrave the shield and they could have been carved soon after the latter.

In terms of our comparative example of bodily features between the site in Kville versus the one in Valdetorres, there are some differences in the way the warriors are presented, for example both figures are static and have hands and feet in Valdetorres 1, while the sword of one warrior is depicted on the waist. However, there are also shared features between the sites, more specifically in how the head and headgear are represented and the general composition of the scene, with two human figures flanking a shield.

The horned warriors on the stela Valdetorres 1 are difficult to date but the sword and spear carved below the shield (and probably simultaneously to it), fit well with metallic correlates dated to the end of Late Bronze Age Wilburton (*c.* 1130–1050 BC) and beginning of the Blackmoor (1050–930 BC) metalworking traditions (Díaz-Guardamino 2010, fig. 210). The shield in Valdetorres belongs to the Herzsprung type with v-shaped notches. A similar shield made of oxen leather (and almost exact replica of the ones depicted on many Iberian warrior stelae, such as Brozas) recovered from a swamp in Cloonbrin, Ireland (Fig. 2.1) yielded a radiocarbon date that would situate its manufacture in the 12th–10th centuries cal BC (1200-931 cal BC, 2 sigma) (Gr-45808, 2880±35 BP; Ucklemann 2012, 159; Díaz-Guardamino *et al.* 2019, table 4, fig. 8). In Valdetorres 1, the termini of the inner notch of the shield seem to extend above the ring. This is a feature observed on many bronze Herzsprung shields including the examples from Fröslunda (Fig. 2.1) (Uckelmann 2014). The dates for such examples range from NBA period IV to V, i.e. 11th–9th century BC (Uckelmann 2012). This means that the two warriors may have been carved during the 11th century or soon after this date, when this symbol had currency in Atlantic Europe (Uckelmann 2014), leaving open the possibility that the Iberian warriors are perhaps somewhat older than the ones in Kville.

In addition to Valdetorres 1, pairs of warrior figures with the same size positioned in parallel/confronted are found in Alamillo, Capilla 8, El Viso 3, El Viso 6, Sao Martinho 1 and Torres Alocaz (Fig. 6.13), all, except the last two, from the Guadiana valley (along with Valdetorres 1). In Alamillo one figure wears a horned headgear while the second does not. Between them there is a sword that seems to belong to the

Figure 6.13. Stelae of Alamillo (0.48 m) and El Viso 3 (0,90 m) from the Guadiana valley (Museum of Ciudad Real and Archaeological and Ethnological Museum of Córdoba, Spain). Photos: Museum of Ciudad Real and Carmen Escobar CC BY 2.0.

horned warrior. The other warrior seems to be associated with a bow. In the stela of El Viso 3 the composition is slightly different. Between the warriors there is another human figure with a large headgear that has been interpreted as a female personage (Galán Domingo 2006). These strong similarities extend beyond the variations in detail and dating of these figures and indicate a relatively long-lasting, formalized narrative about warriors, their gear, and perhaps group solidarity. On the stelae and the bedrock panels a martial idea or myth with specific modes of representation was applied that flourished for a long time in Bronze Age Europe, appearing with more or fewer variations in disparate regions (García Sanjuán 2012; Díaz-Guardamino *et al.* 2022).

The site in Hede, Kville also provides a good comparison for the Iberian stelae in the depiction of a large human figure in an adoring pose, at the lower left section on the panel (Fig. 6.11). This figure shares the general body conception with the rest of the warriors on the panel, including the frame-like body, enlarged calves, etc. While this figure is not accompanied by any weapons other than the closely associated shields, it has hands with clearly carved fingers and earrings. Earrings occur on several warriors, such as the famous warrior in Litsleby and a smaller figure in Finntorp. A similarly large warrior in Brastad shares the raised hand pose which is a relatively frequent occurrence even on smaller figures (see Ling & Unhér 2015).

A strong Iberian parallel with the aforementioned figurative features can be seen on the Iberian stela from Monte Blanco/Olivenza (Badajoz; Fig. 6.14). This stela can be regarded as a composite of the enumerated characteristics of figures with raised hands and warriors with earrings. The warrior is marked out by the shield next to it, the sheathed sword, and the spear above the head. In several instances on the Scandinavian sites it has been observed that the spears had been carved first and then, centuries after this initial carving, warriors including earrings had been placed underneath the spear (Bertilsson 2018; Horn & Potter 2018), a sequence that has not been documented yet in Iberia. Also, contrary to the Iberian tradition, the Scandinavian warriors are usually shown holding the spear and are, thus, not detached from these. A notable exception is the small warrior at another site in Kville (Kville 120:1) that, like the warrior on the stelae from Olivenza, has a cupmark above his head and an unconnected spear. However, in deviation from the Iberian example, this warrior bears a shield, which is a type depicted like a wheel-cross. The spear warrior from Hede, on the other hand, has a loose shield posed next to him and a sheathed sword.

Chariots
There are about 93 depictions of two-wheeled chariots in Scandinavian rock art and likewise 35 from Iberia (Harrison 2004; Mederos Martín 2008; Winther Johannsen 2010; Grahn 2022; Díaz-Guardamino *et al.* in prep.). In terms of Scandinavian sites that depict chariots with Iberian parallels, these can be found widely across southern Sweden: from Frännarp, Scania to Brastad in northern Bohuslän. In Scandinavia the dating of the chariots is much debated, however, most of them seem to derive from

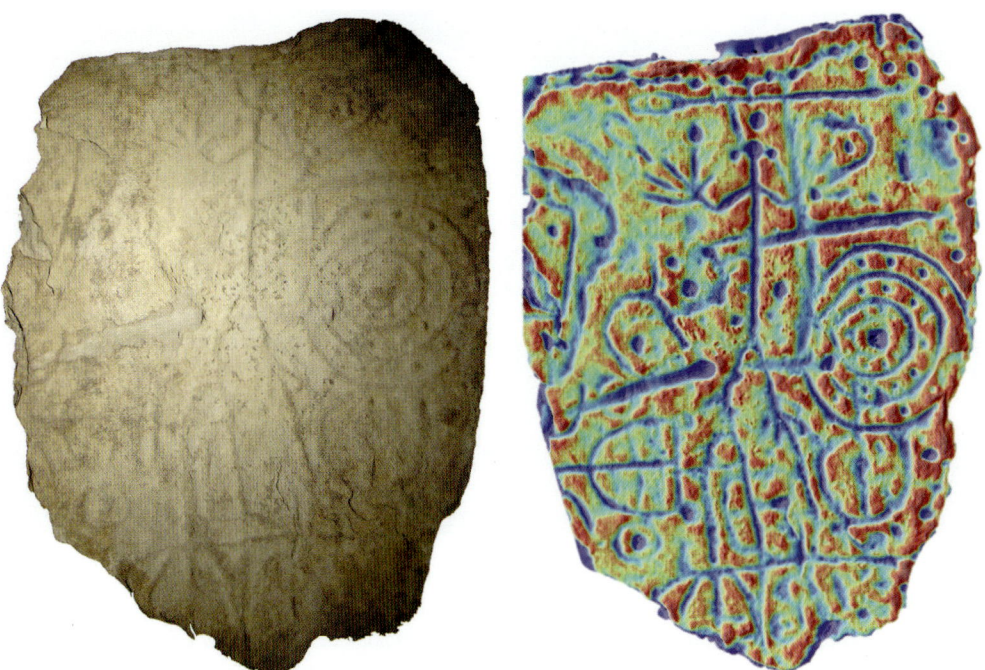

Figure 6.14. Stela of Monte Blanco (1.12 m) (Ethnographic Museum González Santana, Badajoz, Spain). Photo: Ethnographic Museum González Santana. Visualization from laser scan using TVT.

about 1400/1300–900 BC (Winther Johannsen 2010; Grahn 2022) while, in Iberia, they seem to have been inspired by Mycenaean models dated to the Late Helladic IIIB (c. 1300–1200 BC; Mederos 2008). A majority of the chariots depicted on the rocks display two wheels with a central draught pole as well as an axle located behind the cart box and a team of horses (Winther Johannsen 2010; Grahn 2022). Wheels with or without spokes are depicted among the Scandinavian chariot motifs and it has been suggested that this division is meant to represent different types of vehicles, those without spokes representing a coarser disc-wheeled type of chariot (Winther Johannsen 2010). It should be noted, however, that the Iberian chariots similarly include depictions of wheels both with and without spokes and there is no real division in other iconographical details corresponding to wheel type that might suggest that they represent different types of chariot (Mederos Martín 2008, 445–453; Grahn 2022).

One of the most important sites when comparing Iberian and Scandinavian chariot iconography is the Swedish site Frännarp, located in Scania, Southern Sweden (Fig. 6.11, b). This rather large panel includes a total of 17 two-wheeled chariots and is unique in Europe for the sheer number of chariot images on a single panel (Althin 1945; Coles 2002). At least five of the chariots are represented with two draft

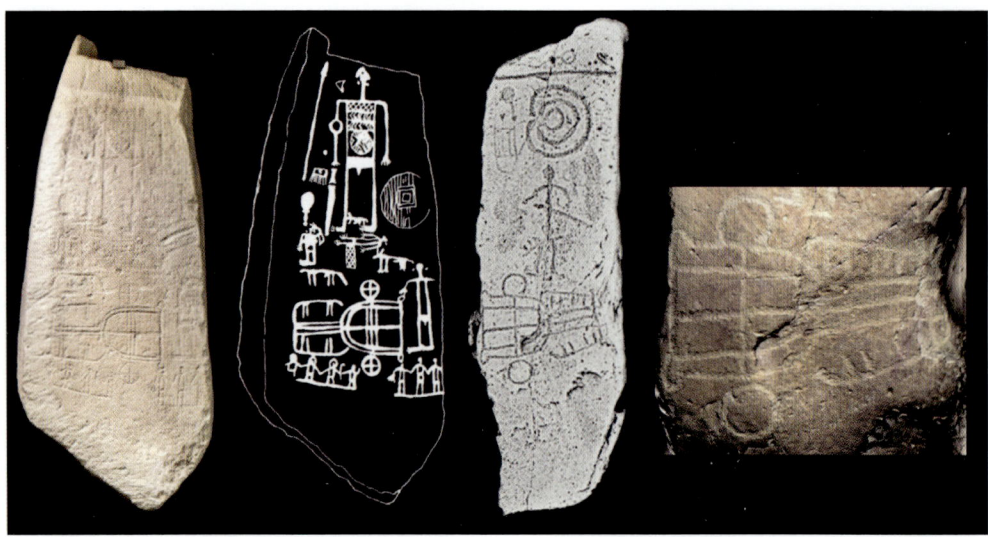

Figure 6.15. Chariots on the stelae of Ategua (1.63 m) (Archaeological and Ethnological Museum of Córdoba, Córdoba, Spain) and Zarza Capilla 1/Los Llanos (1.25 m) (Archaeological Museum of Badajoz, Badajoz, Spain). Images: Archaeological and Ethnological Museum of Córdoba and Marta Díaz-Guardamino. Visualization created with TVT from laser scan and RTI snapshot.

animals each, probably stallions, shown mirroring each other. Two of these are depicted with inward-facing horses, the other three have horses facing outwards and similar depictions of horses can be found in Iberia (Harrison 2004, 147; Grahn 2022). Many parallels could be drawn to the said chariots in Frännarp and the ones found on different stelae in Iberia, for example Ategua, Córdoba; the Zarza Capilla I stela, Badajoz, and Capilla 7, from El Tejadillo (Fig. 6.15; Harrison 2004, fig. 7.16). Thus, the Iberian and Scandinavian chariots share the same stereotypic views of chariot frames, draught poles, and sometimes yokes and reins from above, while the wheels and draught horses are represented turned at 90°. This fact is best explained as a shared tradition of visual culture, rather than a disembodied transmission of heroic concepts but, of course, both aspects could be combined, and these distant communities could have shared ideas and specific ways of displaying them (Díaz-Guardamino et al. 2022).

As similar as they are in their stylistic representation of structural features of the two-horse chariot, it does not seem possible that the Iberian and Scandinavian carved images could be linked only through verbal descriptions or some other disembodied concept of the chariot. It should be stressed that some of the shared iconographic conventions are not exclusive to chariot motifs in Scandinavian and Iberian rock art but are a common mode of depiction across Eurasia and northern Africa (Grahn 2022). However, the sum of all parallels in iconographic details speaks in favour of direct contact and knowledge of the same type of two-wheeled chariots by Iberian and Scandinavian elites (see also Mederos Martín 2008). Additionally, some details are specific to Frännarp and Iberia, such as the Ω-shaped boxes, the 'extensions', 'loops', or 'wings' on the rear sides, as well as the axle being placed towards the centre rather than the rear (Grahn 2022), although this later feature was also common in depictions of chariots on Mycenaean pottery vessels (Mederos Martín 2008). These shared stylistic features include two wheels turned at 90° with spokes and hubs, axles, a chariot body with an open back shown as three parallel horse-shoe shaped lines, a yoke, and a draft pole flanked by two parallel lines representing the reins. Combined, these details amount to a check list, which would hardly have been meaningful to an audience ignorant of sophisticated horse-drawn wheeled vehicles.

Nonetheless, that does not exclude the possibility that the common link between these far-flung regions were representations of chariots in another more portable and perishable medium – such as leather – rather than (or in addition to) the vehicles themselves. Prestigious goods with such imagery made of perishable materials (e.g. leather, wood) could have been in circulation between Scandinavia and Iberia, very much like the Mycenaean chariot kraters (albeit chariots there were depicted following different conventions) that were exchanged as prestige goods in the eastern Mediterranean and deposited in funerary contexts, especially in Cyprus and the Levant (Feldman & Sauvage 2010). The stereotyped, non-naturalistic features shared by the Iberian and Scandinavian representations would certainly be consistent with this alternative possibility. And unless and until similar images turn up in Brittany, Ireland, Britain, or Alpine central Europe, showing all these shared features, this evidence remains most consistent with long-distance transmission, with a specific complex tradition reflected at the terminus points of the network.

Another site of interest for our comparison is Brastad 128:1, west Sweden (Fig. 6.16). It shows many similarities with the Iberian chariots, especially with the one from Ategua, Córdoba (Fig. 6.15), such as the wheels shown with four spokes. In the Swedish example two of the spokes on each wheel are shown as continuing the line of the axle, though this requires the conventional unnaturalistic 90° turning of the wheels. In both the Ategua and Brastad examples a double line follows the curved frame of the chariot, viewed from above. Similarly, the yoke pole is presented in both images as a triple line, representing the pole itself and pair of reins to either side. None of these features is uncommon in the corpora of Bronze Age rock art chariots of Scandinavia or those of the Iberian stelae. For example, many of the chariots on the panel from Frännarp, Scania, share these features (Fig. 6.11).

The two-horse team shown unnaturalistically facing each other on either side of the yoke pole is a universal feature common to both regional sets. Whether these conventions are intended to show each part of the chariot from an ideal angle or were used to represent actual heroic chariot burials in which the horses and disassembled wheels were laid out in this way is a moot point. Frustratingly there is no physical evidence for chariot burial in either region during the Bronze Age (the earliest documented Iberian example being tomb 17 at La Joya, Huelva, dated to c. 8th–7th centuries BC; Garrido & Orta 1978). However, although these two options are not

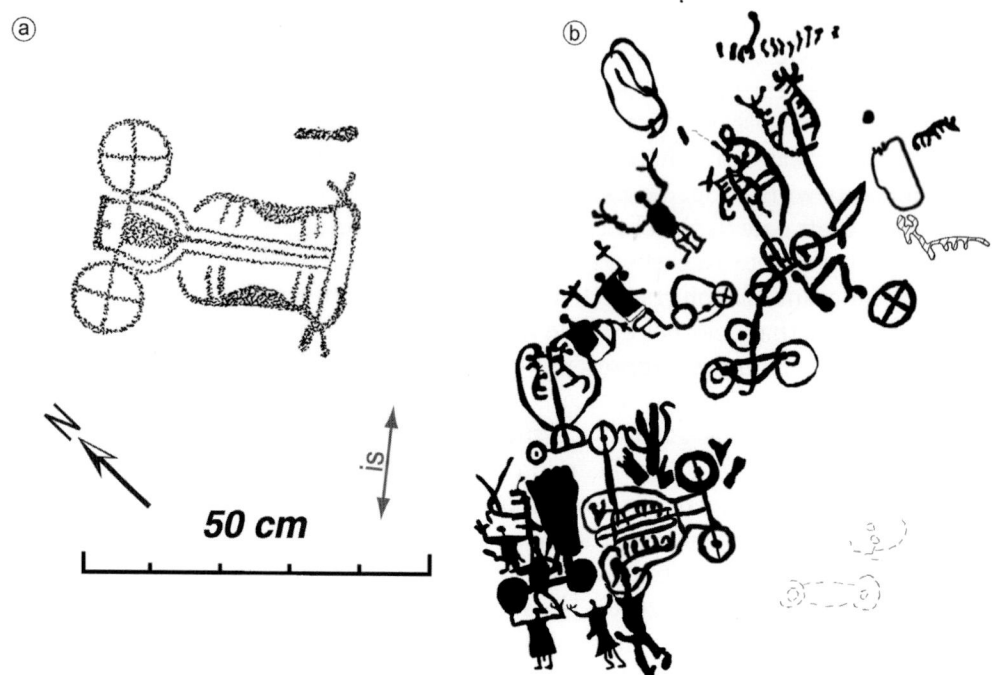

Figure 6.16. Interpretation of sections of the panels in Brastad (RAÄ 128:1) and Brastad (RAÄ 18:1). Visualization of a photogrammetry model using TVT.

mutually exclusive, the fact that no physical remains of chariots have been uncovered in Iberia or Scandinavia before the 8th century BC, suggests that the chariot could have been a concept combining myths and shared ideas rather than a real means of transport during the Late Bronze Age (Galán Domingo 1993; Celestino Pérez 2001a) although in Iberia there is material evidence suggesting the actual use of horse-pulled chariots during the Late Bronze Age (Mederos Martín 2008, 461).

The rock art chariot iconography suggests that chariots were associated with military ideals and activities in Iberian and Scandinavian Bronze Age societies. This is demonstrated by the close connection between chariot and warrior motifs as well as the emphasis on details which shows the functionality of the chariot as a vehicle for transport (Grahn 2022). Iberian chariots are almost exclusively depicted with a centrally placed axle, similar to Aegean chariot depictions (Mederos Martín 2008, 453–454). The centrally located axle served the practical purpose of reducing the stress on the horses (Mazzù et al. 2021). As in Iberia, in the Mycenaean world there is no evidence of actual chariots (only a few material remains related to chariot-riding) but Mycenaean representations on ceramic vessels serve as a helpful source for chariot usage (Feldman & Sauvage 2010, 95–99). Most representations of Mycenaean chariots show them as carriers of elite individuals in processional scenes rather than active combatants in battle (Littauer 1972; Feldman & Sauvage 2010, 95–99). Chariots continued to be used as the warrior class adopted lighter armour because they were significant status symbols. Kristiansen and Larsson (2005, 223–224) argue that Brastad 18:1 (Fig. 6.16) is an example of chariots being used to carry warriors with heavy amour.

Aside from potential military applications, chariots were most likely useful tools for projecting power and identity. Images connected to royalty in the Hittite and Egyptian empires exemplify how the iconography of the chariot was employed throughout the Bronze Age world to portray rank and authority (Mederos Martín 2008; Feldman & Sauvage 2010; Grahn 2022). The association between elites and chariots has also been underlined in connection with the Bronze Age chariot representations in Scandinavia and Iberia (Harrison 2004; Kristiansen & Larsson 2005; Mederos Martín 2008). The clear connection between chariots and burial contexts shown in both Iberian and Scandinavian rock art supports this notion: chariots were displayed as prestige goods and also as elements used in funerary rituals (e.g. Ategua, Fig. 6.15; Celestino 2001a, 229–232; Harrison 2004, 112–114; Mederos Martín 2008).

The two-wheeled war chariot was the fastest and swiftest means for warfare and transportation on land. Its maritime counterpart was the war canoe that could load even more goods and warriors and could overtake war-bands moving on foot where coastal and riverine navigation were possible. It is rather intriguing to see that the chariot as well as the war canoes are depicted in the same context of warrior-related rock art iconography. While several chariots are represented at some sites in Scandinavia, the war canoe was much more frequent.

Even if canoes and chariots refer to correlates used in warrior-related activities (e.g. chariots in battle, war canoes in raids) and are represented on rock art panels and stelae beside warriors or related paraphernalia or activity, these motifs seem to have fulfilled different roles within the rock art canvas. Chariots are represented mostly as passive elements related to the mortuary domain; appearing beside the static image of the body of a warrior in a burial scene in the Iberian stelae or, in the Scandinavian examples, in some cases on panels closely associated with graves. In the context of the stelae, chariots might be seen as a symbol of elite or warrior identity as opposed to an extension of a fighting machine. In any case, it might not apply to the warrior's fighting strategies in the field (in the same way as the comb, lyre, or razor). This could be the reason why depictions of chariots are so passive. Boats, on the other hand, are depicted as elements taking an active part in all kinds of activities; they may be related to funerary activity, mythological tales, or warfare, among others. The comparison between the panel Tossene 926:1, west Sweden, and stela 4 from Cabeza del Buey, Badajoz, could serve as an example of the above (Fig. 6.17). Both display bi-horned warriors with arms but in Sweden the vehicles depicted are war canoes in action, while the stela of Cabeza del Buey 4 shows the warriors next to a passive chariot. Despite this, it is significant that both, chariots and boats, seem to have fulfilled a role as a means of transport to the otherworld, as part of mortuary

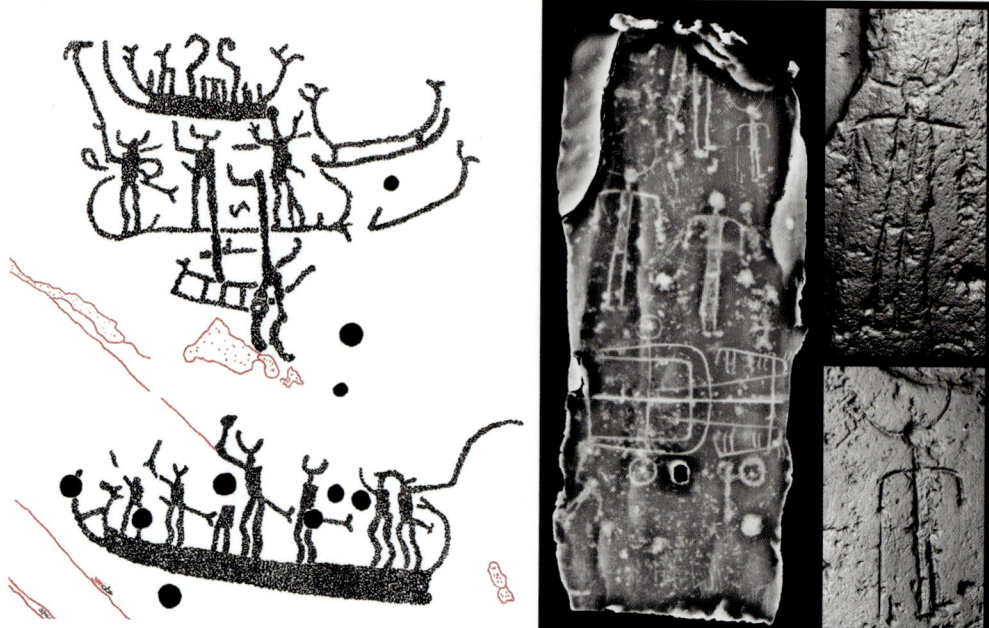

Figure 6.17. Comparison between the panel Tossene 926:1, west Sweden and stela 4 from Cabeza del Buey (1 m) (Archaeological Museum of Badajoz, Spain). Interpretation by project hällristning.se to the left and visualizations using TVT from laser scan to the right and RTI.

passage rites (chariots in depictions in Iberia and probably Scandinavia; boats as rock art depictions and/or funerary containers/tombs in Scandinavia).

6.4. General comparative remarks on stelae, motifs, and themes: Stelae versus outcrops

Motifs

Scandinavian rock art and the Iberian stelae tradition have many shared motifs including mirrors, combs, chariots, weapons, shields, helmets, earrings, and bi-horned warriors, as well as the hand positions of the depicted warriors (Ling & Unhér 2014). The strongest connection is thematic, the very fact that they depict warriors with the aforementioned paraphernalia. The most obvious difference between Scandinavia and Iberia when it comes to rock art is the number of images (Table 6.1). Overall, there are many more sites and motifs in Scandinavia even if we only count human figures that could be interpreted as warriors through the presence of weapons. Around 110 warrior figures could be identified in Iberia whereas in Scandinavia this number is more than 15 times higher (more than 1870). One of the factors that may be influencing these numbers is that of the mobility and perhaps invisibility, of stone stelae in Iberia. In

Table 6.1. Comparison of the number and percentages of key motifs between the rock art traditions of Scandinavia and Iberia

	Scandinavia (sample of 4099)		Iberia (sample of 147)	
	Total	%	Total	%
Warriors	1874	46	110	75
Swords	1268	31	108	73
Shields	514	13	115	78
Exaggerated hands with finger digits	334	8	64	44
Spears	316	8	85	58
Bi-horned warriors	197	5	38	26
Chariots	93	2	35	24
Mirrors	10	0.2	66	45
Combs	0	0	31	21

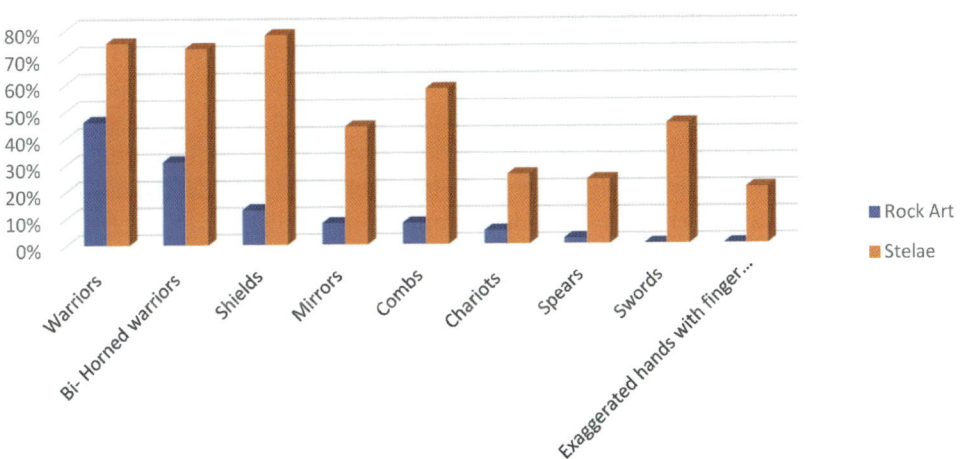

the last few decades, most of the stelae have been discovered through agricultural work with tractors and it is quite possible that many have gone unnoticed, piled up as field clearance, or re-used. Also, it is important to note that, overall, the presence of the warrior archetype in Iberia may have been less intense than that registered in Scandinavia, something that is suggested by the significantly lower occurrence of warrior orientated metalwork, particularly swords, in the Iberian archaeological record (Díaz-Guardamino et al. 2022).

For the following comparison, we used a sample of 147 Iberian warrior stelae. Of these, 96 carry a total of 155 human depictions (this includes warrior figures and other personages). From the Nordic Bronze Age bedrock panels 1874 warrior depictions were included that could be interpreted with sufficient certainty. Since weapons were used to identify warriors, all these images have weapons. A significant number of the Iberian stelae (48) depict weapons but no human body. They were included because they are placed as an assemblage on the stone canvas as if the latter were a surrogate of the human body. Individual weapons were also depicted in Scandinavian rock art. However, the openness and long engraving histories of these panels make it uncertain which objects are directly linked to one another. For this reason, individual weapons were not considered for Scandinavia.

The raw data also show that the Scandinavian material has a much wider variety of combinations of objects and body features linked to the depiction of warriors. In Iberia, 32 distinct features were identified while in Scandinavia there were 65. Among the ten most frequent features the two regions share the presence of shields, swords, spears (Table 6.1), and exaggerated hands with fingers digits. Mirrors, combs, and chariots, which are important features on the stelae, also occur in the Bronze Age rock art of Scandinavia but only rarely with warrior images and more frequently as individual depictions or, in the case of the chariots, they can amass at unique sites like Frännarp in Scania.

There are considerable parallels in the depiction of weaponry between the two regions. Shields and swords are the two most common weapons although they switch places in importance. However, that slightly fewer swords than shields were identified in Iberia could be because of damage to the stelae, since shields are often larger than swords and centrally placed which increases their likelihood of still being identifiable even if they were partially destroyed. In both traditions, spears are perhaps a secondary weapon being the third most frequently depicted weapon. While bows and arrows are not absent in either region they are relatively infrequent. Daggers occur in Iberia (very rarely) and axes in Scandinavia respectively but either seem to be missing in the other region at least on stelae or in close connection to the depiction of warriors (i.e. there is only one possible representation of an axe on a warrior stela). Maces are absent in Iberia and very rare in Scandinavia. Scandinavian rock art makers are seemingly unconcerned with depicting warriors with helmets and it seems that the same happened in Iberia, where there are just a few depictions of headgear (on 45 stelae) albeit sometimes quite detailed (e.g. conic helmets, lyriform horns). However, assuming that horns are not some mythical symbol but, rather, the representation of actual horned headgear in both regions, then helmet repertoires are quite frequent (for Iberia see Brandherm 2008; Villa & De Blas 2021). Importantly, horned warriors also appear in the visual culture of Late Bronze Age Sardinia, this time in the form of bronze cast figurines (*bronzetti*) (Fig. 6.18; Vandkilde *et al.* 2021), whose copper was sourced, at least in large part, from southern Iberian mines (Berger *et al.* 2023). The evidence from Sardinia suggests that there was a careful selection of the ores to cast these

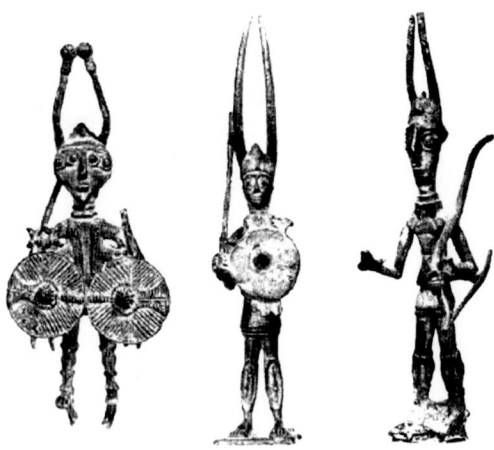

Figure 6.18. Bronzetti from the Uta Abini group in Sardinia (not to scale). Images by Giovanni Lilliu (Araque 2012).

warrior figurines in Sardinia, as the rest of the copper composing Late Bronze Age metalwork and ingots found in Sardinia come from other sources (e.g. Sardinia, Cyprus), suggesting further that the image of the horned warrior was global, moved around, and was appropriated differently in different local or regional settings (e.g. Scandinavia, Iberia, Sardinia).

Vandkilde *et al.* (2021) make interesting points on the representations of the bi-horned iconography, comparing Iberia, Scandinavia, and Sardinia. However, the claims that the Sardinian and Scandinavian examples show greater similarities can be questioned. First, there are far more Scandinavian examples that are not included, especially from Tossene in west Sweden (Ling & Uhnér 2014), that show strong parallels with bi-horned figures from Iberia (Fig. 6.17). Secondly, the Sardinian comparative examples are not rock art, but bronze figurines, which weakens the case for a direct, practice-based transmission. Nonetheless, we should note that there seems to have been a special connection between Sardinia and Iberia because, as mentioned, most of the copper employed to cast the Nuragic *bronzetti* came from Iberia (Berger *et al.* 2023; see also Araque 2023). Thirdly, the study does not consider other important parallels between the Iberian and Scandinavian warrior iconography on the rocks such as details of the human form and gestures or the depiction of associated chariots which also follow the same conventions.

In Scandinavia and Iberia helmets seem to be of medium importance to depicting warriors, although they were more frequently depicted than bow and arrows in both regions. Armour seems to be absent in Scandinavia and only very few examples exist on the Iberian stelae. However, it could be argued that the rectangular depiction of the warrior's body indicated some bulky clothing which is supported by the belts that were often applied to such figures. Although still relatively infrequent, that would mean that armour was at least present in both regions.

Images of mirrors occur in the rock art of both regions, with 66 examples in Iberia, representing the largest group in Europe (Díaz-Guardamino *et al.* in prep.) and ten in Sweden. Mirror depictions occur in at least three sites in west Sweden, in the parishes of Tossene and Kville (Kville 216:1, Tossene 46:1, 427:4; Fig. 6.19). These Scandinavian mirrors are similar to their Iberian counterparts in both shape and size relative to the human figures and other objects depicted with them in the carvings. Albeit in fewer numbers, these mirror representations are found, as in Iberia, in close association

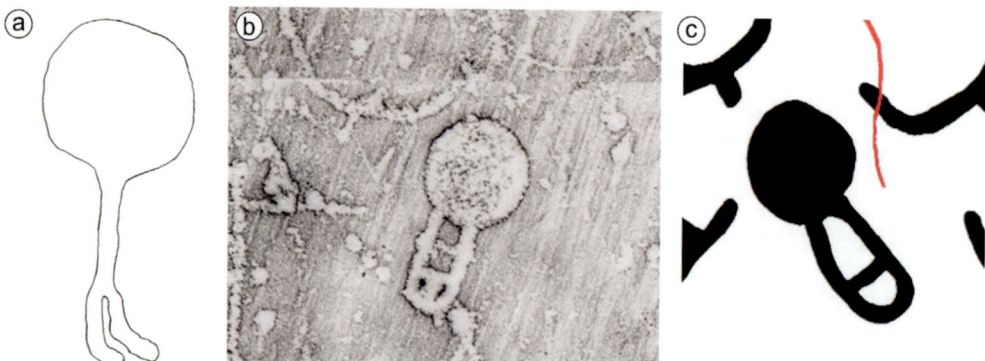

Figure 6.19. Mirrors on (a) Kville (RAÄ 216:1), (b) Tossene (RAÄ 46:1), (c) Tossene (RAÄ 427:4). (a) by Åke Fredsjö, (b) by Stiftelsen för documentation av Bohusläns hällristningar, (c) Broström, Sven-Gunnar and Ihrestam.

with martial motifs such as warriors, bi-horned figures, and war canoes, and are undoubtedly a local articulation of European-wide warrior symbolism (Harrison 2004; Díaz-Guardamino et al. 2022). Shown in martial contexts, they can be understood as an expression of the warrior ideal, including male physical beauty (Treherne 1995; Díaz-Guardamino 2010, 404), or as talismans (Harrison 2004, 107–110). In this light, the site Tossene 427, which includes three depictions of mirrors, also contains some other intriguing motifs, namely depictions of bi-horned helmets near the mirrors in question.

The aesthetics of the pan-European warrior ideal of the Bronze Age and the central places of the war chariot and sea-going vessel in this complex inescapably calls to mind the recurrent themes of the *Iliad* of Homer (Swift 2015). This comparison reminds us that, undoubtedly, there was a dimension of heroic myths and epic storytelling related to this imagery that we have lost. However, the reconstructable vocabulary of the early Indo-European languages of the North and West can give us some idea of the word stock used by the storytellers and epic poets of the Bronze Age to convey the same heroic narratives and ideals that are reflected in the stone carvings. The nine lyres or musical instruments that figure prominently in the layouts of Iberian warrior stelae (Mederos Martín 1996; Harrison 2004, 56, 110, 146, 158–159) strongly imply a central link between the warrior ideal and poetic art. That six of them show carefully carved strings and sounding boards indicates that the crafts of the musicians and stelae carvers were not remote from one another.

Motif combinations

In both Scandinavian and Iberian rock art different weapons can be found depicted together, though with subtle differences in the choice of weapon combinations between the two regions. In Scandinavia, swords and shield were the most frequent pairing, followed by a substantial number of depictions with warriors with swords and spear. The combination of swords and spears without shield plays no role in Iberia.

Instead, combinations of swords, spears, and shields are the most frequent, followed by simultaneous pairings of swords and shields. Here the depiction of warriors on the stelae is much more geared towards the combination of weaponry whereas on the Scandinavian bedrock panels they are often marked with only one weapon. In both regions the combination of sword and shield is the most relevant although often occurring in different positions in relation to the warrior's body.

The combination of the representation of hands with swords was very similar in both regions with 79% and 78% respectively. This goes along with similar hand positions, such as the one hand down over the sword sheath and the other hand up position, discussed earlier (Ling & Unhér 2014). The percentages are distinctly different when it comes to the combination of large hands and spears and shields. They remain prevalent in Iberia but drop off considerably in Scandinavia. The reason for this is simply that warriors with spear and/or shield are often depicted without arms in the latter.

This spear-shield combination on human warriors as it occurs in Scandinavia is interesting though because some human figures including warriors were the outcome of sequential carving actions. One such warrior was discovered in Finntorp.

Figure 6.20. Finntorp panel relief, in Scandinavia, showing the addition of images of warriors in period III (1300–1200 BC). Visualization created using TVT from a laser scan by the County Administrative Board for West Sweden.

Before 1300–1200 BC the image was just a spear placed between a shield and a cupmark, and only later acquired a neck, legs, and phallus (Horn & Potter 2018). This configuration mirrors the typical spear-shield-sword combination found on Iberian stelae, although here the human figure is initially absent. In Iberia, human figures enter the scene slightly later than the basic composition of spear, shield, and sword, by c. 1200 BC (Díaz-Guardamino 2012) and, when they do appear, the schematic human figure is depicted on top of the shield or on its side, ultimately sharing the canvas with it. Thus, it seems like similar ideas about the proper placement of warrior gear were expressed (Fig. 6.20). In the case of Scandinavia, this element was modified at the beginning of period III (1300–1200 BC) to depict a warrior image rather than just warrior gear (Horn & Potter 2018). It is yet unclear how often such transformations took place and whether all similar warriors only emerged after extensive changing of the images. This could also be the case even if the human features were part of the original composition.

Themes

Conceptualizing the associated features in broader themes, i.e. beauty, transport, warfare, death, etc., it is possible to establish broader themes linked to the depiction of warriors. Nine themes were defined: animals, emphasizing body characteristics on otherwise abstract figures, clothing, jewellery, music, other, toiletry, transport, and weaponry. In Iberia, the strongest theme is weaponry. While this may be an outcome of the focus on warriors, it is important to note that in Scandinavia the top concern was with the warrior's body characteristics, especially exaggerated calves, hands, horns, etc. Weaponry – perhaps surprisingly – is only the third strongest theme in the Nordic Bronze Age. While every warrior has at least one weapon, there are, on average, more body characteristics emphasized. Such characteristics, like emphasized hands or toes are the second strongest theme in Iberia followed by toiletry. This theme is almost absent in Scandinavian rock art. However, the concern with the warriors' beauty and grooming their bodies is well-documented in the burial record of Scandinavia where hundreds of razors, tweezers, etc. have been recovered (Treherne 1995). The boat as a means of transport stands out in the Nordic sphere and, thus, is here the second strongest theme. The chariot in Iberia may be seen as an analogous object emphasising the main means of transport for warriors perhaps in battle, to travel to war, or to the otherworld, as part of mortuary rites of passage (Table 6.2). While not a major concern in either region, adorning the body of warriors was somewhat more prevalent in Iberia. Although it is not entirely absent in Scandinavia (for example, with the famous earring wearing warriors in Litsleby and Finntorp), in the mass of images it constitutes only a minor theme. And, as with toiletry, the burial record paints a different picture (Felding *et al.* 2020).

Lastly, it is worth pointing out that the theme of music is less strongly linked to representations of warriors in Scandinavia whereas it occurs frequently on the Iberian warrior stelae, albeit using different symbols for correspondingly different musical instruments. It is possible that this disparity simply reflects a practical/

Table 6.2. Comparative summary of some of the main defining traits of Scandinavian rock art and Iberian warrior stelae

	Scandinavia (Rock art)	Iberia (Warrior stelae)
Landscape setting	Shoreline	Inland
Transport	Boat (maritime)	Chariot (terrestrial)
Place (proximity to)	Water, graves	Water, graves, settlements, pathways
Context	Outcrops (few boulders/slabs)	Sculpted boulders/slabs (exceptionally on outcrops)
Visibility	Horizontal	Vertical (when on outcrops can be horizontal)
Techniques	Petroglyphs	Petroglyphs & occasional painting
Motifs: themes	Warrior & shield+sword+spear	Slab/warrior & shield+sword+spear
Motifs: number	Thousands	Hundreds
Motifs: size	Small (rarely life-size or larger)	1st life-size, 2nd small
Motifs: style	Schematic	Schematic
Scenes	Action (e.g. Combat, …), narrative	1st static (e.g. Burial), 2nd action (narrative, parade)
Composition	Variation in standardised set of figurative elements (e.g. On a warrior for example 'with sheathed sword + phallus', or 'raised spear + phallus')	Standardised (some variation around a limited number of conventions)
Temporality	Long-term use of canvas	Short-lived (mostly), although sometimes re-used
Chronology	1700–500 BC	c. (other stelae and statue-menhirs from 2200) 1400/1250–850 BC

conceptual difference in the use of instruments between the two cultures. While the lurs in Scandinavia could have been used as musical instruments, for entertainment or ritual activities, their strong presence on the rock art boat reliefs (as opposed to the warrior reliefs) indicate an alternative use. For instance, one practical purpose for the presence of lurs aboard a boat could have been to produce signals that would carry further across the water than voices, perhaps announcing a crew's presence to other vessels. On the other hand, the lyres represented on the Iberian warrior stelae would probably not have been used in battle or seafaring contexts. Judging from parallels in Homeric Greece or Migration Period northern Europe, lyres traditionally accompanied poetry telling of the battles and voyages of heroes.

Note
1 All unattributed catalogue nos. can be found in the database of the Swedish Rock Art Research Archives https://shfa.dh.gu.se/

Chapter 7

Linguistic aspects on the warrior iconography in Iberia and Scandinavia[1]

In overview, the Bronze Age rock art of Scandinavia and stelae of Iberia immediately reveal many comparable details. Many of these parallels depict human beings identifiable as warriors because they are shown together with weapons and other warrior paraphernalia, such as chariots and horses (Ling & Koch 2018; Koch 2019b; 2020). If we bring historical linguistics into this comparison, this picture can be amplified and reinforced. The early Indo-European languages from the part of the world we are studying, Northern and Western Europe, provide many examples shared uniquely between them of special words for various kinds of warrior gear and warlike activities (Koch 2020). Drawing these archaeological and linguistic observations together leads naturally to the conclusion that warriors and warfare held a central position – perhaps *the* central position – in the societies being studied. There is no doubt an element of truth in such a conclusion, which can be further supported by hundreds of finds of spearheads, swords, and axes in the wider archaeological record of both regions (Horn & Kristiansen 2018). Nonetheless this interpretation risks being limited and superficial. Moving from the later prehistoric to the early literary periods, we can see that the biography of the warrior hero was often the chosen allegory for the drama of the individual, invested with deeper meaning. It would be naïve to expect that many life stories followed the narrative arc of Achilles, Beowulf, or Cú Chulainn. So, in broadening our study to include words and their meanings alongside rock art iconography, it will be possible to do more than draw together check lists of motifs and words contextualized against snippets of heroic narratives. The details can be placed within a broader framework of evolving concepts of the individual in society and the cosmos.

Regional subsets of Indo-European, that is, words and other features that are limited only to neighbouring branches rather than widely attested across Europe and Asia, can be seen as reflecting later stages than Proto-Indo-European. A particularly large regional subset is that of Indo-European languages of the Northwest: Celtic, Germanic, Italic, Baltic, and Slavic (Mallory & Adams 2006). Within this Northwestern subset of Indo-European languages (the 'NW bloc'), there is strikingly large group, 174 words or innovative developments of words found only in Celtic and Germanic. It is intriguing and surely significant that meanings of many of these Celto-Germanic words can be related to Bronze Age life, social institutions, ideology, and cosmology, as well as artefacts. In the latter category, links can be drawn to the iconography of Scandinavian rock art and the Iberian warrior stelae, including, but not limited to, the examples that follow in this section.

The two places and the period we are focused on here, Bronze Age Iberia and Scandinavia, provide no direct evidence of language in contemporary written records, simply because there is no evidence of written language in either region at so early a date (Koch 2013a). However, there is a link to Celtic evidence in the region of the warrior stelae and Bronze Age copper mines, namely the southwestern Iberian Peninsula, in the immediately succeeding period, the Early Iron Age. As well as the evidence from Herodotus (5th century BC) discussed below, there is a corpus of 90–100 inscribed texts on stone from south Portugal and southwest Spain, several of these found in secondary cist burial contexts (Untermann 1997, 132–133), dating to 800–400 BC (Correia 1993; 1996; Jiménez Ávila 2021, but see Correa & Guerra 2019, who argue for a 6th–5th century BC date). Many Celtic names and other Celtic forms have been identified in these southwestern or 'Tartessian' inscriptions in work over the past 40 years (Koch 2013b; 2019a). These Iron Age stelae also show some direct links to the tradition of the Bronze Age warrior stelae. For example, the stelae of Majada Honda (Cabeza del Buey IV) and Capote, Badajoz, which depict chariots and various human figures, including one with a bi-horned headdress; later these were re-used in the same way, by being fragmented, turned around, and inscribed with Tartessian texts (Koch 2013b, 124; García Sanjuan & Díaz-Guardamino, 2015, 190–192). The stela of Gomes Aires (Abóboda 1), south Portugal, has a text carved around the figure of an armoured warrior brandishing elements that are difficult to interpret, possibly short spears and a shield (Koch 2013b, 73–77). It should be pointed out that the language of the southwestern inscriptions has lately been contested with special vehemence, with arguments tending to refute any and all Celtic evidence from the southwestern Iberian Peninsula earlier than the Late Iron Age (Sims-Williams 2020; García Alonso 2023). Accepting such a revision entails a challenging task of explaining away numerous Celtic-looking forms in the inscriptions, along with other evidence for southwest Iberia in the Early Iron Age pointing towards the same conclusion, such as the names in Herodotus: *Keltoi*, *Kunētes* and the Tartessian king's name *Arganthōnios* (Proto-Celtic *argantom 'silver'). One would also have to reject decades of seminal scholarship on the Palaeo-Hispanic languages (Correa Rodríguez 1989; 1992; Untermann 1997; Villar Liébana 2004; Jordán Cólera 2006; Ballester 2012; Hamp 2013). The intensity of the reaction reflects how much is at stake. If any Celtic was in use in the extreme

7. Linguistic aspects on the warrior iconography in Iberia and Scandinavia

southwest of Europe in the Early Iron Age, the long-established idea that the Celts and their language first spread from west-central Europe in the Hallstatt Iron Age becomes hard to sustain.

The wider knowledge base of linguistics can also be enlisted to explain the background of Bronze Age rock art. Two centuries of painstaking historical linguistic reconstruction has focused with special thoroughness to recover languages that must have been spoken in Europe in later prehistory, including a time depth including the Bronze Age in particular (cf. Mallory 1989; Mallory & Adams 2006). The task is thus narrowed somewhat to determining where exactly in time and space these carefully reconstructed languages were spoken and what archaeological material their speakers made and used. A key anchor point for contextualizing these reconstructed languages is the theory locating the homeland of the common ancestor of the Indo-European languages in the Pontic-Caspian steppe region at about 5000 or 6000 years ago. This 'Steppe Hypothesis' was widely accepted at the beginning of this century, especially amongst linguists (Mallory 1989; Anthony 2007). However, Renfrew's (1987; 2013) alternative 'Anatolian Hypothesis' remained strongly in contention until full-genome sequencing of ancient DNA became feasible more recently (cf. Cunliffe & Koch 2019), which revealed massive gene flow in the 3rd millennium BC from the Pontic-Caspian steppe widely across Western Eurasia, into what was to emerge at the dawn of history as Indo-European-speaking territories. Up to the time we now write the archaeogenetic evidence has provided better support for identifying the Yamnaya cultures of the steppe with the post-Anatolian stage of the proto-language after the most archaic Anatolian branch had split off. Thus, on current evidence, Proto-Indo-European itself might more probably be situated south of the Caucasus (Damgaard *et al.* 2018; Lazaridis 2018; Reich 2018; Koch 2020; Lazaridis *et al.* 2022), owing in this detail something to Renfrew's Anatolian Hypothesis. On the basis of this new understanding, some would now redub the common ancestor of Anatolian and the other branches as 'Indo-Anatolian' or return to the term 'Indo-Hittite' favoured by Sturtevant and Hamp (Lazaridis *et al.* 2022). Although this primal proto-language, datable perhaps to the 5th millennium BC, is now situated nearer geographically and chronologically to the probable epicentre of the first farmers of the European Neolithic, there is *as yet* no compelling case that any subgroup of Europe's agricultural pioneers carried the Caucasian ancestry type or probably spoke an 'Indo-Anatolian' language.

As mentioned above (p. XXX), that a new science has come on the scene with answers to old questions has stirred inevitable and useful controversy (e.g. Klejn *et al.* 2018; Furholt 2019; Hofmann *et al.* 2021). However, any doubt that the seminal archaeogenetic studies had succumbed to simplistic assumptions of a one-to-one correspondence between language and genetic type underrates the strength of genomic evidence and misreads the conclusions as actually formulated. It needs to be remembered that the Steppe Hypothesis won many adherents on just linguistic and archaeological evidence before ancient DNA was found strongly consistent with it. There is now abundant evidence showing that Yamnaya cultures (and their derivatives), post-Anatolian Indo-European, and the genetic steppe cluster often co-occur, but archaeogenetics, properly understood, does not claim or expect that they must be invariably coterminous. The transmission of language with genes is not a biological imperative. They are independent properties of human populations. Life often presents situations in which individuals learn a second language and then pass it on as a first language to their children. Thus 'mismatches' of language and ancestry arise, often cumulatively over the course of centuries. Modern Basque and Finnish people, speakers of non-Indo-European languages (Barbieri *et al.* 2022) and, similarly, some Dravidian-speaking groups, have high levels of steppe ancestry. Such examples are not puzzling when one considers who the neighbours, rulers, and coreligionists of these groups have been through long periods. As the story of the dispersal and diversification of the Indo-European languages and its speakers becomes better understood, the general direction that things evolved – how to draw lines connecting available data points – will sometimes be correctly anticipated on the basis of what we know already, but not always. Expect the unexpected (Koch & Fernández 2019).

Regarding the regions under scrutiny here, the Corded Ware Cultures (CWC) of northern Europe have long been regarded as probably associated with early Indo-European languages, a view which is now consistent with aDNA evidence (Allentoft *et al.* 2015; Haak *et al.* 2015; Malmström *et al.* 2019; Linderholm *et al.* 2020). Similarly, the cradle of Indo-European dialects that evolved into the attested Germanic languages has long been viewed as in and near the territory of the Nordic Bronze Age, in southern Scandinavia, north Germany, and around the western Baltic (e.g. Ringe 2017). And archaeogenetic evidence has done nothing to upset this consensus, thus far. In other words, when we consider the Scandinavian side of the equation we should keep in mind the prehistoric Indo-European dialects that evolved into Germanic, a reconstructed language we may term 'Pre-Germanic'. Encounters in the 3rd millennium BC between the Pitted Ware Culture (PWC) in Scandinavia and groups with pastoral steppe ancestry crossing the Baltic and Kattegat and Skagerrak are likely to represent interaction between Indo-European- and non-Indo-European-speaking groups (Iversen & Kroonen 2017). How did these incoming groups with their very different genetic background assimilate knowledge and tradition from PWC? How did this interaction affect the development of the emerging Indo-European branches, most especially Proto-Germanic in what is often seen as its homeland in southern Scandinavia and lands around the western Baltic? The research of the RAW project and Maritime Encounters programme can potentially throw light on these emerging questions.

For the Atlantic façade, the Archaeogenetic Revolution has provided more of a jolt to established orthodoxies. The story of the Celtic languages has long been presented as entwined with the Hallstatt and La Tène cultures of the European Iron Age and people called Keltoi who Herodotus, writing about 450 BC, located near the source of the Danube and thus where materials of classic Hallstatt and La Tène typology were abundant. It was usually overlooked, downplayed, or explained away that, in the same two passages, Herodotus also told of Keltoi 'beyond the Pillars of Hercules', the same words he used to locate the Phoenician colony at Cádiz, and neighbouring the Kunētes, who we know were in the Algarve. *Kunētes* is Celtic name; probably built on the root meaning 'hound, wolf' hence metaphorically 'warrior, hero', it is the exact cognate of the Ancient Brythonic place-name *Cunētio* and the personal names, Old Breton *Conoit* and Old Welsh *Cunuit* (Koch 2014). There is no indication in Herodotus that either the Keltoi or Kunētes were recent arrivals in Europe's extreme southwest.

The alternative view that the Indo-European that became Celtic reached the Atlantic West as early as the Beaker Copper Age (Dillon & Chadwick 1967; Harbison 1975) and/or was closely associated with the Atlantic Bronze Age (Almagro-Gorbea 1992; 1994) goes back decades. Fresh impetus for this alternative came as Cunliffe's 'Celtic from the West' idea (2001; Cunliffe & Koch 2010). More recently, aDNA sequencing reveals steppe DNA, the Yamnaya-associated cluster, arriving in Ireland, Britain, and the Iberian Peninsula by 2450–2400 BC and ascending to double-digit percentages by 1900 BC (Cassidy *et al.* 2016; Olalde *et al.* 2018; Valdiosera *et al.* 2018; Villaba-Mouco *et al.* 2021). This new evidence sits uncomfortably with earlier ideas of a wholly non-Indo-European Atlantic West through the Bronze Age. In other words, for the western terminus of our network and the transit zone between Iberia and Scandinavia, we should consider possible contact with the Indo-European dialects that gave rise to the attested Celtic languages of these regions, the reconstructed languages that we might term Pre- and Proto-Celtic.

In the standard Hallstatt/La Tène account of the Celts, the Atlantic façade might have remained entirely non-Indo-European-speaking until the mid-1st millennium BC. Suddenly aDNA evidence has tipped decisively against this long-standing idea. As mentioned above (pp. 22–25), a study from Harvard's Reich Lab shows – amongst other important findings – relatively little change in the population of what is now England and Wales in the Iron Age, that is between about 800 BC and the Roman conquest beginning in AD 43. This comparative genetic stability followed a period of dramatic gene flow into southern Britain across the sea from the near continent in the Middle to Late Bronze Age, about 1300–800 BC (Patterson *et al.* 2022).

Patterson *et al.* signals an important advance from the formative 'broad strokes' stage of the archaeogenetic revolution. At first, the history of the population of Europe – and by implication its languages – could be told as the story of three great migratory expansions: first hunter-gatherers repopulating the post-glacial landscape, then the first farmers spreading with an agricultural way of life from Anatolia, and then from about 3000 BC presumably Indo-European-speaking pastoralists expanding widely across Europe and into Central Asia. The mixing of these previously isolated groups was a genetically stark one, similar to that of Europeans first meeting the peoples of the New World in early modern times. But population movement highlighted in the Patterson *et al.* study is not an initial blending of these three primary streams but, rather, of two populations, both of whom had Anatolian farmer and steppe ancestry, but in different proportions. Therefore, we are very possibly dealing with two different

Indo-European-speaking groups. And that in turn raises the question of how far apart their languages might or might not have evolved from one another between the first phase and final phase of the Bronze Age. Also, how complete or partial had been the reduction of contact in the intervening period, about 1900–1300 BC? We have today entered the age of finer grade genetic, archaeological, and linguistic interpretation.

It is important to emphasize in this connection that the chief finding of Patterson *et al.* (2022) is that the steppe component went down in southern Britain between about 1300 and 800 BC, from previous higher levels in the Beaker Period and Early Bronze Age. The genomic clusters associated with Neolithic farmers increased significantly. That is not a finding that would immediately suggest the conclusion that an Indo-European language replaced non-Indo-European during the Late Bronze Age and that non-Indo-European survived longer, where steppe DNA levels remained higher in Scotland and Ireland (cf. Olalde *et al.* 2018; and for Ireland Cassidy *et al.* 2016). Rather, the archaeogenetic data show that a population with high levels of ancestry in common with Indo-European-speaking groups elsewhere had already been established across Ireland and Britain for a thousand years before new movements caused the downward shift in steppe ancestry in southern Britain in the Late Bronze Age. For linguists, this pattern suggests the likelihood of earlier and later varieties of Indo-European entering the British Isles, first about 2450–2000 BC, then about 1300–800 BC. With regards to one specific point of the Patterson *et al.* study, it may be that some early medieval inscriptions from the country of the Picts cannot yet be read, but the persistence of high levels of steppe aDNA in Scotland, from the Early Bronze Age onwards, does not lead to an expectation that Pictland was a non-Indo-European refuge linguistically.

7.1. The horse and wheeled-vehicle package

It will be useful to begin with this domain of meaning for three reasons:

1. This cultural sphere has long been seen as particularly symptomatic of Indo-Europeanization (e.g. Anthony 2007).
2. The category includes several words belonging to Indo-European as a whole (with attestations in the Asiatic languages and/or Anatolian), as well as a later layer showing modifications of form and/or meaning found only in the branches of the North and West, with several of those confined to Celtic and Germanic.
3. Much of this detailed vocabulary names items that are repeatedly represented in the stereotypical iconography of horses and chariots shared by the Bronze Age rock carvings of Scandinavia and Iberia.[2]

Two widespread Indo-European words in this semantic category that are well attested in Germanic and Celtic and can be linked to rock art iconography are *$H_1ékwos$ 'horse' (Old Norse *jór* 'stallion', Old English *eoh* 'war-horse', Old Irish *ech*, Gaulish *epo-* in names, Latin *equus*, Sanskrit *áśva*) and *$yugóm$ 'yoke' (Gothic *juk*, Old Norse *ok*, Old

English *geoc*, Old High German *joh*, Old Welsh *iou*, Latin *iugum*, Greek ζυγόν, Sanskrit *yugá-*, Hittite *i̯uka-*). A universal shared feature of rock art chariots is the pair of horses, usually facing each other, with the prominent line of the yoke joining the pair at their necks.

Horse

In view of the widespread reflexes of Proto-Indo-European *$H_1 éḱwos$* 'horse' in Germanic and Celtic, it is remarkable that a further two words, which mean more-or-less the same thing, are found uniquely in those two branches. A form reconstructable as Pre-Germanic **kankistos** and Pre-Celtic **kanksikā** lie behind • Proto-Germanic **hangistaz ~ *hanhistaz** 'horse, stallion, etc.', giving Ancient Nordic **niu hagestumz** 'nine stallions', Old Norse *hestr* 'stallion', Old English *hengest*, *hengst* 'gelding, horse', Old High German *hengist*, *chengisto* 'gelding'; • Proto-Celtic **kanxsikā-**: Gaulish personal names *Cassicius*, *Cassicia*, Middle Welsh *cassec*, Breton *kazeg* 'mare'. A preform **marko-** became • Proto-Germanic **marhaz** 'horse, steed', giving Old Norse *marr*, Old English *mearh*, Old High German *marah* (cf. East Germanic personal names *Marafredus*, *Marabadus*); • Proto-Celtic **markos** 'horse, steed', whence Gaulish accusative μαρκαν and τριμαρκισα 'a cavalry unit of three riders', *marcosior* 'may I ride', *calliomarcus* glossing 'equi ungula', Old Breton *marh*, Old Cornish *march* glossing 'equus', Middle Welsh *march*, Middle Irish *marc*, cf. Old Irish *marcach* glossing 'eques' 'horseman', Old Welsh *marchauc* < Proto-Celtic **markākos**. In both cases (**kankistos ~ *kanksikā** and **marko-**), it is doubtful whether words have an Indo-European source (Fig. 7.1).

Whether Indo-European or not, the proliferation of words meaning 'horse' in Celtic and Germanic is suggestive. This evidence leads naturally to the conclusion that horses had become more significant in the economies and value systems of North and West Europe during the Bronze Age, i.e. the stage after Proto-Indo-European had begun to break up into regional dialects but while forerunners of Germanic and Celtic remained in close contact or had possibly come back into close contact (cf. Ringe *et al.* 2002). On the level of creativity and sponsorship for creative activities, it is likely that a growing focus on the hero as chariot warrior encouraged Bronze Age stone carvers in Iberia and Scandinavia to repeatedly depict elaborate horse and chariot groups and, at the same time, led poets and storytellers to seek an expanded word stock to vary popular descriptions of the hero's chariot and horses.

Although most of the Celto-Germanic 'horse and wheel-vehicle' vocabulary can be related to Bronze Age rock art iconography, that is not the invariable rule. For example, Germanic and Celtic uniquely share a preform **mongo- ~ *mongā-** for horse's mane, giving Old Norse *makki*, Old English *manu*, Old High German *mana* 'mane'; Old Irish *mong* 'tuft of hair, crest, horse's mane', Old Breton plural *mogou* 'manes', Early Welsh *mwng* 'mane (of horses and other animals)'. Although the manes of horses are not clearly represented in the carved chariot horses of either region, the necks of the horses perpendicular to the line of the yoke are usually carefully carved, and it is possible that the concept of the 'mane' was represented in this way.

Wheeled vehicles and their parts

The Proto-Indo-European root √weĝh- 'move' is the source of words for wheeled-vehicles in several early Indo-European languages, including Greek ὄχος 'chariot' < ϝόχος < *woghos, Sanskrit vāhana 'chariot'. Sanskrit vahítram and Latin vehiculum can be reconstructed as the same Proto-Indo-European suffixed form *weĝhitlom (Mallory & Adams 2006, 247). Pre-Germanic and Pre-Celtic similarly share ***weghnos**, the source of Old Norse vagn, Old English wægn, wegn, Old High German wagan; Old Irish fén (also fénae < ***wegnyā**-). The Gaulish divine epithet **MARTI VEGNIO** (Grevenmacher, Luxembourg), probably belongs here, i.e. 'Mars the chariot driver'. An Ancient Brythonic word for two-wheeled war chariot is couinnus (used for Caledonian war chariots in Tacitus, Agricola) probably from ***ko(m)-wegno-**.*weĝhnos, the same suffixed formation as the Celto-Germanic, will explain Tocharian B yakne, but the meaning of that word is 'way, manner' suggests that *weĝhnos developed the specific narrow sense 'wheeled vehicle' only in Celto-Germanic.

It is possible that Proto-Indo-European *(H)rótH$_2$-o/eH$_2$- originally meant 'wheel' rather than 'wheeled vehicle'. But this is uncertain as both meanings are attested, and this word has been formed from the Proto-Indo-European verb √retH$_2$- 'run', which could lead to nouns of various meanings (Mallory & Adams 2006, 248). So, for example, Sanskrit rátha- 'war chariot', Avestan raθa- 'wagon, chariot' may preserve the basic meaning. In the northwestern languages, the form became ***rotos ~ *rotā**, which gives Old Frisian reth, Old High German rad, hrad; the Gaulish place-name Rotomagus, Old Irish roth 'wheel', Middle Welsh rot 'wheel'; Lithuanian rãtas 'wheel, circle, ring, (plural) cart'. It is possible that Latin rota 'wheel, chariot' similarly goes back to Proto-Italic ***rotā**; however, Latin rota may be a loanword from Celtic (Olander 2019), cf. Latin petorritum 'four-wheeled Gaulish carriage', from Gaulish *petru-rotom. It is Latin radius 'spoke' that probably preserves the native Italic word in a formation cognate with Vedic ráthya- 'belonging to a chariot' < Proto-Indo-European *(H)rotH$_2$-yo-. The root √H$_2$ek̂s-i- 'axle' is Proto-Indo-European: Sanskrit ákṣa- 'axle', Avestan aša- 'arm-pit', Greek ἄξων 'axle'. However, the suffix with *-(V)l- with the meaning 'axle' is uniquely shared by Pre-Celtic/Pre-Germanic: ***aksil- ~ *aks̥l-**, as the source of Old Norse ǫxull 'axle'; Middle Welsh echel, also achel 'axle-tree, axle, axis, pivot', Middle Breton ahel 'axle'. A clearly carved axle is a standard feature of the carved chariots of both Iberia and Scandinavia, similarly represented as deeply carved straight line linking the hubs of the two wheels (represented as turned outwards 90°), parallel to the line of the yoke and perpendicular to that of the draught pole (Fig. 7.1; Table 7.1).

Riding

Reconstructable for both Germanic and Celtic is a verb ***reidh-**, meaning 'to ride a horse or a horse-drawn vehicle', giving Old Norse ríða 'to ride', Old English rīdan, Old High German rītan; Gaulish is the probable source of Latin rēda 'travelling carriage with four wheels', cf. Gaulish uerēdus 'steed' (para-uerēdus, the source of German Pferd), Old Irish réidid 'rides (a horse or a horse-drawn chariot)', cf. Middle Welsh gorwyδ 'steed, mounted horse'. It is important to note that in both Germanic and Celtic the derivatives of **reidh-** signify rising on the back of horse, as well as riding in a wheeled vehicle, and that this is probably a shared innovation in meaning pointing to a cultural innovation shared by the two groups. The same verb is found with a similar, but less specialized meaning in Baltic: Lithuanian *riedéti* 'rolling', reflecting northwest Indo-European √(H)reidh-e- 'roll'. That Baltic comparison suggests that the meaning linked with the wheeled vehicle is more original and the sense of horseback riding secondary.

Particularly close interaction between the ancestors of Germanic and Celtic is indicated by several two-element close compounds with exactly parallel formations in the two language families. One of these corresponding compounds belongs to the 'horse and wheeled vehicle' field. We can reconstruct for Pre-Germanic and Pre-Celtic at close compound **ekwo-reidho-** 'horse'+'ride', as reflected by Old Norse personal name *Jó-reiðr*, Old English *ēo-red* 'troop, band (of retainers)'; the Gaulish personal

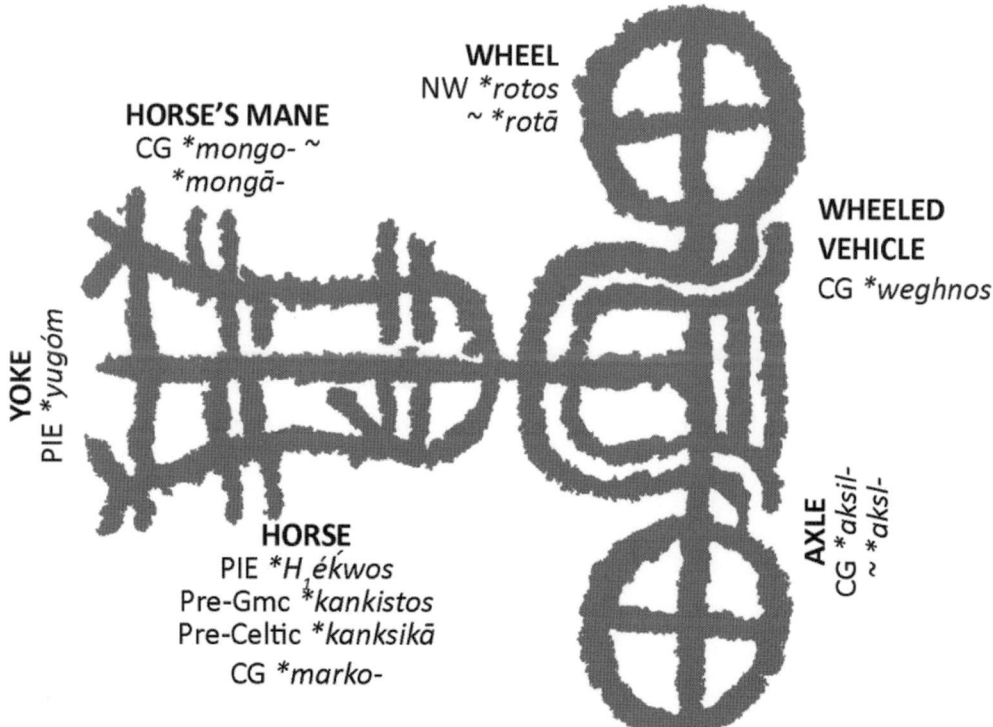

Figure 7.1. Drawing of a Scandinavian rock art chariot (panel in Frännarp (Gryt 1:1)), Scania, showing inherited Celto-Germanic and Northwest Indo-European vocabulary for its components as repeatedly depicted in Scandinavian rock art and Iberian stelae. Interpretation based on a visualization from photogrammetry by Christian Horn and Rich Potter.

name *Epo-rēdo-rīx* 'horse-ride+king' (Caesar, *Bello Gallico* §7.38) = Galatian Ἐπορηδοριξ (Freeman 2001, 55), cf. Middle Welsh *ebrwyδ* 'quick, swift, sudden'.

In the vocabulary of the horse and wheeled-vehicle discussed above, each item corresponds to 'stock' features repeatedly depicted in the Bronze Age rock carvings of Scandinavia and Iberia. In interpreting a three-way correspondence of material culture (actual domestic horses and warrior-associated wheeled vehicles) and their reflection, on the one hand, in visual arts and, on the other, in language, it should not necessarily be assumed that material culture is primary with independent reflections in art and language. As a possible analogy, we may turn to the medieval Irish heroic tales that comprise the so-called 'Ulster Cycle', a literary corpus written and copied in a time and place, i.e. early medieval Ireland, in which the chariot no longer figured in warfare. Nonetheless, the Ulster Cycle tales have numerous examples of formulaic descriptions of war chariots and their many parts with repetitive use of stock vocabulary (Greene 1972; Mallory 1998; Karl 2003; Stifter 2009). This analogy alerts us to the possibility that formulaic enumerations of the parts of the chariots of heroes might be a common source of shared vocabulary in this semantic domain and the visual representation of chariots that can be broken

Table 7.1. *Inherited Celto-Germanic and northwest Indo-European vocabulary for components of the horse and wheeled vehicle package*

		HORSE AND WHEELED VEHICLE PACKAGE		
Proto-language	Reconstruction	Meaning	Attestations	PIE derivation
CG	*aksil- ~ *aks̯l-	axle	ON *ǫxull* 'axle'; MW *echel, achel*, MB *ahel* 'axle'	√H_2eks-i- 'axle'
CG	*ekwo-reidho-	horse+ride	ON *Jó-reiðr*, OE *ēo-red* 'troop, band'; Galatian Ἐπορηδοριξ	*H_1ékwos 'horse'
CG	*kankistos ~ *kanksikā	horse	ON *hestr* 'stallion', OE *hengest* 'gelding, horse', OHG *hengist* 'gelding'; MW *cassec*, B *kazeg* 'mare'	
CG	*marko-	horse	ON *marr*, OE *mearh*, OHG *marah*; Gaul μαρκαν, MIr *marc*, OB *marh*, OC *march* 'equus', MW *march* 'horse, stallion'	
CG	*mongo- ~ *mongā-	horse's mane	ON *makki*, OE *manu*, OHG *mana*; OIr *mong*, MW *mwng*	
CG	*reidh-	to ride a horse or horse-drawn vehicle	ON *ríða* 'ride', OE *rīdan*, OHG *rītan*; OIr *réidid* 'rides (a horse or horse-drawn chariot)'	NW √(H)reidh-e- 'roll'
NW	*rotos ~ *rotā	(spoked?) wheel	OHG *rad*; OIr *roth*, MW *rot*; Lat *rota*?; Lith *rātas* 'wheel, circle'	*(H)rótH$_2$o/eH$_2$-
CG	*weghnos	wheeled vehicle	ON *vagn*, OE *wægn*, OHG *wagan*; OIr *fén*	√weĝh- 'move'

down as standardized arrangement of isolated parts. As a creative *tour de force*, the detailed description or visual representation of a chariot and horses could attract an appreciative audience; not just carriage makers would be familiar with all the parts, but anyone who used, assembled, disassembled, repaired, or trained and harnessed horses to pull wheeled vehicles. Such an underlying check list could help to explain why horses, wheels, axles, etc. are not shown in rock art in correct spatial relationship to one another, but so that each element could be most easily recognized separately.

7.2. The 'warrior's panoply'

The 'horse and wheeled-vehicle package' canvassed above can be understood as a subset of the 'warrior's panoply', which once again lends itself to detailed check lists for comparing Iberian stelae and Scandinavian rock art and likewise vocabulary items unique to the North and West of the Indo-European world. A selection of comparable items is set out below (Fig. 7.2; Table 7.2).

Spear

The spear is prominent in the rock carvings of both regions. There are two distinctly Celto-Germanic words for 'spear'. A reconstruction ***ghaisó-** is implied by Old Norse *geirr*, Old English *gār*, and Old High German *gēr* in Germanic, and Gaulish *gaesum* and Old Irish *gae* for Celtic. This word is also the first element of shared compound name, meaning 'Spear-king': *Gaisericus* king of the Vandals (~AD 389–477) and *Gaesorix* the Celtic name of the chief of the Cimbri captured by the Romans in 101 BC. A second Celto-Germanic word for 'spear' lies behind Old Norse *ljóstr* 'fish-spear' and Middle Irish *los* 'end, butt, foot, point of a staff, stick', Middle Welsh *llost* 'tail, spear, lance, javelin' (English *leister* 'fish-spear' is a Scandinavian loanword).

Axe

Ubiquitous in Bronze Age material, but somewhat ambiguous as both a tool and a weapon, a shared word for 'axe' can be traced to a formation of inherited elements, Proto-Indo-European √bheiH- 'strike' + instrument suffix *-tlo-, hence 'striking implement', as implied by Old Norse *bíldr* 'axe', Old High German *bīhal*, Old Irish *biáil*, Middle Welsh *buyall*, Middle Breton *bouhazl*. Axes are prominent in Scandinavian rock art, less so in Iberian stelae.

Bow and arrow

A word ***arkʷo-** meaning 'bow and arrow' can be reconstructed for Germanic, Celtic, and Italic, but no other Indo-European language: thus, Gothic *arƕazna*, Old Norse *ǫr*, Old English *arwe, earh*, all meaning 'arrow'; the very common Hispano-Celtic name *Arquius* 'bowman', feminine *Arcea*, place-name *Arco-brigā* 'bow-shaped hill' (Koch 2016; Koch & Fernández Palacios 2019); Latin *arcus*, genitive *arquī* 'bow, arch'. The earlier meaning of the word is probably reflected in Greek ἄρκευθος, Latvian *ērcis*, Russian *rakíta* 'juniper', a wood suitably flexible for making bows.

Shield

The primary words for 'shield' present an interesting case: the prehistoric form behind the Germanic word resembled the Italic, Balto-Slavic, and most especially the Celtic words, but they are not actually cognates. Thus, Gothic *skildus*, Old Norse *skjǫldr*, Old English *scyld*, Old High German *scilt* can be reconstructed as Proto-Germanic **skelduz** from an earlier (before the operation of the Germanic change known as 'Grimm's Law') **skel(H)-tú-**. Old Irish *scíath*, Old Welsh *scuit*, Old Breton *scoit* go back to Proto-Celtic **skēto-** < **skeito**. Latin *scūtum* implies Proto-Italic **skoitom**. Compare also Old Prussian *staytan*, *scaytan* 'shield', Russian *ščit* 'shield' from Proto-Balto-Slavic **skóitum**. The actual cognate Pre-Celtic **skeito-** 'shield' came to mean 'sheath' in Germanic: Old Norse *skíði*, Old English *scēað*, Old High German *sceida*. It is not surprising to sound-alikes shifting meaning within a shared sphere of meaning like this.

Club

A Celto-Germanic word, with no clear Indo-European source, designating a primitive and basic weapon, lies behind Old Norse *lurkr* 'club, thick stick'; Old Irish *lorg* 'staff, stick, rod, club, cudgel', Archaic Welsh *llory* 'hunter's club, cudgel'.

Sword

Negative evidence is not always significant, especially when we are hunting for an old word with a particular meaning. All languages change and all words are therefore subject to random loss over time. Thus far, research in the RAW project has not turned up a Celto-Germanic word for sword, though this is a prominent weapon in the Bronze Age archaeological record and rock art iconography of both regions. In this case – more than that of the spear or bow and arrow, for example – technological changes leading to changes in sword-fighting technique between the Bronze and Iron Ages could easily have led to obsolescence of vocabulary. It is also worth noting that over much of West-central Europe the sword went largely out of fashion in the Hallstatt D period (~600–475 BC) to be followed by a very different type in the La Tène Iron Age. It would therefore be unremarkable if the old word had been lost. Nevertheless, there is an intriguing correspondence. Anyone surveying the corpus of Scandinavian rock art will notice how relatively rarely the sword is depicted in action but, more often, warriors are depicted with swords projecting behind them and an erect penis to the front at the same level, creating some visual ambiguity as to whether what is actually represented might be the hilt of the sword. In an intriguing Celtic parallel, medieval Irish has two common words for sword: *claideb* and what was arguably the older word referring to an older type of weapon (a stabbing sword or rapier) *colg* or *calg*. That second word was also the base of the name of the Caledonian leader who fought Agricola in AD 84, *Calgācus* 'the swordsman'. In Brythonic, on the other hand, this word occurs as Middle Welsh *caly* and Middle Breton *calch*, but that means 'penis'; the meaning 'sword' had been lost before the earliest attestations. Therefore, it is likely that the sword was the weapon most associated metaphorically with sex – what goes into a

7. Linguistic aspects on the warrior iconography in Iberia and Scandinavia   95

Table 7.2. Inherited Celto-Germanic and Northwest Indo-European vocabulary for accoutrements of the warrior. Consisting mostly of weapons, these items feature prominently in both Scandinavian rock art and Iberian stelae

		WEAPONS, WARRIOR'S PANOPLY		
Proto-language	Reconstruction	Meaning	Attestations	PIE derivation
ICG	*arkʷo-	bow and arrow	Goth arḥv-azna, ON ǫr, OE arwe, earh 'arrow'; HC Arquius, Arcea 'bow(wo)man', Arco-brigā 'bow-shaped hill'; Lat arcus 'bow, arch'	cf. Greek ἄρκευθος 'juniper'
CG	*bhei(a)tlo-	axe	ON bíldr, OHG bīhal 'axe'; OIr biáil, MW buyall, MB bouhazl 'axe'	√bheiH- 'strike' + *-tlo-
CG	*dhelgo- ~ *dholgo-	brooch, dress fastener	ON dálkr 'brooch, clasp, pin, dagger', OE dalc, dolc 'clasp, bracelet, brooch, buckle'; OIr delg 'pin fastening mantel, brooch; thorn', OC delc 'necklace, collar'	cf. Lith dìlgė 'nettle'
CG	*ĝhaisó-	spear	ON geirr, OE gār, OHG gēr; Gaulish gaesum, OIr gae	√ĝhi- 'throw', cf. Skt. héṣas- 'missile'
CG	*Ghaiso-rīg-s	Spear-king	Gaisericus of the Vandals, Gaesorix of the Cimbri	
Proto-Celtic	*kalgo- ~ *kalgā-	sword, penis	OIr colg or calg, Pictish Calgācus 'swordsman', MW caly, MB calch 'penis'	
CG	*leust- ~ *lustā-	spear	ON ljóstr 'fish-spear'; MIr los 'end, butt, foot, point of a staff, stick', MW llost 'tail, spear, lance, javelin'	√leuH$_x$ 'hunt, release, cut off'
CG	*lurgā-	club	ON lurkr 'club, thick stick'; OIr lorg 'staff, stick, rod, club, cudgel', MW llory 'hunter's club, cudgel'	
NW	*skel(H)-tú ~ *skeito- ~ *skoitom	shield (sheath)	Goth skildus, ON skjǫldr, OE scyld, OHG scilt 'shield'; OIr scíath, OW scuit, OB scoit 'shield'; Lat scūtum; OP scaytan 'shield', Russian ščit 'shield'	

sheath – and most especially in this sense early types of sword that were stabbing weapons, rather than edge weapons.

Brooch, dress pin

The direct evidence of personal possessions show that Bronze Age warriors valued displays of status and beauty, as well as equipment for combat. Such aesthetic values carry over into rock art. For example, prominent mirrors, represented in similar ways occur as stock motifs in both regions. If there was a shared word for these, we have

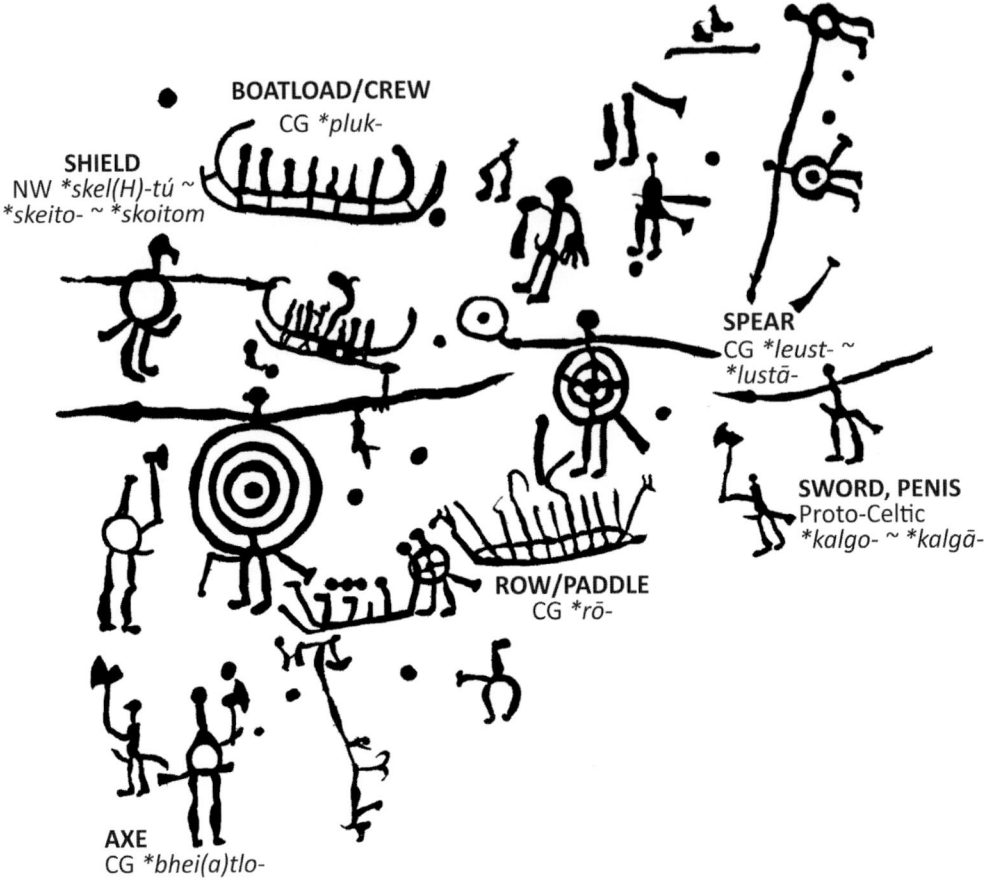

Figure 7.2. Rock art panel from Sweden (Panel in Finntorp (Tanum 89:1)), Bohuslän, labelled with the corresponding Celto-Germanic and Northwest Indo-European vocabulary items. Interpretation based on a visualization from photogrammetry by Christian Horn and Rich Potter.

yet to find it. On the other hand, disproportionately large brooches were sometimes carved alongside warrior figures, and we can relate these to Celto-Germanic ***dhelgo- ~ *dholgo-**, whence Old Norse *dálkr* 'brooch, clasp, pin, dagger', Old English *dalc, dolc* 'clasp, bracelet, brooch, buckle'; Old Irish *delg* 'pin fastening mantel to the breast, brooch, thorn, spike, peg', Old Cornish *delc* 'necklace, collar'. Lithuanian *dilgė* 'nettle' points to an earlier sense 'pointed piercing object' and a semantic development in dress ornaments from simple pins to more complex fasteners with moving parts.

7.3. Combat, warfare, violence

Battle
As well as specific items of warrior's gear, a theme characteristic of Scandinavian and Iberian iconography in general and likewise Celto-Germanic vocabulary in general is

the domain of combat, warfare, and violence. With the Iberian stelae, the figures are represented in a static posture, the combat is offstage, but implicit in the detailed attention to preparation for it. A long list of synonyms and near synonyms can be compiled, including but not limited to the following, of words meaning broadly 'battle, fighting, combat' and confined to our corner of the Indo-European world: Celto-Germanic ***bhodhwo-** reflected as Old Norse *boð*, Old English *beadu*, Old High German *batu-*; Gaulish personal names *Boduo-gnatus, Ateboduus, Atebodua, Boduognatus, Boduacus, Boduogenus, Boduos*; Ancient Brythonic **BODVOCI**, Middle Irish *bodb, badb* 'war-god(dess), scald-crow', the Gaulish goddess name **[C]ATHUBODVAE**, Old Breton Personal name *Catuuodu*; Celto-Germanic ***katu-** reflected as Ancient Nordic **haþu**, Old Norse *hǫð*, Old English *heaðo-*, Old High German *hadu*; Gaulish group name *Catuslugi*, Gaulish and Ancient Brythonic *Catuvellauni*, OIr. *cath*, Old Welsh *cat* 'battle'; Celto-Germanic ***weik- ~ *wik-** reflected as Gothic *weihan*, Ancient Nordic **uuigaz** 'warrior', Old Norse *vega* 'kill, fight', Old English and Old High German *wīhan* 'fight'; Gaulish *Eburo-uices* 'Yew-fighters', *Lemo-uices* 'Elm-fighters', Ancient Brythonic *Ordo-uices* 'hammer fighters', Old Irish *fichid* 'fights', *fecht* 'military expedition', Old Welsh *gueith* 'battle'; Celto-Germanic ***nīt-** giving Gothic *neiþ* 'envy, jealousy, enmity', *andaneiþa* 'enemy', Old English *nīþ*, Old High German *nīd* 'battle-rage, hate, envy'; Old Irish *níth* 'fighting, combat, battle, pugnacity, anger, resentment'; Celto-Germanic ***nant-** as the source of Gothic *ana-nanþjan* 'to take courage', Old English *nēþan* 'to venture, to risk', Old High German *gi-nenden, nanta* 'to apply oneself, to have courage'; Old Irish *néit* 'battle, combat, fighting', *Néit* 'god of battle, husband of the war-goddess Nemain or Badb'; Celto-Germanic ***bhēgh- ~ *bhōgh-**, giving Old Norse *bægjast* 'quarrel, strive', Old High German *bāgēn* 'quarrel, fight'; Old Irish *bág* 'fight, contest, striving, act of contending', *bágaid* 'fights, boasts', cf. Middle Welsh *kymwyat* 'fighter; Celto-Germanic ***bhrest-** giving Old Norse *bresta*, Old English *berstan* 'to burst, damage, injure, harm'; Old Irish *bres* 'fight, blow, effort', *brissid* 'breaks, smashes, destroys, defeats in battle, routs, overthrows', Middle Breton *bresel* 'war'; also Celto-Germanic ***slak-** 'strike (in battle)', Gothic *slahan* 'strike', Old Norse *slá* 'strike', Old English *slēan* 'to strike to death', *slege* 'blow, stroke', Old High German *slahan* 'to slay'; Middle Irish *slachta* 'struck', *slacc* 'sword'.

Particularly close contacts between speakers of the languages ancestral to Celtic and Germanic are indicated compounds shared uniquely between these branches, several of which have to do with combat: ***Katu-mōros ~ *Katu-mēros** 'great/famous in battle' becoming Old High German *Hadumâr*; Galatian **ΚΑΤΟΜΑΡΟΣ**, Gaulish *Catumaros*, Archaic Welsh *Catmor*; ***katu-wl̥kʷo- ~ *katu-wolkʷo-** 'Battle-wolf/predator' reflected in Ancient Nordic **haþuwulafz**, Gaulish *Catuvolcus* and the Middle Welsh epithet *katwalch* 'hero, champion, warrior'; ***Seghi-mēros ~ *Segho-mōros** 'great/famous in victory', whence Ancient Germanic Σεγιμερος = *Segimēros* (Strabo), Ancient Nordic **sigimaraz**, Old Norse *Sigimarr*, Old English *Sigemær*, Old High German *Sigimar*; Hispano-Celtic **SEGVMARVS**, Gaulish (Gallo-Greek) **ϹΕΓΟΜΑΡΟϹ**. A Celtic Germanic compound verb for triumphant fighting, ***uper-weik- ~ *uper-wik-** is the source Old High German *ubarwehan* 'to overcome' and Old Irish *for-fich* 'conquered'.

Hillfort

A related development less overt in rock art iconography – though possibly undetected in its symbolism – is the rise of the elite fortified settlement. And this is a development that can be traced in the evolution of Proto-Indo-European towards the Germanic and Celtic subfamilies. For example, the Proto-Indo-European root √bherĝh- 'be high, hill', in its zero-grade as Celto-Germanic **bhr̥gh-** came to mean 'fortified settlement, hillfort': Gothic *baurgs* 'town(s)', Old Norse *borg* 'town, citadel, small hill', Old English *burg* 'city, fortified town', Old High German *burg* 'town'; Hispano-Celtic and Gaulish *brigā* 'fortified town, hillfort' (Table 7.3).

A related formation had religious significance in Proto-Indo-European, and then gave rise to the name of powerful tribes and tribal confederations as uniquely Celto-Germanic **Bhr̥ghn̥tes**, which became Old Norse *Burgundar*, Old English *Burgendas*, the name of the powerful East Germanic-speaking group, the Burgundians, a name also preserved in the Baltic island name *Bornholm*, Old Norse *Burgundarholmr*. The corresponding Celtic group name Βριγαντες occurs in Ptolemy's *Geography* for groups in southeast Ireland and north Britain. The group name Βριγαντιοι occurred also in southern Germany and Galicia. The corresponding divine name is Romano-British *Brigantia* (Falileyev *et al.* 2010, 12), as well as the Old Irish name of the saint and goddess *Brigit*, called 'dea poetarum' in Cormac's Glossary. The Indo-European origin of this goddess is confirmed by Vedic *br̥hatī́* 'the high one' (<*bhr̥ĝhn̥tī́), an epithet of Uṣás, the goddess of the dawn. As Ptolemy's Βριγαντες were located in the regions where the cults of goddess Brigantia and St Brigit flourished, it is likely that the group name arose as 'people of the sky goddess', rather than 'hillfort people'.

Wound, injure

Another long list words unique to our regions can be grouped under the meaning 'wound, injure' (Table 7.4): Celto-Germanic **bhreus-**, the source of Old English *brȳsan* 'bruise'; Old Irish *bruïd* 'breaks in pieces, smashes, crushes', *bronnaid* 'injures, damages', Middle Welsh *briw* noun 'wound, hurt, injury, bruise, sore', Cornish *brew* 'wound'; **kneit-** ~ **knit-** giving Old Norse *hníta* 'wound to death', Old English and Old Saxon *hnītan* 'thrust, stab'; Old Irish *cned* 'a wound, sore'; **aghlo-**, the source of Gothic *agliþa*, *aglo* 'affliction', *agljan* 'treat badly, harm', Old English *eglan* 'to harass, afflict'; Middle Irish *álad* 'wound', Middle Welsh *aelet* 'pain, suffering, affliction, grief', *aelawt* 'grief, affliction'; **gʷhen-** ~ **gʷhon-**, reflected in Gothic *banja* 'strike, wound', Old Norse *ben*, Old English *ben(n)* 'slayer, murderer', Old High German *bano* 'death, bringer of death, bane, killer'; Old Irish *guin* 'wound, injury', Welsh *gwaniad* 'stab, thrust, prick, wound'; Celto-Germanic **koldo-**, giving Gothic *halts*, Old Norse *haltr*, Old English *healt*, Old High German *halz* 'lame, crippled, limping'; Old Irish *coll* 'destruction, spoiling, injury, loss, castration, deflowering', Middle Welsh *coll* 'loss, damage, hurt, destruction, harm caused by loss'; **kre(n)g-** ~ **krog-**, the source of Old Norse *hrekja* 'to drive away, worry, vex, damage, abuse'; Old Irish *crécht* 'wound, ulcer', Old Breton *creithi* 'ulcera', Middle Welsh *creith* 'scar, wound'; Celto-Germanic

Table 7.3. Celto-Germanic inherited vocabulary related to fighting and warfare

COMBAT, WARFARE, VIOLENCE

Proto-language	Reconstruction	Meaning	Attestations	PIE derivation
CG	*bhēgh- ~ *bhōgh-	fighting, combat, battle	ON bǽgjast 'quarrel, strive', OHG bāgēn 'quarrel, fight'; OIr bág 'fight, contest', bágaid 'fights, boasts'	
CG	*bhodhwo-	fighting, combat, battle	ON boð, OE beadu, OHG batu- 'battle'; Gaul personal names Boduacus, Boduos; AB BODVOCI, MIr bodb, badb 'war-god(dess), scald-crow'	
CG	*bhrest-	fighting, combat, battle	ON bresta, OE berstan 'to burst, damage, injure, harm'; OIr bres 'fight, blow, effort', brissid 'breaks, smashes, destroys, defeats in battle', MB bresel 'war'	
CG	*bhr̥gh-	hillfort, fortified settlement	Goth baurgs 'town(s)', ON borg 'town, citadel, small hill', OE burg 'city, fortified town', OHG burg 'town'; HC & Gaul brigā 'fortified town, hillfort'	√bherĝh- 'be high, hill'
CG	*katu-	fighting, combat, battle	AN haþu, ON hǫð, OE heaðo, OHG hadu 'battle'; Gaul group name Catuslugi, Gaul & AB Catuvellauni, OIr cath, OW cat 'battle'	cf. OCS kotora 'fight'
CG	*Katu-mōros ~ *Katu-mēros	great/famous in battle	OHG Hadumâr; Galatian ΚΑΤΟΜΑΡΟΣ, Gaul Catumaros, OW Catmor	
CG	*katu-wolkʷo-	battle-wolf/predator	AN haþuwulafz; Gaul Catuvolcus, MW katwalch 'hero, champion, warrior'	
CG	*nant-	fighting, combat, battle	Goth ana-nanþjan 'to take courage', OE nēþan 'to venture, to risk', OHG gi-nenden 'to have courage'; OIr néit 'battle, combat, fighting'	
CG	*nīt-	fighting, combat, battle	Goth neiþ 'envy, jealousy, enmity', OE nīþ, OHG nīd 'battle-rage, hate, envy'; OIr níth 'fighting, combat, battle, anger'	
CG	*Seghi-mēros ~ *Segho-mōros	great/famous in victory	Ancient Gmc Σεγιμερος, AN sigimaraz, ON Sigimarr, OE Sigemǽr, OHG Sigimar; HC SEGVMARVS, Gaul ΣΕΓΟΜΑΡΟΣ	
CG	*slak-	strike (in battle)	Goth slahan, ON slá 'strike', OE slēan 'to strike to death', OHG slahan 'to slay'; MIr slachta 'struck', slacc 'sword'	
CG	*uper-weik- ~ *uper-wik-	conquer, overcome	OHG ubarwehan 'to overcome'; OIr for-fich 'conquered'	
CG	*weik- ~ *wik-	fighting, combat, battle	Goth weihan 'to fight', AN uuigaz 'warrior', ON vega 'kill, fight', OE & OHG wīhan 'fight'; Gaul Eburo-uices 'Yew-fighters', Lemo-uices 'Elm-fighters', AB Ordo-uices 'hammer fighters', OIr fichid 'fights'	cf. Lat vincō 'conquer', Lith apveikiù 'defeat', Rus vek 'force'

Table 7.4. Celto-Germanic inherited vocabulary relating to 'wounding, injury'

WOUNDING, INJURY

Proto-language	Reconstruction	Meaning	Attestations	PIE derivation
CG	*aghlo-	wound, injure	Goth *agliþa* 'affliction', OE *eglan* 'to harass, afflict'; MIr *álad* 'wound', MW *aelet* 'pain, affliction, grief', *aelawt* 'grief, affliction'	Cf. Skt *aghalá-* 'terrible'
CG	*bhreus-	wound, injure	OE *brȳsan* 'bruise'; OIr *bruïd* 'breaks in pieces, smashes', *bronnaid* 'injures, damages', MW *briw* noun 'wound, hurt, injury, bruise, sore'	Cf. Lat *frustum* 'piece'
CG	*gʷhen- ~ *gʷhon-	wound, injure	Goth *banja* 'strike, wound', ON *ben*, OE *ben(n)* 'slayer, murderer', OHG *bano* 'death, bane, killer'; OIr *guin* 'wound, injury, killing'	√*gʷhen-* 'strike'
CG	*kneit- ~ *knit-	wound, injure	ON *hníta* 'wound to death', OE *hnītan* 'thrust, stab'; OIr *cned* 'a wound, sore'	
CG	*koldo-	wound, injure	Goth *halts*, ON *haltr*, OE *healt*, OHG *halz* 'lame, crippled, limping'; OIr *coll* 'destruction, spoiling, injury, loss, castration', MW *coll* 'loss, damage, hurt, destruction'	
CG	*kre(n)g- ~ *krog-	wound, injure	ON *hrekja* 'to drive away, damage, abuse'; OIr *crécht* 'wound, ulcer', OB *creithi* 'ulcera', MW *creith* 'scar, wound'	
CG	*sai-	wound, injure	Goth *sair*, ON *sár* 'wound, pain', OIr *saeth* 'trouble, hardship, distress', MW *hoet* 'longing, sorrow, grief'	√*seH₄i-* 'pain'

*sai-, whence Gothic *sair*, Old Norse *sár* 'wound, pain', Old English *sār* 'pain, wound, suffering', Old High German *serō* 'painfully'; Old Irish *saeth* 'trouble, hardship, distress, disease, illness', Middle Welsh *hoet* 'longing, sorrow, grief, vexation'.

7.4. Maritime vocabulary

As the working hypothesis of the RAW project involves long-distance contact by sea between metal consuming Bronze Age Scandinavia and the metal-producing Atlantic West, both images and words indicating interest in seafaring at this period hold special significance. As far as images go, though there are similarities between some images of vessels carved on stone in western Iberia and those of Scandinavian rock art, there is a great contrast between these regions in the numbers of surviving carvings.

7. Linguistic aspects on the warrior iconography in Iberia and Scandinavia

Over 20,000 vessel images have been identified in Scandinavian rock art but relatively few from Bronze Age Iberia. This observation is consistent with the premise that, much as in the Viking Age 2000 years later, the primary ship-builders and instigators of long-distance expeditions were base in Scandinavia. This Bronze Age/Viking Age parallelism is an important cornerstone of the maritime mode of production interpretive model applicable to both periods (Ling *et al.* 2018). It does not necessarily follow that at either period that the far-ranging crews were exclusively recruited from groups of Scandinavian background. Suggestive maritime vocabulary that can be lined up with rock art iconography (Table 7.5; Fig. 7.3) include: 'row, paddle' as a primary verb, Celto-Germanic ***rō-**, whence Old Norse *róa* 'to row', Old English *rōwan* 'to go by water, sail, swim'; Old Irish *ráïd* 'rows, sails, voyages' and the Middle Irish compound *imm·rá* 'travels by boat, navigates' (cf. Hyllested 2010); ***kŭp-, *kup-s-**, which had originally meant any sort of curved container or specifically a beehive (English *hive*), acquiring the meaning 'boat, boat's hull' only in Celtic and Germanic, as seen in Old Norse *húfr* 'hull of a ship', Middle Welsh *cwch* 'boat, beehive'; Celto-Germanic ***kapono-** 'harbour, shelter for vessels', giving Old Norse *hǫfn*, Old English *hæfen*, Old High German *havan*; Middle Irish *cúan* 'haven, harbour, port, bay, gulf'; a Celto-Germanic ***pluk-** 'boatload' (from Proto-Indo-European √*pleu-* 'float, swim, wash') can be reconstructed as the common source of Old Norse *flokkr* 'troop, host, flock', Old English *flocc* 'flock, company, troop' (cf. Middle Dutch *vluycken* 'to transport

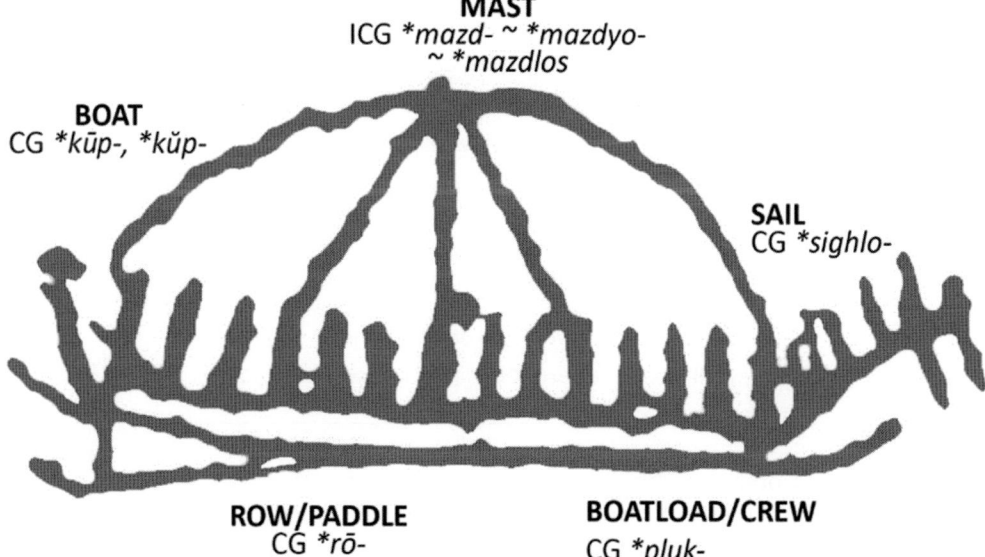

Figure 7.3. Drawing of a rock art image of sizable boat with crew and rigging from Sweden (panel in Järrestad (Järrestad 13:1)), Scania, labelled with inherited Celto-Germanic and Italo-Celtic/Germanic inherited vocabulary items corresponding to items depicted or implied in the image. Interpretation by Christian Horn based on a photograph by Catarina Bertilsson.

Table 7.5. Celto-Germanic and Italo-Celtic/Germanic inherited vocabulary relating to the maritime sphere and watercraft

			MARITIME WORDS, NAVIGATION	
Proto-language	Reconstruction	Meaning	Attestations	PIE derivation
CG	*kapono-	harbour, shelter for vessels	ON *hǫfn*, OE *hæfen*, OHG *havan*; MIr *cúan* 'haven, harbour, port, bay, gulf'	
CG	*kŭp- ~ *kup-s-	boat, also beehive	ON *hýfr* 'hull of a ship', OE *hȳf* 'bee-hive', MW *cwch* 'boat, beehive', Breton *kouc'h* 'beehive'	Skt. *kū́pa-* 'pit, hole', Lat. *cūpa, cŭppa* 'cask, barrel, tub', Gk *kupsélē* 'chest, box, beehive'
CG	*mazd- ~ *mazdyo- ~ *mazdlos	mast	ON *mastr*, OE *mæst*, OHG *mast*; MIr *maide* 'post, stick; mizen mast', MW *meithlyon* 'masts'?; Lat *mālus* 'ship's mast'	
ICG	*peisko- ~ *pisko-	fish	Goth *fisks*, ON *fiskr*, OE *fisk*, OHG *fisc*; OIr *íasc*; Lat *piscis*	cf. Skt *picchā-* 'calf of the leg'
CG	*pluk-	boatload	ON *flokkr* 'troop, host, flock', OE *flocc* 'flock, company, troop'; Gaul *luxtos* 'load of pottery', OIr *lucht* 'class of people, occupants, category, boat's crew, ship's cargo', OW *luidt*, MW *llwyth* 'tribe, lineage, kin group, faction, (full) load, ship's cargo'	√*pleu-* 'float, swim, wash, pour'; cf. M Dutch *vluycken* 'transport over water', ON *fley* 'ship'
CG	*reinos	river way, Rhine	OE, MHG *Rīn* 'Rhine'; Lat *Rhēnus* < Celtic, MIr *rían* 'sea, ocean, course, route, path'	Cf. Skt *ri̇́yate, riṇā́ti* 'flows', OCS *riṇǫti sę* 'flows', OE *rīð* 'stream', Lat *rīvus* 'river'
CG	*rō-	row, paddle (primary verb)	ON *róa* 'to row', OE *rōwan* 'to go by water, sail, swim'; OIr *ráïd* 'rows, sails, voyages', MIr *imm·rá* 'travels by boat, navigates'	cf. Skt *aritár-*, Gk *erétē* 'rower'
CG	*sighlo-	sail	ON *segl*, OE *seg(e)l*, OHG *segal*; OIr *séol*, OW *huil*	

over water', Old Norse *fley* 'ship'); Gaulish *luxtos* 'load of pottery', Old Irish *lucht* 'class of people, occupants, category, boat's crew, ship's cargo', Old Welsh *luidt*, Middle Welsh *llwyth* 'tribe, lineage, kinship group, faction, clan, occupants, inhabitants, (full) load, ship's cargo'; Celto-Germanic **sighlo-** 'sail', reflected in Old Norse *segl*, Old English *seg(e)l*, Old High German *segal*; Old Irish *séol*, Old Welsh *huil* 'sail' (cf. Bengtsson 2017). The word 'mast', reconstructable as **mazd- ~ *mazdyo- ~ *mazdlos**, is shared uniquely between Germanic, Celtic, and Italic: Old Norse *mastr*, Old English *mæst*,

Old High German *mast*; Middle Irish *maide* 'post, stick; mizen mast, (figuratively) leader', probably also Archaic Welsh word *meithlyon* 'masts'; Latin *mālus* 'ship's mast' < ?**mazdlos**; for a case for masts in Bronze Age Scandinavia, see Bengtsson (2017). Note also that the word 'fish', reconstructable as **peisko-** ~ **pisko-**, is confined to Germanic, Celtic, and Italic: Gothic *fisks*, Old Norse *fiskr*, Old English, Old Frisian *fisk*, Old High German *fisc*; Old Irish *íasc*; Latin *piscis*.

The river name 'Rhine' occurs as Old English *Rīn* and Middle High German *Rīn*. Latin *Rhēnus* and Greek 'Ρῆνος 'Rhine' are borrowed from Celtic. These can be related to Sanskrit *ríyate, riṇáti* 'flows', Old Church Slavonic *rinǫti sę* 'flows', Old English *rīð* 'stream', Latin *rīvus* 'river'. The corresponding Middle Irish *rían* means 'sea, ocean, course, route, path', which can be explained as a change of meaning that occurred when speakers of Indo-European, who had previously migrated following rivers, took to the sea to settle new lands.

7.5. Human beings, gods, and the cosmos

In both Bronze Age rock art traditions we are considering, human beings are central and the human form is represented with comparable simplicity. 'Stick figures' is often an apt description. However, there are differences: notably the Scandinavian figures often convey an attitude of action but the Iberian figures are more static. Despite this disparity, there are often detailed points of comparison. For example, bi-horned warriors recur in both traditions, reminiscent of the Nuragic *bronzetti* or the Shardana warriors as represented in Egyptian relief scenes. An example of strikingly similar gestures can be seen in the Ervidel II stela from Portugal and Kville panel from Sweden. Both of these can be grouped within larger subsets in which five oversized, splayed fingers – and sometimes also toes – have been carefully carved. Certainly these gestures signify something – and most probably the same thing – in both far-flung locations. From the linguistic side, it also worth noting that there is shared Celto-Germanic word ***gʷistis**, meaning 'digit, finger, toe, twig', whence Old Norse *il-kvistir* 'toes', *kvistr* 'branch'; Old Cornish *bis, bes*, Middle Welsh *bys*, Breton *biz* 'finger, toe'; cf. the rare Middle Irish dative plural *bissib ega* 'icicles'.

As well as the proliferation of vocabulary for individuals within their increasingly complex social context, the emerging Indo-European branches of the North and West formed words and meanings reflecting new notions of the human being in ideological, cosmological, and mythological settings. An innovative word to express the concept of the 'self' can be detected in Germanic, Celtic, and Italic: Gothic *silba* 'self', Old Norse *sjalfr* 'self', Old English *self, seolf*, Old High German *selb* 'self'; Old Irish *selb* 'property, appurtenance, ownership', Middle Welsh *elw, helw* 'profit, possession'; Venetic **sselboi-sselboi** 'to oneself'. A particularly interesting and meaningful innovation was shared by the forerunners of Germanic, Celtic, Italic, and Baltic: thus, in these languages we find new words for 'human being' created from an inherited a Proto-Indo-European word meaning 'the earth' (**dhéĝhm̥*, genitive **dhĝhmós* 'earth, land', as reflected by

Hittite *tēkan*, genitive *taknaš* 'land', Greek χθών 'earth, ground, land, region', Vedic *kṣám*, genitive *kṣmás* 'earth, ground'). These innovative forms are widely attested, including Gothic *guma* 'man', Old Norse *gumi*, Old English *guma*, Old High German *gomo*; Old Irish *duine* 'person, human being', Old Breton *don*, *den*, Old Cornish *den* 'homo', Middle Welsh *dyn*; Latin *homō*, Oscan nominative plural **humuns**, Umbrian dative plural *homonus*; Old Prussian *smunents*, *smūnets* 'man', Old Lithuanian *žmuō* 'human being'.

It is clear from comparative evidence that the speakers of Proto-Indo-European had thought of some gods as located in the sky. Thus, Proto-Indo-European **deiwós*

Table 7.6. *Celto-Germanic and Northwest Indo-European inherited vocabulary relating to human beings, gods, and the cosmos*

Proto-language	Reconstruction	Meaning	Attestations	PIE derivation
		HUMAN BEINGS AND GODS		
CG	*Bhr̥ǵhn̥tes	high ones, people of the sky goddess	ON *Burgundar*, OE *Burgendas* 'Burgundians' ON *Burgundarholmr* 'Bornholm'; Ancient Celtic Βριγαντες, cf. OIr *Brigit* 'dea poetarum'	√*bherǵh-* 'be high, hill'
PIE	*deiwós ~ *dyēus	god, sky god	ON *Týr*, OE *Tīw*, OIr *día*, MW *duw*, Lat *deus*, Lith *diēvas*, Skt *dēvá-*, Hittite *sius*	√*dei-* 'shine'
NW	*dhgh(e)m- ~ *dhghom-	human being < earthling	Goth *guma*, ON *gumi*, OE *guma*, OHG *gomo* 'man'; OIr *duine* 'human being', OB *don*, *den*, Old Cornish *den* 'homo', MW *dyn*; Lat *homō*; OP *smunents*, 'man', OLith *žmuō* 'human being'	*dhéǵhm̥, gen. *dhǵhmós 'earth, land'
CG	*gʷistis	digit, finger, toe, twig	ON *il-kvistir* 'toes', *kvistr* 'branch'; OC *bis*, *bes*, MW *bys*, B *biz* 'finger, toe', cf. MIr *bissib ega* 'icicles'	
CG/BS	*meldh-	hammer of the thunder god	ON *Mjǫllnir* (Thor's hammer); MW *mellt* 'lightning', Gaulish god MELDIO; OP *mealde* 'lightning', Latv *milna* 'hammer of the thunder god', OCS *mlъni* 'lightning'	√*melH₂-* 'grind'
CG/BS	*Perkʷunos	thunder god	ON gods's names *Fjǫrgyn*, *Fjǫrgynn* (father of Frigg); Gaul *(silva) Hercynia*; Lith *perkūnas* 'thunder, god of thunder', Old Russian *Perunъ* 'god of thunder'	NW *perkʷús* 'oak'
ICG	*selbho- ~ *selwo-	possession, self	Goth *silba*, ON *sjalfr*, OE *self*, OHG *selb* 'self'; OIr *selb* 'property, appurtenance, ownership', MW *elw*, *helw* 'profit, possession'; Venetic *sselboi-sselboi* 'to oneself'	√*sel-* 'seize, take possession'
CG	*ton(a)ros ~ *tn̥ros	thunder, thunder god	ON *þórr*, OE *þunor*, *þuner*, OHG *donar*; Gaul divine names *Taranis*, *Taranucnos*, OIr *torann*, MW, OC *taran* 'thunder'	√*(s)tenH₂-* 'thunder'

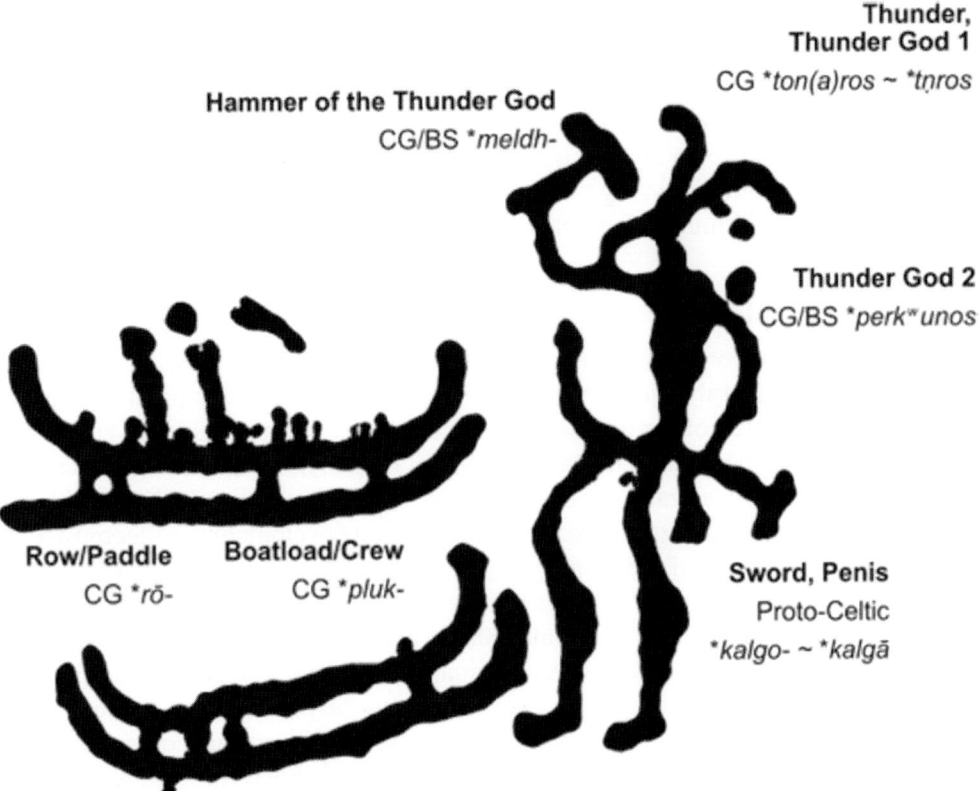

Figure 7.4. Drawing of detail of a rock art panel from Sweden (panel in Lövåsen (Tanum 321:1, Bohuslän)), labelled with the corresponding Celto-Germanic and northwest Indo-European vocabulary items. Interpretation based on a visualization from photogrammetry by Christian Horn and Rich Potter.

'god' and **dyēus* 'sky, sky god' based on the root √*dei-* 'shine' can be related to widely attested names for gods, often simply the word for 'god', including Old Norse *Týr*, Old English *Tīw*, Old Irish *día*, Welsh *duw*, Latin *deus*, Lithuanian *diēvas*, Sanskrit *dēvá-*, Hittite *sius*. On the other hand, a clearly formulated opposition of immortal sky dwellers versus mortal earthlings is only well attested in NW and not more widely across Indo-European. A useful example is the bilingual Latin/Cisalpine Gaulish inscription from Vercelli, in which the same contrasting cognate words occur in the parallel texts: Latin DEIS AT HOMINIBVS 'to gods and men' and Celtic **teuo-xtonio-** 'gods and human beings' (Fig. 7.4; Table 7.6).

Although **deiwós* 'god (of the bright sky)' is Proto-Indo-European, a younger layer of divine sky gods is confined to the North and West. For example, Celto-Germanic ***ton(a)ros ~ *tṇros** 'thunder, thunder god' is reflected in Old Norse *þórr*, Old English *þunor, þuner*, Old High German *donar*; Gaulish divine names *Taranis, Taranucnos, Taranucnus*, Old Irish *torann* 'thunder, noise', Middle Welsh *taran* '(peal of) thunder, Old Cornish *taran* 'tonitruum' 'thunder'. A Celto-Germanic/Balto-Slavic word for 'hammer of the thunder god' ***meldh-** can be reconstructed on the basis of Old Norse *Mjöllnir* (Thor's hammer); Middle Welsh *mellt* 'lightning', the Gaulish god's name (dative) **MELDIO**; Old Prussian *mealde* 'lightning bolt', Latvian *milna* 'hammer of the thunder god', Old Church Slavonic *mlъni* 'lightning'. Another thunder god ***Perkʷunos** can be seen behind Old Norse *Fjǫrgyn* (mother of Thor), *Fjǫrgynn* (father of Frigg), Old English *firgen* 'mountain', Old High German *Firgunnea*; Latinized Gaulish *silva Hercynia*; Lithuanian *perkūnas* 'thunder, god of thunder', Old Russian *Perunъ* 'god of thunder'.

7.6. Social complexity

Big-picture overviews of the Bronze Age (e.g. Kristiansen & Larsson 2005; Ling *et al.* 2018) recognize in the general trajectory of the period a rise of social complexity together with an intensification of status stratification. In decoding the social role and status of individuals and their attributes as depicted in rock art, historical linguistics may be of special value. Once again, the evidence that is likely to be especially valuable for this period is that vocabulary that post-dates common developments reflected across eastern and western Indo-European branches but pre-date the earliest attestations of Germanic and Celtic (Table 7.7). Words unique to these two branches, or more widely being also reflected in Italic and/or Balto-Slavic, are numerous and include a range of subtly distinct terms for persons of subordinate status, low status, or lacking status within the recognized social group: the compound ***alyo-morgi-** ~ ***alyo-mrogi-** 'foreigner', giving Ancient Nordic **aljamarkiz**, the Gaulish group name *Allobroges*, Middle Welsh *allfro* 'foreigner(s)', Italo-Celto-Germanic ***ghostis** 'guest', reflected in Ancient Germanic personal name **harigasti** 'guest of the war-band' (Negau B helmet ~200–50 BC), similarly Ancient Nordic personal names **hlewagastiz** 'famous-guest' (Gallehus horn ~AD 400), **widugastiz** 'wood' + 'guest', Gothic *gasts*, Old Norse *gestr*, Old English *giest*, Old High German *gast*; the Lepontic personal name **UVAMOKOZIS** < **U(p)amo-gostis* 'supreme guest'; Latin *hostis* 'foreigner, enemy';[3] ***gheisslo-** 'hostage', reflected in Ancient Nordic **asugisalas** = **ansu-gīsᵃlas** genitive singular, Old Norse *gísl*, Old English *gīsel*, Old High German *gīsal*; Old Irish *gíall* 'human pledge, hostage', Middle Welsh *gwystyl* 'pledge, surety, hostage'; cf. Gaulish genitive personal name **CONGEISTLI** 'co-hostage' (Noricum); ***m̥bhakto-** ~ ***m̥bhaktā-** 'person sent back and forth on behalf of a superior', is reflected in Gothic *andbahts* 'servant, minister', Old Norse *ambátt* 'bondwoman, concubine', Old English *ambiht* 'office, service, commission, officer', Old High German *ambaht* 'servant, employee, official'; common Hispano-Celtic name *Ambatos*, feminine *Ambata*, Gaulish **AMBACTVS, AMBACTOS** 'vassal, minister', Middle Welsh *amaeth* 'ploughman' (the Germanic reflects a prehistoric borrowing from Proto-Celtic); ***maghus** 'son, youth', gives Ancient Nordic dative **magōz** 'son', accusative **magu**, Gothic *magus* 'boy, son', Old Norse *mǫgr* 'son, youth', Old English *magu* 'child, son, young man'; Old Irish *mug* 'male slave, servant, monk'.

At the lowest level of the social pyramid there is Italo-Celto-Germanic ***kaptós** 'made captive, bound, slave', reflected by Gothic *hafts* 'joined, bound', Old Norse *haptr* 'captive', Old English *hæft* 'bond, fetter, made prisoner, captive', Old Saxon, Old High German *haft* 'made prisoner, captive'; Old Irish *cacht* 'servant, person in bondage, slave, confinement'; Old Cornish *cait* 'servus', Middle Welsh *caeth* 'bond, bound, captive, captured, slavish, restricted'; Latin *captus* 'thing or person taken'. As argued by Ling *et al.* (2018), unfree labour is likely to have had an important place in the exchange networks of the Bronze Age:

> As a bulk commodity of high value, slaves would have been desired by Bronze Age communities in Scandinavia as well as farther away in urban palace societies of the eastern Mediterranean and elsewhere. Blonde northern slaves are shown in Etruscan wall paintings (Briggs-Nash 2006), representing perhaps a continuing practice already established in the Early Bronze Age. As described comparatively for Viking, Haida, and Philippine maritime societies, wealth in captive human bodies could have derived from local interchiefdom wars and from raids into coastal and riverine settlements along voyaging routes. The importance of slaves in the Viking case provides the likely homology. When individuals from a defeated population were not killed, 'they had forfeited their right to be free' … (Ling *et al.* 2018, 502)

The autobiographical *Confessio* (§§16–18) and *Epistola* (§10) of St Patrick remind us of how the rise of advanced seafaring created special opportunities for the slave trade: as a youth abducted to Ireland by seaborne raiders, Patrick could not simply run home to Britain, rather only at great risk did he eventually find another barbarian ship and pledge loyalty to its captain (see Hood 1978).

At the other end of the social spectrum there is a range of specialized Post-Proto-Indo-European vocabulary for those admitted to the in-group with conferred status of varying degrees: ***priyo-** ~ ***priyā-** 'free', the source of Gothic *freis*, Old English *frēo*, Old High German *frī*; Old Breton *rid* 'free', Middle Welsh *ryð* 'free, not in slavery, having civil and legal rights, unrestricted'; contrast this word's earlier meaning seen in Vedic *priyá-*, Avestan *friia-* 'beloved' < Proto-Indo-European $*priH_xós$ 'beloved, of one's own'; related to the previous word is Celto-Germanic ***priyānt-** 'relative, friend', giving Gothic *frijonds* 'friend', Old Norse *frændi, frjándi* 'relative, friend', Old English *frēond* 'friend, loved one, relative' Old High German *friunt* 'friend, loved one'; Welsh *rhiaint* 'parents, ancestors, elders'; ***weni-** 'friend, relative', becoming Ancient Nordic **uiniz** 'friend', Old Norse *vinr*, Old English *wine*, Old High German *wini* 'friend, beloved'; Old Irish *fine* 'a group of persons of the same family'; ***orbho-** 'heir' (<Proto-Indo-European $*H_3orbh$-o- 'bereaved, orphan'), whence Ancient Nordic **arbijano** 'of heirs', Old High German *arbeo, erbeo*; Old Irish *orb*; ***orbhyom** 'inheritance', giving Ancient Nordic **arbija**, Old Norse *arfr* 'inheritance, patrimony', Old English *ierfe* 'inheritance', Old High German *arbi, erbi* 'inheritance'; Old Irish *orbe* 'inheritance, legacy'.

The key concept – determining the position of both free and unfree, insiders and outsiders – is the nation or tribe, for which the word reflected in Germanic, Celtic, Italic, and Baltic is ***teutā**, whence Gothic *þiuda*, Old Norse *þjóð*, Old English *þéod*, Old High German *diota*; Gaulish personal names **TOVTIA, TOVTIVS**, Old Irish *túath*, Old Welsh and Old Breton *tut*; in Italic Oscan *touto* 'ciuitas' 'community, city', Venetic *teuta* 'ciuitas'; Old Prussian *tauto*, Lithuanian *tauta* 'land', Latvian *tàuta* 'people'.

The apex of the society of the ***teutā** is designated by a word attested as *-rix* in many Gaulish and Ancient Brythonic personal names, Old Irish *rí* 'king, leader', Old Welsh singular *ri*; Latin *rēx*, genitive *rēgis* < Proto-Indo-European **H₃rḗĝ-s* 'ruler, leader of ritual'. Although found also in Italic and Indic (Sanskrit *rāj-* 'king'), the long **ī* n the Germanic forms imply a prehistoric borrowing from Celtic: Gothic *reiks* 'king; rich, powerful', Old Norse *ríkr* 'ruler, king', Old English *rice*, Old High German *rīhhi*. This borrowing brought with it related ideologically significant words, showing the same characteristically Celtic vowel (but the Germanic consonant shift): Gothic *reiki*

Table 7.7. Celto-Germanic and Northwest Indo-European inherited vocabulary relating to social organization

Proto-language	Reconstruction	Meaning	Attestations	PIE derivation
		THE INDIVIDUAL IN SOCIETY		
CG	*altro-	nurturer, one acting as a parent	OE *ealdor* 'parent, ancestor, master, chief', Swedish *föräldrar*; MIr *altru* 'foster father, nourisher', MW *athro* 'teacher, tutor, foster parent', OB *altro(u)* 'foster father', C *altrou* 'stepfather'	
CG	*alyo-morgi- ~ *alyo-mrogi-	foreigner	AN *aljamarkiz*, Gaul group name *Allobroges*, MW *allfro* 'foreigner(s)'	
CG	*drūto-	joker, fool	ON *trúðr* 'juggler, fool', OE *trūð* 'trumpeter, actor, buffoon'; MIr *drúth* 'professional jester, fool; idiot'	
CG	*gheisslo-	hostage	ON *gísl*, OE *gīsel*, OHG *gīsal*; OIr *gíall* 'human pledge, hostage', MW *gwystyl* 'pledge, surety, hostage'	
ICG	*ghostis	guest	Ancient Gmc name *harigasti*, AN names *hlewagastiz*, *widugastiz*, Goth *gasts*, ON *gestr*, OE *giest*, OHG *gast*; Lepontic UVAMOKOZIS; Lat *hostis* 'foreigner, enemy'	
ICG	*kaptós	captive, bound, slave	Goth *hafts* 'joined, bound', ON *haptr* 'captive', OE *hæft* 'bond, fetter, captive', OHG *haft* 'captive'; OIr *cacht* 'servant, slave', OC *cait* 'servus', MW *caeth* 'captive, slavish'; Lat *captus* 'thing or person taken'	√*kap-* 'seize'
CG	*lēgi-	healer, physician, leech	Goth *lekeis* 'doctor', ON *lækir*, OE *lǣce* 'doctor, leech', OHG *lāhhi*, *lāchi*; OIr *lieig*, *liaig* 'physician, healer, leech'	
CG	*maghus	son, youth	AN dat *magōz* 'son', acc *magu*, Goth *magus* 'boy, son', ON *mǫgr* 'son, youth', OE *magu* 'child, son, young man'; OIr *mug* 'male slave, servant, monk'	possibly non-IE

(Continued)

7. Linguistic aspects on the warrior iconography in Iberia and Scandinavia

Table 7.7. (Continued)

		THE INDIVIDUAL IN SOCIETY		
Proto-language	Reconstruction	Meaning	Attestations	PIE derivation
CG	*m̥bhakto- ~ *m̥bhaktā-	one sent back and forth	Goth *andbahts* 'servant, minister', ON *ambátt* 'bondwoman, concubine', OE *ambiht* 'office, service', OHG *ambaht* 'servant, official'; HC *Ambatos, Ambata*, Gaul AMBACTOS 'vassal, minister', MW *amaeth* 'ploughman'	compound verb *H_2m̥bhi + *H_2eĝ- 'drive back and forth'
CG	*orbho-	heir	AN *arbijano* 'of heirs', OHG *arbeo, erbeo*; OIr *orb*	*H_3orbh-o- 'bereaved, orphan'
CG	*orbhyom	inheritance	AN *arbija*, ON *arfr* 'inheritance, patrimony', OE *ierfe*, OHG *arbi, erbi* 'inheritance'; OIr *orbe* 'inheritance, legacy'	*H_3orbh-o- 'bereaved, orphan'
CG	*priyānt-	relative, friend	Goth *frijonds* 'friend', ON *frœndi, frjándi* 'relative, friend', OE *frēond* 'friend, loved one, relative', OHG *friunt* 'friend, loved one'; W *rhiaint* 'parents, ancestors, elders'	*priH$_x$ós 'beloved, of one's own'
CG	*priyo- ~ *priyā-	free	Goth *freis*, OE *frēo*, OHG *frī*; OB *rid*, MW *ryδ* 'free, not in slavery, having civil and legal rights, unrestricted'	*priH$_x$ós 'beloved, of one's own'
CG	*rektu- ~ *rekto-	legally right, just, correct	ON *réttr* 'right, legal order, straight, correct', OE *riht* 'right', OHG *reht* 'straight, good, right'; OIr *recht* 'law, rule, authority', MW *reyth* 'law, sermon, jury, verdict'	*H_3reĝ-tu- and *H_3reĝ-to- 'straight, direct'
ICG	*rīg-s < *rēg-s	king, ruler of a *teutā	Goth *reiks* 'king; rich, powerful', ON *ríkr* 'ruler, king', OE *rice*, OHG *rīhhi*; AB RIX, OIr *rí*, OW *ri*; Lat *rēx, rēgis*	*H_3réĝ-s 'ruler, leader of ritual'
CG	*rīgyā < *rēgyā	kingship, sovereignty	Goth *reiki* 'authority', ON *ríki*, OE *rīce*, OHG *rīhhi*; OIr *ríge* 'ruling, kingship, sovereignty', MW *rieδ* 'glory (of God), majesty, kingship, sovereignty'	*H_3réĝ-s 'ruler, leader of ritual'
NW	*teutā	nation, tribe	Goth *þiuda*, ON *þjóð*, OE *þeod*, OHG *diota*; Gaulish personal names TOVTIA, TOVTIVS, OIr *túath*, OWB *tut*; Oscan *touto*, Venetic *teuta* 'ciuitas'; OP *tauto*, Lith *tauta* 'land', Latv *tàuta* 'people'	
CG	*teuto-rīg-	king of the tribe/nation	Goth *Þiudareiks*, ON *Þjóðrikr*, OE *Ðeodric*, German *Dietrich*; Gaulish TOVTIORIGI, OW *Tutir, Tutri*	
CG	*weni-	relative, friend	AN *uiniz* 'friend', ON *vinr*, OE *wine*, OHG *wini* 'friend, beloved'; OIr *fine* 'a group of the same family'	

'authority', Old Norse *ríki*, Old English *rīce*, Old High German *rīhhi*; Old Irish *ríge* 'ruling, kingship, sovereignty', Middle Welsh *rieδ* 'glory (of God), majesty, kingship, sovereignty'. A Celto-Germanic name ***teuto-rīg-** 'king of the people' compounds the two words: Gothic 'Theodoric', Old Norse *Þjóðrikr*, Old English *Ðeodric*, German *Dietrich*; probably the Gaulish Latinized divine epithet **APOLLINI TOVTIORIGI**, Old Welsh *Tutir, Tutri*.

Etymologically, this word for 'king' *$H_3rḗĝ$- derives from a Proto-Indo-European action word √$H_3reĝ$- 'to stretch out straight'. The related Proto-Indo-European *$H_3reĝ$-tu- and *$H_3reĝ$-to- had originally meant simply 'straight, direct', but meanings of legality and justice come to predominate in Germanic and Celtic: Old Norse *réttr* 'right, legal order, straight, correct', Old English *riht* 'right', Old High German *reht* 'straight, good, right'; Old Irish *recht* 'law, rule, authority, ordinance, scripture', Middle Welsh *reyth* 'law, sermon, jury, verdict'. So we see that as society evolved what had been an abstract principal became a code with a mechanism for enforcement.

Words unique to Germanic and Celtic referring to specific social roles include: ***lēgi-** 'healer, physician, leech', the source of Gothic *lekeis* 'doctor', Old Norse *lækir*, Old English *lǣce* 'doctor, leech', Old High German *lāhhi, lāchi*, cf. Gothic *lekinon* 'to heal'; Old Irish *lieig, liaig* 'physician, healer, leech'; ***drūto-** 'joker, fool', Old Norse *trúðr* 'juggler, fool', Old English *trūð* 'trumpeter, actor, buffoon'; Middle Irish *drúth* 'professional jester, fool; legally incompetent, idiot'; ***altro-** 'nurturer, person acting as a parent', reflected in Old English *ealdor* 'parent, ancestor, master, chief', cf. Swedish *föräldrar*; Middle Irish *altru* 'foster father, nourisher', Middle Welsh *athro* 'teacher, tutor, foster parent', and its variant *alltraw* 'godparent, sponsor' (feminine *elltrewyn*), likewise Old Breton *altro(u)* 'foster father', Cornish *altrou* 'stepfather'.

In their different ways, historical linguistics and the study of rock art iconography open windows onto the Bronze Age. Recent advances in archaeogenetics and the archaeological science of metal sourcing provide a new basis for bringing rock art and language together within a specified framework of times and places. The RAW Project and new study of Patterson *et al.* (2022) coincide auspiciously in refocusing attention on the same region and period: the intensity of north-west-southwest interaction in Western Europe in the Late Bronze Age. We can now begin to tell a new story to fill in that long gap between Proto-Indo-European spreading with people from the steppe and the early attested languages at the dawn of history.

Notes

1 Abbreviated linguistic terms used in tables in alphabetical order: AB = Ancient Brythonic; acc = accusative; AN = Ancient Nordic (from runes in the older futhark); B = Modern Breton; C = Cornish; CG = Celto-Germanic; dat = dative; Gaul = Gaulish; gen = genitive; Gmc = Germanic; Goth = Gothic; HC = Hispano-Celtic; ICG = Italic/Celto-Germanic; Lat = Latin; Latv = Latvian; Lith = Lithuanian; MB = Middle Breton; MIr = Middle Irish; MW = Middle Welsh; non-IE = non-Indo-European; NW = North-west Indo-European (not attested outside the subset Celtic, Germanic, Italic, Baltic, and Slavic); OB = Old Breton; OC = Old Cornish; OCS = Old Church Slavonic; OE = Old English; OHG = Old High German; OIr = Old Irish; OLith = Old Lithuanian; ON = Old Norse; OP = Old Prussian; OW = Old Welsh; OWB = Old Welsh and Old Breton; PIE = Proto-Indo-European; Skt = Sanskrit; W = Modern Welsh

2 To avoid cluttering text by citing the same reference works repeatedly, the main sources used in compiling the examples below are Mallory & Adams (2006) for Proto-Indo-European roots and the subset limited to the northwestern branches; Hyllested (2010) for CG words; Kroonen (2013), Ringe (2017), and Fulk (2018) for Germanic; LEIA and Matasović (2009) for Celtic; de Vaan (2008) for Italic; ALEW and Derksen (2015) for Balto-Slavic. The forms and meanings of Old and Middle Irish words are based on eDIL, and those of Welsh on GPC. The readings of runes in the older futhark follow Antonsen (1975). For ancient Celtic place-names, the main compilations consulted are Talbert (2000), Koch *et al.* (2007), Falileyev *et al.* (2010), and Delamarre (2012).
3 Old Church Slavonic *gostъ*, Russian *gost'* 'guest', these are possibly borrowed from Germanic.

Chapter 8

Bronze Age contacts between Scandinavia, Iberia, and the Atlantic communities

In the sections above, we have considered evidence for metal trade, shared motifs in rock art and stelae, and developments shared uniquely by the early languages of Northern and Western Europe, all of which point to previously unrecognized ties between Scandinavia and Iberia. However, it is critical to examine more closely the specific nature and extent of these connections and how they evolved over time. We shall now conclude, beginning with a summary overview of the subject. Then, building on that, we will provide more indirect data that may help lead to a better understanding of the maritime relationship between these distant regions in the Late Bronze Age. This includes data on sites that could have functioned as maritime landing places along the route between Iberia and Scandinavia during this period, on the Atlantic façade. In the final section that follows we will discuss and model aspects of social institutions connected to rock art and long-distance trade of metals.

Over the years many scholars have stressed Atlantic connections in the Late Bronze Age. However, only a few included Scandinavia in this framework (Nordén 1925; MacWhite 1951; Eogan 1995; Kristiansen 1998). Nordén was the first of these, drawing attention to both Scandinavian rock art and the Iberian double-looped palstave found in Sweden. Gordon Childe was seemingly inspired by Nordén's thesis and made the first map showing the distribution of these axes, extending from Iberia in the south to Scandinavia in the north, thus indicating an Atlantic system that included Scandinavia (Childe 1939). Somewhat later, Gräslund (1967) published a paper with a map showing the distribution of the Herzsprung shields, including Sweden in the north, Iberia, and the eastern Aegean world in the south that indicated maritime connections not only within the Atlantic system but also links to Sardinia and the eastern Mediterranean. Along similar lines, Almagro Basch noted formal parallels between some chariot depictions in Iberia and Scandinavia, as well as parallels between the shields depicted on Iberian warrior stelae and shields found elsewhere, primarily in the eastern Mediterranean and Northwest Europe, including Scandinavia (Almagro Basch 1966, 156–170).

After the discovery of Europe's largest hoard of Herzsprung shields in Fröslunda, Sweden, in 1985, Gräslund's map was more often referred to; for example, Kristiansen (1998) updated it with the new evidence of Herzspung shields from Ireland as well as the Iberian warrior iconography that clearly depicted the same type. Another significant contribution was made by Eogan (1995), who argued that small neck-rings and torques of bronze and gold should be recognized as connecting Iberia, Ireland, and Scandinavia in the Late Bronze Age. In Iberia there are golden torcs that are thought to have been imported from Ireland (see also Delibes de Castro et al. 1995), while other torcs of gold seem to have been inspired by Nordic prototypes (Berrocal Rangel 1987; Díaz-Guardamino 2010, 240–250). Moreover, Eogan argued that some Irish metalwork derived from Nordic prototypes during this phase and also highlighted the fact that Ireland had revealed many more finds of Baltic amber during this phase than had England. All in all, this indicated an Atlantic system that included Iberia in the south and Sweden in the north (Eogan 1995). When seen in the light of the long-distance linkages recently revealed by the outcomes of recent projects, all these formal links take on enhanced importance. One of these research initiatives has shown that Baltic amber made its way to Iberia during the Late Bronze Age (Murillo-Barroso & Martinón-Torres 2012). Interestingly, these researchers do not favour the hypothesis that Baltic amber was transported via the Atlantic system. A second study (Ling et al. 2014; 2019), which looked at the lead isotope and chemical analysis of bronze metalwork samples from southern Scandinavia, found that the copper has an isotopic signature that matches southern Iberian ores from Los Pedroches, the Alcudia valley, and the upper Guadalquivir region. A third recent study that acknowledges that ingots of copper as well as bronze alloys found among the Middle and Late Bronze Age Salcombe 'shipwrecks' contained copper from the same Iberian sources as indicated for sampled Scandinavian objects (Berger et al. 2022). Finally, the analyses of a few of bronze alloys from Ireland that date from 1400–900 BC point to Iberian sources (O'Brien 2022).

Overall, these data indicate that the communities engaged in warrior stelae making in western Iberia were also involved in copper mining and in the distribution of copper through inter-regional, long-distance exchange networks that reached Scandinavia (Ling & Uhnér 2014; Vandkilde et al. 2021; Díaz-Guardamino et al. 2022). Still, much remains to be explained about this trade. What was its volume? When and why did it begin and end? What areas and communities were directly involved? What was the balance of long-distance direct exchange and trans-shipment though intermediate hubs? In fact, few studies have discussed in detail where and how exactly exchange could have taken place between the communities engaged in long-distance trade along the Atlantic façade.

8.1. Strategic landing sites, indirect exchange, and trans-shipment though intermediate hubs

There is a strong likelihood that certain strategic landing sites could have worked as meeting places between groups travelling from Iberia and Scandinavia along the Atlantic façade (Fig. 8.1). Bradley (2022) has recently pointed out several locations in Britain and Ireland with attributes auspicious for this function. Of special interest are those from which bun ingots have been recovered that potentially could be of Iberian origin, such as those found in Salcombe (Berger *et al.* 2022). Long-distance maritime encounters with planked-built boats like the Hjortspring might cover 80–100 km per day (Ling *et al.* 2018). However, the distance between Scandinavia and Iberia is about 3000 km, which raises the possibility that groups from Iberia and Scandinavia regularly met halfway. Nonetheless, the ethnographic analogy of the indigenous island dwelling Haida people of the Canadian Pacific should be pointed out. The Haida were known to cross open waters over great distances with their large seagoing canoes, made from enormous red cedars and manned by large crews of paddling warriors. The Haida were known to conduct raids ranging from Sitka, Alaska, to the Fraser River on the Canadian mainland, but also as far south as southern California, a distance of over 2500 km (Jenness 1934, 243).

Already back in 2014 we stressed the fact that groups from Iberia and Scandinavia could have directed long-distance journeys through Britain due to demand for Cornish tin on the part of the same patrons.

> In any case, the British Isles would have had a very strategic position in this north-south network and the strong connections between British Isles and the west Mediterranean World in the Bronze Age is therefore of greatest importance ... An important observation in the context of the connections between the British Isles and Scandinavia is the consistency of the lead isotope composition of the tin ingot from Vårdinge in Sweden (T1:60) with the ores from Cornwall. Actually the availability of tin might be the reason why several copper producing areas directed their 'copper routes' to pass the British Isles during the Bronze Age. Probably, 'traders' were in many cases not searching separately for tin and copper, but were receiving the two metals from nearby ports, stressing the possibility that ports in the British Isles acted as transit centres for copper from other parts of Europe as well as providing local tin ore. This theory is further supported by the evidence from Cliffs End ... (Ling *et al.* 2014, 126–127)

In the context of maritime interaction between Iberia and Scandinavia several scholars have recently highlighted Cliffs End on the Isle of Thanet which had been a true island during the Bronze Age (in fact until the Middle Ages).

> Larger islands could take on specialised roles in production and exchange. One was Thanet which was separated from the mainland of Kent by a channel that has since been drained. It provided a sheltered route between the Strait of Dover and the Thames Estuary, both of which are associated with large amounts of metalwork. (Bradley 2022, 133)

The most dramatic discoveries at the Cliffs End site are strontium and oxygen isotope data on human bone from a few of the graves that included individuals who must

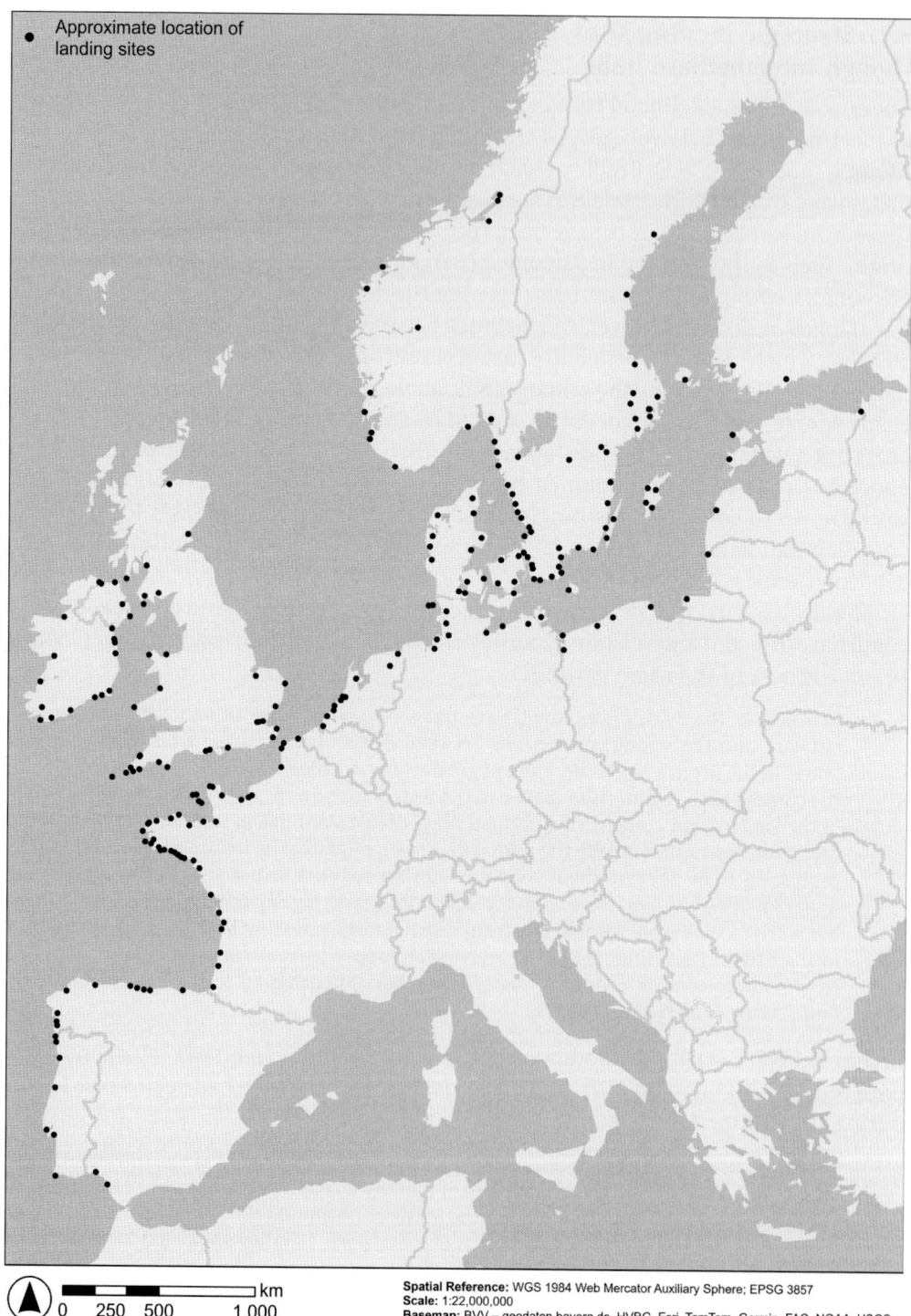

Figure 8.1. Selection of strategic landing sites along the Atlantic façade. Map by Ashely Green.

8. Bronze Age contacts between Scandinavia, Iberia, and the Atlantic communities

had travelled very long distances. Some analysed human remains show signatures consistent with Scandinavian geology, while others point to Iberia (McKinley *et al.* 2013; 2015; Millard 2015). Furthermore, Cliffs End has been interpreted as an important Late Bronze Age and Early Iron Age site for long-distance maritime interaction and exchange, as indicated by finds, such as bun ingots and Baltic amber. According to Bradley:

> The island was especially important during the Late Bronze Age when a series of hoards was deposited along the coast. There is direct evidence that metals were being worked here (Bradley 2022, 133).

In the archaeogenetic study of Patterson *et al.* (2022), Cliffs End highlights two Late Bronze Age genomes dated to 1011–860 cal BC (2 sigma) (PSUAMS-7671, 2795±20 BP) and 1014–836 cal BC (2 sigma) (GrA-37751, 2790±30 BP). These are both extreme outliers, agreeing with neither the Early Bronze Age or Late Bronze Age genetic norms in Britain, so very possibly newcomers from overseas. Similar results were returned for somewhat earlier individuals from Margetts Pit, also in Kent: 1391–1129 cal BC (2 sigma) (SUERC-49774, 3019±31 BP) and 1261–1019 cal BC (2 sigma) (SUERC-49769, 2956±28 BP). This DNA shows significant parallels with genomes from central European Urnfield Knovíz sites of ~1300–1025 BC (Patterson *et al.* 2022, 591). Unlike the Iron Age French and Tartessian individuals used to model possible sources for new population entering southern Britain in the Middle to Late Bronze Age, the Urnfield genomes pre-date Cliffs End. They are therefore more auspicious as proxies for a source population for the Kentish outliers.

There is also some potentially relevant linguistic evidence for the area of Thanet and Cliffs End (Fig. 8.2). The former island has two pre-English names: *Tanatos* whence Thanet, of uncertain origin, and Old Welsh *Ruim*. In Modern Welsh spelling there are two words *rhwyf*: one meaning 'oar, rudder' borrowed from Latin *rēmus*, and a native Celtic word meaning 'chief, foremost, furthest forward', probably cognate with Latin *prīmus*. Thanet is the first land mariners saw approaching southeast Britain from the east. Facing Thanet from mainland Kent at the mouth of the river Stour is Richborough, the ancient *Rutupias*, where the Claudian invasion landed in AD 43. That name has long been connected with Middle Welsh *rwt* 'rust, oxide, corrosion, sediment, dirt' (e.g. Rivet & Smith 1979, 448–450), note also Old Breton *rod* glossing *eruginem* 'corrosion'. Though not straightforward cognates, these Celtic words are reminiscent in form and meaning of Old Dutch *arut* 'ore',

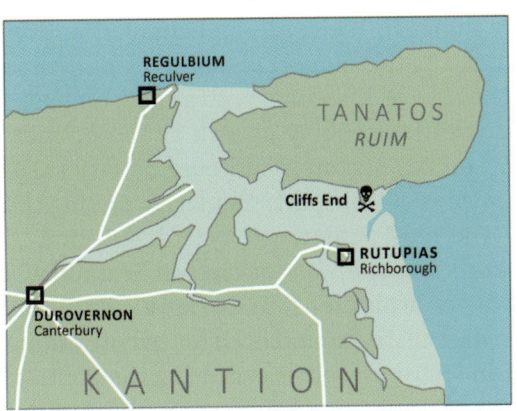

Figure 8.2. The Isle of Thanet, Richborough, and Cliffs End Farm with the region's ancient place-names. Image: John Koch.

Old High German *aruz, ariz, aruzi, arizi*: 'ore', Latin *raudus, rūdus, rōdus*: 'lump of ore, piece of copper or brass, piece of copper used as a coin', all pointing to a repeatedly borrowed trade word of non-Indo-European origin: cf. Sumerian *urudu, uruda, urud*: 'copper, metal' (Halloran 2006; 2020; Iversen & Kroonen 2017; Koch 2020, 110). Thus, before the Romans landed, this part of coastal Kent was possibly known as a source of raw metal.

We have now discussed Cliffs End as a potential meeting point in the Late Bronze Age between groups of trading warriors along the Atlantic façade. But there are of course other sites of interest, with plano-convex ingots of copper dated to the Late Bronze Age, both in Ireland and Britain but also in France, that could indicate Iberian origin. Some of the ingots from these sites will be analysed within the new Maritime Encounters programme. In Britain and the Channel Islands, there are various places with ingots that are potential candidates for maritime interaction, such as Sark off the coast of Normandy, Mount Batten (Plymouth, nowadays a peninsula but probably an island in late prehistory), and St Michael's Mount in southwest England (Needham 2009; Bradley 2022, 133–134).

8.2. Warriors, secret societies, and long-distance exchange in Atlantic Europe

Varied forms of ranked societies, chiefdoms, and social complexity based on production, transportation, or consumption of metals can be modelled in Bronze Age Europe (Earle *et al.* 2015; Kristiansen & Earle 2022). Here, we can exemplify this with Scandinavia and Iberia, two regions with decentralized chiefdoms located at the terminus zones of Atlantic Europe, at the gateways to the Baltic and Mediterranean. In Scandinavia, elites created maritime institutions to control the consumption of metals by monitoring the means of trade, namely boats and warriors. In Iberia, elite individuals with aspirations to warrior ideals controlled the production of the mines, the transportation of the copper from the mines to the coast, and circulation over interior areas, in some contexts probably aided by the support of emerging part-time 'warriors'. Both societies were ranked, in the case of Scandinavia stratified, and both were dependent on control of both the domestic economy as well as the political economy, that in turn were connected to two key sectors, the house or farmstead sector versus the sector for boats or other means of transport, regularly crossing the boundaries of small-scale local societies. The most important social institution to realize the connections between these sectors was the warrior class in Scandinavia or the 'agent of metal circulation' (with warrior aspirations) in Iberia (Vilaça 1998a; 1998b). Such elite individuals and warriors were instrumental both for tribute taking and controlling the domestic economy/farm sector as well as executing the political economy by controlling exchange by means of transportation, meeting the demand for captives as farm labour and territorial defence and expansion by warfare or by establishing alliances for economic expansion and trade. The Bronze Age warrior, or any individual embodying that identity even temporarily for that matter, has been characterized by a high degree of social exposure due to their ambivalent (possibly fluid) position (i.e. liminal state) in society (Horn 2023). The warrior is literally the figure on the border, essential to defending and extending the territory on which the agro-pastoral economy of the segmentary group, simple or complex chiefdom was based. This means that the warrior must strive to attain a recognized high social position. Advertising can serve as an important strategy in this context and it is tempting to see warrior iconography in Iberia and Scandinavia as a manifestation of this strategy.

The common association between warriors and secret societies would have been particularly attractive for Bronze Age adventurers because society rituals offered supernatural protection for individuals who were engaging in the risks of long-distance journeys and combat, thus to ensure success (Hayden 2018; Chacon *et al.* 2020). As documented in many geographical areas including North America, Oceania, and Africa, the interaction of secret society members on regional or greater geographic scales is one of their major features (Hayden 2018). It may be especially important to understand the regional and supra-regional dimension of rock art in Iberia and Scandinavia (Chacon *et al.* 2020). The secret societies not only provide a motivation for regional interaction and exchange but also the motivation and ability for creating rock art as well as the means for safeguarding passage to distant communities. The depicted warriors with horned helmets in Iberia and Scandinavia may have been part of the ritual paraphernalia that was supposed to confer supernatural powers in combat or at least in ritualized contests. Seafaring in island environments is another likely association with secret societies due to the dangers involved in excursions made to attend regional rituals, procure exotic ritual paraphernalia, or to control trade in valuable materials (Chacon *et al.* 2020). Warrants of supernatural protection could have been given for all such sea ventures.

It is worth noting in this connection that a word of high ideological significance that is found throughout the Germanic and Celtic languages, but absent from all the other Indo-European branches, is ***rūn-**. Its attested forms consistently mean 'secret' and 'secret knowledge' in all the early Germanic and Celtic languages, such as Old Norse *rún* and Old Irish *rún*. Though it would be impossible to prove, the fact that this word came to refer to the specialist script used to carve Germanic languages on stone in the Migration Period and Viking Age suggests that ***rūn-** had in preliterate times been used for the rock carvings and their secret meanings known to the initiated.

8.3. Concluding remarks: An integrated recapitulation

The concept of the secret is an apt one on which to draw this book to a close. While many secrets of the warrior iconography of Bronze Age Scandinavia and Iberia must remain for future researchers, and some possibly forever, it is hoped that at least part of the enigma has been dispelled. That closely comparable motifs occur in the rock carvings of two regions about 3000 km apart becomes immediately less puzzling once new geochemical and isotopic evidence is adduced for a sizable trade network in which copper extracted in the Iberian terminus zone was consumed in the Scandinavian. Zooming into the scale of the two localities, it can be seen: 1) that the Iberian mines and warrior stelae were in close enough proximity to be outputs of the same communities or communities in intimate contact, and 2) that the societies of the northern consumers were organized for the maritime mode of production and so ideally placed for boat-building and recruiting crews for long-distance expeditions, a finding consistent with the 30,000 images of vessels and crews known in Scandinavian rock art. Coming at the same time as the intensified long-distance movement of metal, recent breakthroughs in archaeogenetics reveal large-scale two-way movement of people between the Atlantic North (specifically southern Britain) and lands to its south in the period 1300–800 BC, a gene flow that tapered to a trickle after about 800 BC. Prior to that downturn, southern Britain's natural harbours, such as Salcombe, and offshore islands, such as Thanet, evidently provided key midway stations in this traffic. Linguistic reconstruction provides 174 items of inherited prehistoric vocabulary shared by Germanic and Celtic, but no other Indo-European language, implying that the Indo-European branches of the North and West remained in contact, or came back into contact, in the Late Bronze Age before the operation of Grimm's Law. Anthropological analogy strongly suggests that the 'trader-raiders' of the Nordic and Atlantic Bronze Age would have pledged themselves to their high-risk expeditions through initiation into secret societies and that this is possibly the setting in which the rock art was executed and its meanings were transmitted. Viewed from the vantage points of the several disciplines involved here, the parallel warrior iconography of Scandinavia and Iberia can be understood as symptomatic of a climactic stage of the European Bronze Age that came to an end at the Bronze–Iron Transition.

Bibliography

ALEW = Hock, W., Bukevičiūtė, E.-J., Schiller, C., Fecht, F., Feulner, A. H., Hill, E. & Wodtko, D. S. 2015 *Altlitauisches etymologisches Wörterbuch*. Hamburg, Baar.

Allentoft, M. E., Sikora, M., Sjögren, K.-G., Rasmussen, S., Rasmussen, M., Stenderup, J., Damgaard, P. B. *et al.* 2015 Population genomics of Bronze Age Eurasia. *Nature* 522, 167–172.

Almagro Basch, M. 1966 *Las estelas decoradas del Suroeste Peninsular*. Madrid, Consejo Superior de Investigaciones Científicas.

Almagro Gorbea, M. 1977 *El Bronce Final y el período Orientalizante en Extremadura*. Madrid, Consejo Superior de Investigaciones Científicas.

Almagro Gorbea, M. 1992 El origen de los celtas en la Península Ibérica: protoceltas y celtas. *Polis* 4, 5–31.

Almagro Gorbea, M. 1994 'Proto-Celtes' et Celtes dans la Péninsule Ibérique. *Aquitania* 14, 283–296.

Alonso, N. & Pérez-Jordà, G. 2023 The origins of millet cultivation (*Panicum miliaceum* and *Setaria italica*) along Iberia's Mediterranean area from the 13th to the 2nd century BC. *Agronomy* 13 (2), 584. https://doi.org/10.3390/agronomy13020584

Althin, C.-A. 1945 *Studien zu den bronzezeitlichen Felszeichnungen von Skåne*. Lund, Gleerup.

Angelbeck B. & Grier, C. 2012 Anarchism and the archaeology of anarchic societies: resistance to centralization in the Coast Salish region of the Pacific Northwest coast. *Current Anthropology* 53 (5), 547–587.

Anthony, D. W. 2007 *The Horse, the Wheel, and Language: How Bronze-Age riders from the Eurasian steppes shaped the modern world*. Princeton NJ, Princeton University Press.

Antonsen, E. H. 1975 *A Concise Grammar of the Older Runic Inscriptions*. Tübingen, Max Niemeyer.

Aragón, E., Montero-Ruiz, I., Polzer, M. E. & van Duivenvoorde, W. 2022 Shipping metal: Characterisation and provenance study of the copper ingots from the Rochelongue underwater site (seventh–sixth century BC), West Languedoc, France. *Journal of Archaeological Science: Reports* 41, 103286. https://doi.org/10.1016/j.jasrep.2021.103286

Araque, R. 2012 Sardinian bronze figurines in their Mediterranean setting. *Praehistorische Zeitschrift* 87 (1), 83–109.

Araque, R. 2023 From the Atlantic to the Mediterranean and back: Sardinia, Iberia, and the transfer of knowledge in Late Bronze Age networks. *Open Archaeology* 9 (1), 20220314. https://doi.org/10.1515/opar-2022-0314

Araque, R., Asmus, B., Baptista, P., Mataloto, R., Paniego Díaz, P., Rammelkammer, V., Richter, A., Vintrici, G. & Rafael Ferreiro, M. 2023 Stone-working and the earliest steel in Iberia: Scientific analyses and experimental replications of final bronze age stelae and tools. *Journal of Archaeological Science* 152, 105742. https://doi.org/10.1016/j.jas.2023.105742

Arboledas, L., Alarcón, E., Contreras, F., Moreno, A., & Padilla, J. J. 2015 La mina de José Martín Palacios-Doña Eva (Baños de la Encina, Jaén): la primera explotación minera de la Edad del Bronce documentada en el sureste de la Península Ibérica. *Trabajos De Prehistoria* 72 (1), 158–175. https://doi.org/10.3989/tp.2015.12149

Armada, X.-L. 2013 Big Men showing off: The ideology and practice of social inequality in the Atlantic Late Bronze Age of Iberia. In *The Prehistory of Iberia: Debating early social stratification and the state*, eds M. Cruz Berrocal, L. García Sanjuán & A. Gilman, 267–291. New York, Routledge.

Armada, X.-L., Comendador Rey, B., Faro, M. G. & Lackinger, A. 2023 El cobre y sus aleaciones en la prehistoria reciente del Noroeste Ibérico. *De Re Metallica* 40, 33–52.

Artioli, G., Angelini, I., Nimis, P. & Villa, I. M. 2016 A lead-isotope database of copper ores from the southeastern Alps: A tool for the investigation of prehistoric copper metallurgy. *Journal of Archaeological Science* 75, 27–29.

Artioli, G., Canovaro, C., Nimis, P. & Angelini, I. 2020 LIA of prehistoric metals in the central Mediterranean area: a review. *Archaeometry* 62, Suppl. 1, 53–85. https://doi.org/10.1111/arcm.12542

Artursson, M. 2009 *Bebyggelse och samhällsstruktur: Södra och mellersta Skandinavien under senneolitikum och bronsålder 2300-500 f. Kr.* Gothenburg, Gothenburg University.

Artursson, M. 2015 The long-house as a transforming agent: Emergent complexity in Late Neolithic and Early Bronze Age southern Scandinavia 2300–1300 BC. In *The Bell Beaker Transition in Europe. Mobility and Local Evolution during the 3rd Millenium BC*, eds M.P. Prieto Martínez & L. Salanova, 69–76. Oxford, Oxbow Books.

Aubet, M. E. 1975 *La Necrópolis de Setefilla en Lora del Río, Sevilla.* Barcelona, Consejo Superior de Investigaciones Cientificas.

Aubet, M. E. 1978 *La Necrópolis de Setefilla en Lora del Río, Sevilla: (túmulo B).* Barcelona, Departamento de Prehistoria y Arqueología.

Aubet, M. E., Serna, M. R., Escacena, J. L. & Ruiz Delgado, M. M. 1983 *La Mesa de Setefilla. Lora del Río (Sevilla). Campaña de 1979. Excavaciones Arqueológicas en España.* Madrid, Ministerio de Cultura.

Austvoll, K. I. 2021 *Seaways to Complexity: A study of sociopolitical organisation along the coast of northwestern Scandinavia in the Late Neolithic and Early Bronze Age. New directions in anthropological archaeology.* Sheffield, Equinox.

Ballester, X. 2012 *Falas Indo-Europeias e Anindo-Europeias na Hispânia Pré-Romana.* Lisbon, Apenas Livros.

Barbieri, C., Blasic, D. E., Arango-Isaza, E., Sotiropoulos, A. G., Hammarström, H., Wichmann, S., Greenhill, S. J., Gray, R. D., Forkel, R., Bickel, B. & Shimizu, K. K. 2022 A global analysis of matches and mismatches between human genetic and linguistic histories. *PNAS* 119(47), e2122084119. https://doi.org/10.1073/pnas.2122084119

Barceló, J. A. 1992 Una interpretación socioeconómica del bronce final en el sudoeste de la Península Ibérica. *Trabajos De Prehistoria* 49, 259–275. https://doi.org/10.3989/tp.1992.v49.i0.545

Bengtsson, B. 2017 *Sailing Rock Art Boats. A Reassessment of Seafaring Abilities in Bronze Age Scandinavia and the Introduction of the Sail in the North.* Oxford, British Archaeological Report S2865.

Bengtsson, L. 2004 *Bilder vid vatten: Kring hällristningar i Askum sn, Bohuslän.* Gothenburg, Gotarc Serie C, Arkeologiska Skrifter 51.

Berger, D., Wang, Q., Brügmann, G., Lockhoff, N., Roberts, B. & Pernicka, E. 2022 The Salcombe metal cargoes: new light on the provenance and circulation of tin and copper in later Bronze Age europe provided by trace elements and isotopes. *Journal of Archaeological Science* 138, 105543. https://doi.org/10.1016/j.jas.2022.105543

Berger, D., Matta, V., Nørgaard, H. W., Salis, G. & Vandkilde, H. 2023 Origin and mixing of metals for Nuragic bronzetti studied with isotopes and trace elements. In *Contacts and Exchanges between Sardinia, Continental Italy and North-Western Europe in the Bronze Age (18th-11th c. BC): The "Copper Route", The "Amber Route", The "Tin Route". Proceedings of the Fifth Festival of the Nuragic Civilization (Orroli, Cagliari)*, eds M. Perra & F. Lo Schiavo, 241–259. Cagliari, Arkadia Editore.

Bergerbrant, S. & Wessman, A. 2018 Women on the move in the Nordic Bronze Age: A case study based on rock art and costume. In *Giving the Past a Future: Essays in archaeology and rock art studies in honour of Dr. Phil. HC Gerhard Milstreu*, eds J. Dodd & E. Meijer, 121–134. Oxford, Archaeopress.

Bergerbrant, S., Kristiansen, K., Allentoft, M. E., Frei, K. M., Price, T. D., Sjögren, K.-G. & Tornberg, A. 2017. Identifying commoners in the Early Bronze Age: Burials outside barrows. In *New Perspectives on the Bronze Age. Proceedings of the 13th Nordic Bronze Age Symposium held in Gothenburg 9th to 13th June 2015*, eds S. Bergerbrant & A. Wessman, 37–64. Oxford, Archaeopress.

Bertilsson, U. 2015 Examples of application of modern digital techniques and methods structure for motion (SfM) and multiview stereo (MVS) for three-dimensional documentation of rock carvings in Tanum creating new opportunities for interpretation and dating. In *Prospects for*

Prehistoric Rock Art Research. XXVI Valcamonica Symposium 2015, ed. F. Troletti, 57–62. Capo di Ponte: Edizione del Centro.

Bertilsson, U. 2018 'In the beginning there was the spear': Digital documentation sheds new light on Early Bronze Age spear carvings from Sweden. In *Prehistoric Warfare and Violence. Quantitative and Qualitative Approaches*, eds A. Dolfini, R. J. Crellin, C. Horn & M. Uckelmann, 129–148. New York & Cham, Springer.

Bertilsson, U., Ling, J., Bertilsson, C., Potter, R. & Horn, C. 2017 The Kivik tomb – Bredarör enters into the digital arena – documented with OLS, SfM and RTI. In *New Perspectives on the Bronze Age, Proceedings of the 13th Nordic Bronze Age Symposium held in Gothenburg 9th to 13th June 2015*, eds S. Bergerbrant & A. Wessman, 289–306. Oxford, Archaeopress.

Berrocal Rangel, L. 1987 El antropomorfo del Bodonal (Badajoz): Ensayo de interpretación de las estelas-guijarro y sus relaciones atlánticas. *Arqueologia (Porto)* 16, 83–94.

Berrocal Rangel, L, Mederos Martín, A., Caso Amador, R. & Rodriguez Rastrojo, M. 2023 Un paisaje funerario singular de la Edad del Bronce del Suroeste: la necrópolis y la estela del Alto de la Cruz de Piedra (Jerez de los Caballeros, Extremadura). *Complutum* 34(34), 129–143.

Bettencourt, A. M. S. 1998 O conceito de Bronze Atlântico na Península Ibérica. In *Existe uma Idade do Bronze Atlântico? Trabalhos de Arqueologia* 10, ed. S. O. Jorge, 18–39. Lisbon, IPA.

Bettencourt, A. M. S. 2001 Aspectos da metalurgia do bronze no Entre-Douro e-Minho, no quadro da Proto-História do Noroeste Peninsular. *Arqueologia* 26, 13–40.

Bettencourt, A. M. S. 2010 La Edad del Bronce en el Noroeste de la Península Ibérica: Un análisis a partir de las prácticas funerarias. *Trabajos De Prehistoria* 67 (1), 139–173. https://doi.org/10.3989/tp.2010.10034

Bettencourt, A. M. S. 2013 O Bronze Final no Noroeste Português: Uma rede complexa de lugares, memórias e ações. *Estudos Arqueológicos de Oeiras* 20, 157–172.

Bettencourt, A. M. S. 2017 Gravuras rupestres do Noroeste português para além das artes atlântica e esquemática. In *Arqueología em Portugal, 2017: Estado da Questão*, eds J. M. Arnaud & A. Martins, 1053–1068. Lisbon, Associação dos Arqueólogos Portugueses

Blanco-González, A. 2011 From huts to 'the house': The shift in perceiving home between the Bronze Age and the Early Iron Age in Central Iberia (Spain). *Oxford Journal of Archaeology* 30, 393–410. https://doi.org/10.1111/j.1468-0092.2011.00373.x

Blanco-González, A. 2018 De cabañas a casas. Estrategias sociales en la prehistoria final de la Meseta (1400-400 AC). In *Más allá de las casas. Familias, linajes y comunidades en la protohistoria peninsular*, eds A. Rodríguez Díaz, I. Pavón Soldevila & D. Duque Espino, 295–326. Cáceres, Universidad de Extremadura.

Bottaini, C., Vilaça, R., Osório, M., Montero-Ruiz, I. & Mack, P. 2022 New data on the Late Bronze Age/Early Iron Age metallurgy in central Portugal: The contribution of Vila do Touro (Sabugal, Guarda). *Munibe Antropología-Arkeologia* 73, 135–148. https://doi.org/10.21630/maa.2022.73.16

Bradley, R. 2022 *Maritime Archaeology on Dry Land: Special sites along the coasts of Britain and Ireland from the first farmers to the Atlantic Bronze Age*. Oxford, Oxbow Books.

Bradley, R., Jones, A., Myhre, L. N. & Sackett, H. 2002 Sailing through stone: Carved ships and the rock face at Revheim, southwest Norway. *Norwegian Archaeological Review* 35 (2), 109–118. https://doi.org/10.1080/002936502762389738

Brandherm, D. 2003 *Die Dolche und Stabdolche der Steinkupfer- und der älteren Bronzezeit auf der Iberischen Halbinsel*. Stuttgart, Prähistorische Bronzefunde 12.

Brandherm, D. (with Rovira Llorens, S.) 2007 *Las espadas del Bronce Final en la Península Ibérica y Baleares*. Stuttgart, Prähistorische Bronzefunde Abteilung IV, 16.

Brandherm, D. 2008 The warriors new headgear. *Antiquity* 82 (316), 480–484. https://doi.org/10.1017/S0003598X00096964

Brandherm, D. 2013 Mediterranes, Atlantisches und Kontinentales in der bronze- und ältereisenzeitlichen Stelenkunst der Iberischen Halbinsel. In *Petasos: Festschrift für Hans Lohmann*

(*Mittelmeerstudien*), eds G. Kalaitzoglou, G. Lüdorf, F. Paderborn & B. Schöningh, 131–148. Leiden, Wilhelm Fink.

Brandherm, D. 2016 Stelae, funerary practice, and group identities in the Bronze and Iron Ages of SW Iberia: a moyenne durée perspective. In *Celtic from the West 3: Atlantic Europe in the metal ages — questions of shared language*, eds J. T. Koch7 B. W. Cunliffe, 179–216. Oxford: Celtic Studies Publications 19.

Brandherm, D. & Krueger, M. 2017 Primeras determinaciones radiocarbónicas de la necrópolis de Setefilla (Lora del Río) y el inicio del periodo orientalizante en Andalucía occidental. *Trabajos De Prehistoria* 74 (2), 296–318. https://doi.org/10.3989/tp.2017.12196

Broström, S.-G. & Ihrestam, K. 2015 *Hagbards galge, RAÄ 17 i Asige socken, Halland*. https://www.academia.edu/21377683/HAGBARDS_GALGE

Burenhult, G. 1980 *Götalands hällristningar (utom Göteberg och Bohus län samt Dalsland)*. Stockholm, Stockholm University.

Cameron, C. M. 2016 *Captives: How stolen people changed the world*. Lincoln NE & London: University of Nebraska Press.

Capelle, T. 1972 Felsbilder in Nordwestdeutschland. *Acta Archaeologica* 43, 229–238.

Cassidy, L. M., Martiniano, R., Murphy, E. M., Teasdale, M. D., Mallory, J., Hartwell, B. & Bradley, D. G. 2016 Neolithic and Bronze Age migration to Ireland and establishment of the insular Atlantic genome. *Proceedings of the National Academy of Sciences* 113 (2), 368–373.

Cattin, F., Guénette-Beck, B., Curdy, P., Meisser, N., Ansermet, S., Hofmann, B., Kündig, R. et al. 2011 Provenance of Early Bronze Age metal artefacts in western Switzerland using elemental and lead isotopic compositions and their possible relation with copper minerals of the nearby Valais. *Journal of Archaeological Science* 38 (6), 1165–1394.

Celestino Pérez, S. 2001a *Estelas de guerrero y estelas diademadas. La precolonización y formación del mundo tartésico*. Barcelona, Bellaterra.

Celestino Pérez, S. 2001b Los santuarios de Cancho Roano: del indigenismo al orientalismo arquitectónico. In *Arquitectura Oriental y Orientalizante en la Península Ibérica*, eds D. Ruiz Mata & S. Celestino, 17–57. Madrid, CEPO-CSIC.

Celestino Pérez, S. & Salgado Carmona, J. A. 2011 Nuevas metodologías para la distribución espacial de las estelas del Oeste peninsular. In *Estelas e estátuas-menires: da Pré à Protohistória Actas das IV Jornadas Raianas*, ed. R. Vilaça, 417–448. Sabugal, Câmara Municipal do Sabugal.

Chacon, R., Ling, J., Hayden, B. & Chacon, Y. 2020 Understanding Bronze Age Scandinavian rock art: The value of interdisciplinary approaches. *Adoranten* 51, 74–95.

Chan, T. W. 2011 The War Ethos and Practice in Ancient Greece. Unpublished PhD dissertation, Chinese University of Hong Kong.

Childe, V. G. 1939 Double-looped palstaves in Britain. *Antiquaries Journal* 19 (3), 321–323.

Coles, J. M. 1962 European Bronze Age shields. *Proceedings of the Prehistoric Society* 28, 156–190. https://doi.org/10.1017/S0079497X0001570X

Coles, J. M. 2002. Chariots of the Gods? Landscape and imagery at Frännarp, Sweden. *Proceedings of the Prehistoric Society* 68, 215–246.

Coles, J. M. 2005 *Shadows of a Northern Past: rock carvings of Bohuslän and Østfold*. Oxford, Oxbow Books.

Comendador Rey, B. 1999 Cambios en la escala de la producción metalúrgica durante las fases finales de la Edad del Bronce en el noroeste peninsular. *Revista de Guimarâes. Volumen especial* 2, 515–537.

Comendador Rey, B. & Bettencourt, A. M. S. 2011 Nuevos datos sobre la primera metalurgia del Bronce en el Noroeste de la Península Ibérica: la contribución de Bouça da Cova da Moura (Ardegães, Maia, Portugal). *Estudos do Quaternário* 7, 19–31. https://hdl.handle.net/1822/45739

Comendador Rey, B. & González Insua, F. 2017 Rock art in the upper Támega Valley (Galicia, Spain). In *Recorded Places, Experienced Places: The Holocene rock art of the Iberian Atlantic north-west*, eds A. M. S. Bettencourt, M. Santos Estevez, H. Sampaio & D. Cardoso, 49–62. Oxford: British Archaeological Report S2878.

Comendador Rey, B., Meunier, E., Figueiredo, E., Lackinger, A., Fonte, J., Fernandez Fernandez, C., Lima, A., Mirao, J. & Silva, R. J. C. 2017 Northwest Iberian tin mining from Bronze Age to modern times: An overview. In *The Tinworking Landscape of Dartmoor in a European Context - Prehistory to 20th century*, ed. P. Newman, 133–153. Yelverton, Dartmoor Tin Working Research Group.

Correa Rodríguez, J. A. 1989 Posibles antropónimos en las inscripciones en escritura del SO. (o tartesia). *Veleia* 6, 243–252.

Correa Rodríguez, J. A. 1992 La epigrafía tartesia. In *Andalusien zwischen Vorgeschichte und Mittelalter*, eds D. Hertel & J. Untermann, 75–114. Cologne, Böhlau.

Correa Rodríguez, J. A., & Guerra, A. 2019 The epigraphic and linguistic situation in the south-west of the Iberian peninsula. In *Palaeohispanic Languages and Epigraphies*, eds A. G. Sinner & J. Velaza, 109–137. Oxford, Oxford University Press. DOI: 10.1093/oso/9780198790822.003.0005

Correia, V. H. 1993 As necrópoles da Idade do Ferro do Sul de Portugal: arquitectura e rituais. *Trabalhos de Antropologia e Etnologia* 33 (3–4), 351–370.

Correia, V. H. 1996 *A epigrafia da Idade do Ferro do Sudoeste da Península Ibérica*, Porto, Edições Etnos.

Costa Caramé, M. E. 2013 Las estelas del Suroeste en el valle del Guadalquivir y Sierra Morena: Distribución espacial y nuevas perspectivas de investigación. *Trabajos De Prehistoria* 70 (1), 76–94. https://doi.org/10.3989/tp.2013.12103

Cunliffe, B. 2001 *Facing the Ocean. The Atlantic and its Peoples 8000 BC–AD 1500*. Oxford, Oxford University Press.

Cunliffe, B. 2013 *Britain Begins*. Oxford, Oxford University Press.

Cunliffe, B. & Koch, J. T. 2010 *Celtic from the West. Alternative Perspectives from Archaeology, Genetics, Language, and Literature*. Oxford, Oxbow Books/Celtic Studies Publications.

Cunliffe, B. & Koch, J. T. 2019 A dialogue at the crossroads. In *Exploring Celtic Origins: New ways forward in archaeology, linguistics, and genetics*, Celtic Studies Publications 22, eds B. Cunliffe & J. T. Koch, 192–206. Oxford, Oxbow Books.

Dalsgaard, K. & Westergaard Nielsen, M. 2018 Were the Bronze Age fields at Bjerre 4 manured?: A survey of the phosphorus content and a comment on the cultivation potential. In *Bronze Age Settlement and Land-use in Thy, Northwest Denmark*, eds J.-H. Bech, B. V. Eriksen & K. Kristiansen, 459–468. Aarhus, Aarhus University Press.

Damgaard, P. de Barros, Martiniano, R., Kamm, J., Moreno-Mayar, J. V., Kroonen, G., Peyrot, M., Barjamovic, G. et al. 2018 The first horse herders and the impact of early Bronze Age steppe expansions into Asia. *Science* 360 (6396). doi:10.1126/science.aar7711

De Blas, M. A. 2014 El laboreo del cobre en la Sierra del Áramo (Asturias) como referente cardinal de la minería prehistórica en la región cantábrica. *Cuadernos de Prehistoria y Arqueología de la Universidad de Granada* 24, 45–84. https://revistaseug.ugr.es/index.php/cpag/article/view/4088

De Blas, M. A. & Suárez, M. (eds) 2022 *Las explotaciones de cobre en la Sierra del Aramo (Riosa, Asturias), ca. 2500-1400 a. de C.* Oviedo, Instituto de Estudios Asturianos.

Delamarre, X. 2012 *Les noms de lieux celtiques de l'Europe ancienne*. Paris, Errance.

Delgado Hervás, A. 2013 Households, merchants, and feasting: Socioeconomic dynamics and commoners, agency in the emergence of the Tartessian world (eleventh to eighth centuries, BC). In *The Prehistory of Iberia: Debating early social stratification and the state*, eds M. Cruz Berrocal, L. García Sanjuán & A. Gilman Guillén, 311–336. London, Routledge.

Delibes de Castro, G., Elorza, J. C. & Castillo, B. 1995 ¿La dote de una princesa irlandesa? A propósito de un torques aúreo de la Edad del Bronce hallado en Castrojeriz (Burgos). In *Homenaje al Profesor Martín González*, ed. J. R. Blanco, 51–61. Valladolid, Universidad de Valladolid.

Delibes de Castro, G., Fernández Manzano, J., Fontaneda Pérez, E. & Rovira Llorens, S. 1999 *Metalurgia de la Edad del Bronce en el Piedemonte Meridional de la Cordillera Cantábrica. La Colección Fontaneda*. Castilla y León, Junta de Castilla y León.

Derksen, R. 2015 *Etymological Dictionary of the Baltic Inherited Lexicon* (ed. A. Lubotsky). Leiden, Indo-European Etymological Dictionary Series 13.

de Vaan, M. 2008 *Etymological Dictionary of Latin and the other Italic Languages* (ed. A. Lubotsky), Leiden, Indo-European Etymological Dictionary Series, Volume 7.

Díaz-Guardamino, M. 2010 Las estelas decoradas en la Prehistoria de la Península Ibérica, Unpublished PhD Thesis, Universidad Complutense de Madrid, Madrid. https://eprints.ucm.es/id/eprint/11070/

Díaz-Guardamino, M. 2011 Iconografía, lugares y relaciones sociales: Reflexiones en torno a las estelas y estatuas-menhir atribuidas a la Edad del Bronce en la Península Ibérica. In *Estelas e Estátuas-menir: da Pré à Proto-história*, ed. R. Vilaça, 63–88. Sabugal: Câmara Municipal do Sabugal, Universidades de Coimbra e Porto.

Díaz-Guardamino, M. 2012 Estelas decoradas del Bronce Final en la Península Ibérica: Datos para su articulación cronológica. In *Sidereum Ana II, El río Guadiana en el Bronce Final*, ed. J. Jiménez Ávila, 389–415. Mérida CSIC, Instituto de Arqueología de Mérida.

Díaz-Guardamino, M. 2014 Shaping social identities in Bronze Age and Early Iron Age western Iberia: The role of funerary practices, stelae, and statue-menhirs. *European Journal of Archaeology*, 17 (2), 329–349. https://doi.org/10.1179/1461957114Y.0000000053

Díaz-Guardamino, M. 2020 Rock art as process: Iberian Late Bronze Age warriorstelae in-the-making. In *Images in-the-making: Art, process, archaeology*, eds I.-M. Back Danielsson & A. M. Jones, 73–89. Manchester, Social Archaeology and Material Worlds. https://doi.org/10.7765/9781526142856.00014

Díaz-Guardamino, M. 2023 Rock art technology, reflectance transformation imaging and experimental archaeology: Recent research on Iberian Late Bronze Age warrior stelae. *Complutum* 34 (special issue), 147–164. https://dx.doi.org/10.5209/cmpl.85238

Díaz-Guardamino, M., Garcia Sanjuan, L., Wheatley, D. & Rodríguez Zamora, V. 2015 RTI and the study of engraved rock art: A re-examination of the Iberian Late Bronze Age stelae of Setefilla and Almadén de la Plata 2. *Digital Applications in Archaeology and Cultural Heritage* 2 (2–3), 1–45. https://doi.org/10.1016/j.daach.2015.07.002

Díaz-Guardamino, M., Ling, J., Koch, J., Schulz Paulsson, B. & Horn, C. 2022 The local appropriation of warrior ideals in Late Bronze Age Europe: A review of the rock art site of Arroyo Tamujoso 8 and the warriorstela of Cancho Roano (Badajoz, Spain). *Trabajos de Prehistoria*. 79 (2), 329–345. https://doi.org/10.3989/tp.2022.12302

Díaz-Guardamino, M., García-Sanjuán, L., Wheatley, D. W., Lozano-Rodríguez, J. A., Rogerio-Candelera, M. Á & Casado-Ariza, M. 2020 Late prehistoric stelae, persistent places and connected worlds: A multi-disciplinary review of the evidence at Almargen (Lands of Antequera, Spain). *Cambridge Archaeological Journal* 30, 69–96.

Díaz-Guardamino, M., García Sanjuán, L., Wheatley, D. W., Lozano Rodríguez, J. A., Rogerio Candelera, M.Á., Krueger, M., Hunt Ortiz, M., Murillo-Barroso, M. & Balsera Nieto, V. 2019 Rethinking Iberian warriorstelae: A multidisciplinary investigation of Mirasiviene and its connection to Setefilla (Lora del Río, Seville, Spain). *Archaeological and Anthropological Sciences* 11, 6111–6140.

Dillon, M. & Chadwick, N. K. 1967 *The Celtic Realms*. New York, New American Library.

Domergue, C. 1987 *Catalogue des mines et des fonderies antiques de la Péninsule Ibérique*. Madrid, Casa de Velázquez-Diffusion de Boccard.

Domínguez de la Concha, C., González Bornay, J. M. & De Hoz Bravo, J. 2005 *Catálogo de estelas decoradas del Museo Arqueológico Provincial de Badajoz (Siglos VIII–V a.C.)*. Badajoz, Consejería de Cultura, Junta de Extremadura.

Drennan, R. D. & Peterson, C. E. 2012 Challenges for comparative study of early complex societies. In *The Comparative Archaeology of Complex Societies*, ed. M. E. Smith, 62–87. Cambridge, Cambridge University Press

Drescher, H. 1958 *Der Überfangguß: Ein Beitrag zur vorgeschichtlichen Metalltechnik*. Mainz, Rudolf Habelt.

Earle, T. K. 1997 *How Chiefs Come to Power. The Political Economy in Prehistory*. Stanford CA, Stanford University Press.

Earle, T. K. 2002 *Bronze Age Economics: The beginnings of political economies*. London, Routledge.
Earle, T. K. 2017 Chiefs, chieftaincies, chiefdoms, and chiefly confederacies: Power in the evolution of political systems. In *Chiefdoms: Yesterday and today*, eds R. Carneiro, L. Grinin & A. Korotayev, 233–256. New York, Eliot Werner.
Earle, T. K., Ling, J., Uhnér, C., Stos-Gale, Z. & Melheim, L. 2015 The political economy and metal trade in Bronze Age Europe: Understanding regional variability in terms of comparative advantages and articulations. *European Journal of Archaeology* 18 (4), 633–657.
eDIL = *Electronic Dictionary of the Irish Language.* http://www.dil.ie/
Effenberger, H. 2018 The plant economy of the Northern European Bronze Age: More diversity through increased trade with southern regions. *Vegetation History and Archaeobotany* 27 (1), 65–74. https://doi.org/10.1007/s00334-017-0621-3
Ehrenreich, R. M., Crumley, C. L. & Levy, J. E. (eds) 1995 *Heterarchy and the Analysis of Complex Societies.* Arlington TX, Archaeological Papers of the American Anthropological Association 6.
Engels, F. 1972 *The Origin of the Family, Private Property, and the State: In the light of Lewis H. Morgan.* New York, International Publishers
Enríquez-Navascués, J. J. 2006 Arqueología Rural y Estelas del SO (desde la Tierra, para la Tierra y por la Tierra). *Trabajos de Arqueología Navarra* 14, 151–175.
Eogan, G. 1995 Ideas, people and things. Ireland and the external world during the Late Bronze Age. *Ireland in the Bronze Age. Proceedings of the Dublin Conference, April 1995*, eds J. Waddell & E. S. Twohig, 128–135. Dublin, Stationery Office.
Fábrega-Álvarez, P., Fonte, J. & González García, F. 2011 Las sendas de la memoria. Sentido, espacio y reutilización de las estatuas-menhir en el noroeste de la Península Ibérica. *Trabajos de Prehistoria* 68 (2), 313–330. http://dx.doi.org/10.3989/tp.2011.11072
Fábregas Valcarce, R. & Rodríguez-Rellán, C. 2015 Walking on the stones of years. Some remarks on the north-west Iberian rock art. In *Picturing the Bronze Age*, eds P. Skoglund, J. Ling & U. Bertilsson, 47–64. Oxford, Swedish Rock Art Series 3.
Fábregas Valcarce, R., Martínez Cortizas, A., Blanco Chao, R. & Chesworth, W. 2003 Environmental change and social dynamics in the second–third millennium BC in NW Iberia. *Journal of Archaeological Science* 30 (7), 859–871. https://doi.org/10.1016/S0305-4403(02)00264-9
Falileyev, A., Gohi, A. E. & Ward, N. 2010 *Dictionary of Continental Celtic Place-Names. A Celtic Companion to the Barrington Atlas of the Greek and Roman World*. Aberystwyth, CMCS.
Feinman, G. M. 2017 Multiple pathways to large-scale human cooperative networks: A reframing. In *Feast, Famine or Fighting? Multiple Pathways to Social Complexity*, eds R. J. Chacon & R. G. Mendoza, 459–478. New York & Cham, Springer.
Felding, L., Reiter, S., Frei, K. M. & Vandkilde, H. 2020 Male social roles and mobility in the Early Nordic Bronze Age. A perspective from SE Jutland. *Danish Journal of Archaeology* 9, 1–167. https://doi.org/10.7146/dja.v9i0.117955
Feldman, M. H. & Sauvage, C. 2010 Objects of prestige? Chariots in the Late Bronze Age eastern Mediterranean and Near East. *Ägypten und Levante* 20, 67–181.
Freeman, P. M. 2001 *The Galatian Language: A comprehensive survey of the language of the ancient Celts of Greco-Roman Asia Minor*. Lampeter, Ancient Near Eastern Texts and Studies 13.
French, C. 2010 The palaeo-environments of Bronze Age Europe. In *Organizing Bronze Age Societies. The Mediterranean, Central Europe, and Scandinavia Compared*, eds T. K. Earle & K. Kristiansen, 34–56. Cambridge, Cambridge University Press.
Frieman, C. J. & Hofmann, D. 2019 Present pasts in the archaeology of genetics, identity, and migration in Europe. A critical essay. *World Archaeology* 32, 1–18. https://doi.org/10.1080/00438243.2019.1627907
Frieman, C., Brück, J., Rebay-Salisbury, K., Bergerbrant, S., Montón Subías, S., Sofaer, J., Knüsel, C. J., Vankilde, H., Giles, M. and Treherne, P. 2017 Aging well: Treherne's 'Warrior's Beauty' two decades later. *European Journal of Archaeology* 20 (1), 36–73. doi:10.1017/eaa.2016.6

Fulk, R. D. 2018 *A Comparative Grammar of the Early Germanic Languages*. Amsterdam/Philadelphia PA, John Benjamins.

Furholt, M. 2019 Re-integrating archaeology: A contribution to aDNA studies and the migration discourse on the 3rd millennium BC in Europe. *Proceedings of the Prehistoric Society* 85, 115–129. doi:10.1017/ppr.2019.4

Fyllingen, H. 2003. Society and violence in the Early Bronze Age: An analysis of human skeletons from Nord-Trøndelag, Norway. *Norwegian Archaeological Review* 36 (1), 27–43.

Galán Domingo, E. 1993 *Estelas, paisaje y territorio en el bronce final del suroeste de la Península Ibérica*. Madrid, Universidad Complutense de Madrid.

Galán Domingo, E. 2006 Las estelas del suroeste: ¿historias de gentiles damas y poderosos guerreros? In *Acercándonos al Pasado. Prehistoria en 4 Actos* Madrid, Ministerio de Cultura.

Galan Huertos, E. & Mirete Mayo, S. 1979 *Introducción a los minerales de España*. Madrid, Instituto Geológico y Minero de España.

García-Alix, A., Jimenez-Espejo, F. J., Lozano, J. A., Jiménez-Moreno, G., Martinez-Ruiz, F., García Sanjuán, L., Aranda Jiménez, G., García Alfonso, E., Ruiz-Puertas, G. & Anderson, R. S. 2013 Anthropogenic impact and lead pollution throughout the Holocene in Southern Iberia. *The Science of the Total Environment* 449, 451–460. https://doi.org/10.1016/j.scitotenv.2013.01.081

García Alonso, J. L. 2023 The south-west of ancient Hispania in its linguistic and epigraphic context. *Journal of Celtic Linguistics* 24, 35–84.

García Sanjuán, L. 2006 Funerary ideology and social inequality in the late prehistory of the Iberian south-west (*c.* 3300–850 cal BC). In *Social Inequality in Iberian Late Prehistory*, eds P. Díaz del Río & L. García Sanjuán, 149–170. Oxford, British Archaeological Report S1525.

García Sanjuán, L. 2012 The Warrior Stelae of the Iberian South-west: Symbols of Power in Ancestral Landscapes. In *Atlantic Europe in the First Millennium BC: Crossing the Divide*, eds T. Moore & X. L. Armada, Oxford, Oxford University Press. https://doi.org/10.1093/acprof:osobl/9780199567959.003.0025

García Sanjuán, L. & Díaz-Guardamino, M. 2015 The outstanding biographies of prehistoric monuments in Iron Age, Roman, and medieval Spain. In *The Lives of Prehistoric Monuments in Iron Age, Roman, and Medieval Europe*, eds M. Díaz-Guardamino, L. García Sanjuán & D.W. Wheatley, 183–204, Oxford, Oxford University Press.

García Sanjuán, L., Wheatley, D. W., Fábrega Álvarez, P., Hernández Arnero, M. J. & Polvorinos del Río, A. 2006 Las estelas de guerrero de Almadén de la Plata (Sevilla). Morfología, Tecnología y Contexto. *Trabajos de Prehistoria*, 63 (2), 135–152. https://doi.org/10.3989/tp.2006.v63.i2.21

Garrido, J. P. & Orta, E. M. 1978 *Excavaciones en la necrópolis de La Joya, Huelva (3ª, 4ª Y 5ª Campañas)*. Madrid, Excavaciones Arqueológicas en España 96.

Gilman, A. 1995 Prehistoric European chiefdoms: Rethinking 'Germanic' societies. In *Foundations of Social Inequality: Fundamental issues in archaeology*, eds T. D. Price & G. M. Feinman, 235–251. Boston MA, Springer. https://doi.org/10.1007/978-1-4899-1289-3_9

Glob, P. V. 1969 *Helleristninger i Danmark*. Copenhagen, Gyldendal.

Goldhahn, J. 2007 Dödens hand: En essä om brons-och hällsmed. In *Rituelle spesialister i bronse- og jernalderen*, eds J. Goldhahn & T. Østigård, 21–373. Gothenburg, GOTARC Serie C, Arkeologiska skrifter.

Goldhahn, J. 2013 *Bredarör på Kivik: En arkeologisk odysse*. Simrishamn, Kalmar studies in archaeology IX.

Goldhahn, J. 2016 *Sagaholm: North European Bronze Age rock art and burial ritual*. Oxford, Oxbow Books.

Goldhahn, J. & Ling, J. 2013 Bronze Age rock art in Northern Europe: Contexts and interpretations. In *The Oxford Handbook of the European Bronze Age*, eds H. Fokkens & A. Harding, 270–290. Oxford, Oxford University Press. https://doi.org/10.1093/oxfordhb/9780199572861.013.0015

Gomes, M. V. 1994 *A Necrópole De Alfarrobeira (S. Bartolomeu de Messines) E A Idade Do Bronze No Concelho De Silves*. Silves: Museu Arqueológico de Silves.

González Bornay, J. M. & Domínguez García, A. 2021 *Catálogo de estelas decoradas del Museo de Cáceres*. Cáceres: Junta de Extremadura.

González-Rabanal, B., Marín-Arroyo, A. B., Cristiani, E., Zupancich, A. & González-Morales, M. R. 2022 The arrival of millets to the Atlantic coast of northern Iberia. *Science Reports* 12, 18589. https://doi.org/10.1038/s41598-022-23227-4

GPC = *Geiriadur Prifysgol Cymru, A Dictionary of the Welsh Language*. Caerdydd, Gwasg Prifysgol Cymru, 1950–2002. http://welsh-dictionary.ac.uk/gpc/gpc.html

Grahn, H. B. 2022 Chariots of the Atlantic Warriors: A comparative study of chariot motifs on Scandinavian and Iberia rock art. Unpublished MA dissertation. University of Gothenburg.

Gräslund, B. 1967 The Herzsprung shield type and its origin. *Acta Archaelogica* 38, 59–71.

Greene, D. 1972 The chariot as described in Irish literature. In *The Iron Age in the Irish Sea Province*, ed. C. Thomas, 59–73. London, Council for British Archaeology Research Report 9.

Gron, K. J., Larsson, M., Gröcke, D. R., Andersen, N.H., Andreasen, M., Bech, J. H., Henriksen, P. S. *et al.* 2021 Archaeological cereals as an isotope record of long-term soil health and anthropogenic amendment in southern Scandinavia. *Quaternary Science Reviews* 253, 106762. https://doi.org/10.1016/j.quascirev.2020.106762

Guerra, A. 2005 Povos, cultura e língua no ocidente peninsular: uma perspectiva, a partir da toponomástica. *Acta Palaeohispanica IX/Palaeohispanica* 5, 793–822.

Gutiérrez, C., Muñoz, P., Pereira, J. & Chapa, T. 2020 Las estelas de guerrero del valle medio del Tajo. Recreación experimental del proceso de elaboración. In *Anejos a CuPAUAM 4. Docendo discimus. Homenaje a la profesora Carmen Fernández Ochoa*, eds L. Berrocal Rangel & A. Mederos Martín, 93–104. Madrid, Universidad Autónoma de Madrid.

Haak, W., Lazaridis, I., Patterson, N., Rohland, N., Mallick, S., Llamas, B., Brandt, G. *et al.* 2015 Massive migration from the steppe was a source for Indo-European languages in Europe. *Nature* 522, 207–211. https://doi.org/10.1038/nature14317

Hakenbeck, S. E. 2019 Genetics, archaeology and the far right: an unholy Trinity. *World Archaeology* 9 (3), 1–11.

Halloran, J. A. 2006 *Sumerian Lexicon: A dictionary guide to the ancient Sumerian language*. Los Angeles CA, Logogram.

Halloran, J. A. 2020 *Sumerian Lexicon: Version 3.0*. https://www.sumerian.org/sumerian.pdf, accessed 26 February 2020

Hamp, E. P. (with Adams, D. Q.) 2013 *The Expansion of the Indo-European Languages: An Indo-Europeanist's evolving view*. Philadelphia PA, Sino-Platonic Papers 239.

Harbison, P. 1975 The coming of Indo-European to Ireland: An archaeological viewpoint. *Journal of Indo-European Studies* 3, 101–119.

Harding, A. 2007 *Warriors and Weapons in Bronze Age Europe*. Budapest, Archaeolingua.

Harrison, R. J. 2004 *Symbols and Warriors. Images of the European Bronze Age*. Bristol, Western Academics & Specialist Press.

Harrison, R. J. & Mederos, A. 2000 Patronage and clientship: A model for the Atlantic Final Bronze Age in the Iberian Peninsula. In *Metals Make the World Go Round: The supply and circulation of metals in Bronze Age Europe*, ed. C. Pare, 133–150. Oxford, Oxbow Books.

Hayden, B. 2018 *The Power of Ritual in Prehistory: Secret societies and origins of social complexity*. Cambridge, Cambridge University Press.

Hedeager, L. 1994 Warrior economy and trading economy in Viking-Age Scandinavia. *Journal of European Archaeology* 2 (1), 130–137.

Hencken, H. 1950 Herzsprung shields and Greek trade. *American Journal of Archaeology* 54, 295–309.

Heyd, V. 2017 Kossinna's smile. *Antiquity* 91 (356), 348–359. https://doi.org/10.15184/aqy.2017.21

Hofmann, D., Hanscam, E., Furholt, M., Bača, M., Reiter, S., Vanzetti, A., Kotsakis, K. *et al.* 2021 Forum: Populism, identity politics, and the archaeology of Europe. *European Journal of Archaeology* 24 (4), 519–555. doi:10.1017/eaa.2021.29

Hood, A. B. E. (ed. & trans.) 1978 *St. Patrick: His writings and Muirchu's life*, London & Chichester, Arthurian Period Sources 9.

Höppner, B., Bartelheim, M., Hujsmans, M., Krauss, R., Martinek, K. P., Pernicka, E. & Schwab, R. 2005 Prehistoric copper production in the Inn Valley (Austria) and the earliest copper in Central Europe. *Archaeometry* 47 (2), 293–315.

Holst, M. K., Rasmussen, K., Kristiansen, K. & Bech, J.-H. 2013 Bronze Age 'herostrats': Ritual, political, and domestic economies in Early Bronze Age Denmark. *Proceedings of the Prehistoric Society* 79, 265–296.

Horn, C. 2013 Weapons, fighters and combat: Spears and swords in Early Bronze Age Scandinavia. *Danish Journal of Archaeology* 2 (1), 20–44.

Horn, C. 2014 *Studien zu den europäischen Stabdolchen*. Bonn, Universitätsforschungen zur Prähistorischen Archäologie 246.

Horn, C. 2016 Nothing to lose: Waterborne raiding in southern Scandinavia. In *Comparative Perspectives on Past Colonisation, Maritime Interaction and Cultural Integration*, eds H. Glørstad, A. Z. Tsigaridas Glørstad & L. Melheim, 109–127. Sheffield, Equinox.

Horn, C. 2018 Warfare vs. exchange?: Thoughts on an integrative approach. In *Warfare in Bronze Age Society*, eds C. Horn & K. Kristiansen, 47–60. Cambridge, Cambridge University Press.

Horn, C. 2019 Showmen and fighters: Bronze Age rock art and weaponry in Scandinavia. In *Materialisierung von Konflikten/Materialisation of Conflicts. Beiträge der Dritten Internationalen LOEWE-Konferenz vom 24. bis 27. September 2018 in Fulda/Proceedings of the Third International LOEWE Conference, 24-27 September 2018 in Fulda*, eds S. Hansen & R. Krause, 45–65. Bonn, Rudolf Habelt.

Horn, C. 2021 Trouble in paradise? Violent conflict in Funnel-Beaker societies. *Oxford Journal of Archaeology* 40 (1), 43–64.

Horn, C. 2022 Most deserve to be forgotten: Could the southern Scandinavian rock art memorialize heroes? In *Rock Art and Memory in the Transmission of Cultural Knowledge*, ed. L. F. Zubieta, 125–146. New York & Cham, Springer.

Horn, C. 2023 Warriors as a challenge: Violence, rock art, and the preservation of social cohesion during the Nordic Bronze Age. *European Journal of Archaeology* 26 (1), 57–80.

Horn, C. & Kristiansen, K. (eds) 2018 *Warfare in Bronze Age Society*. Cambridge, Cambridge University Press.

Horn, C. & Potter, R. 2018 Transforming the rocks: Time and rock art in Bohuslän, Sweden. *European Journal of Archaeology* 21 (3), 361–384. https://doi.org/10.1017/eaa.2017.38

Horn, C., Potter, R. & Peternell, M. 2022 Water flows and water accumulations on bedrock as a structuring element of rock art. *Journal of Archaeological Method and Theory* 30, 828–854. https://doi.org/10.1007/s10816-022-09578-2

Horn, C., Austvoll, K. I., Ling, J. & Artursson, M. forthcoming *Nordic Bronze Age Economies*. Cambridge, Cambridge University Press.

Hornblower, S. 2007 Warfare in ancient literature: The paradox of war. In *The Cambridge History of Greek and Roman Warfare*, eds P. Sabin, H. Van Wees & M. Whitby, 22–53. Cambridge: Cambridge University Press. doi:10.1017/CHOL9780521782739.003

Hunt Ortiz, M. 2003 *Prehistoric Mining and Metallurgy in South West Iberian Peninsula*. Oxford, British Archaeological Report S1188.

Hunt Ortiz, M. 2019 Estudio arqueometalúrgico. In *La explotación tartésica del estaño en San Cristóbal de Logrosán (Cáceres, España)* eds A. Rodríguez Díaz, I. Pavón Soldevila & D. M. Duque Espino, 223–266. Oxford, Archaeopress.

Hunt Ortiz, M. & Ling, J. 2023 Minería y metalurgia en el Bronce Final y el Tarteso: Evolución e innovación. (Tarteso. Nuevas fronteras). *Mytra* 12, 273–290.

Hyllested, A. 2010 The precursors of Celtic and Germanic. In *Proceedings of the 21st Annual UCLA Indo European Conference*, ed. S. W. Jamison, H. C. Melchert & B. Vine, 107–128. Bremen, Hempen.

IBERLID = García De Madinabeitia, S., Gil Ibarguchi, J. I. & Santos Zalduegui, J. F. 2021 IBERLID: A lead isotope database and tool for metal provenance and ore deposits research. *Ore Geology Reviews*. https://doi.org/10.1016/j.oregeorev.2021.104279

Iversen, R. & Kroonen, G. 2017 Talking Neolithic. Linguistic and archaeological perspectives on how Indo-European was implemented in southern Scandinavia. *American Journal of Archaeology* 121 (4), 511–525.

Janson, S., Lundberg, E. B. & Bertilsson, U. (eds) 1989 *Hällristningar och hällmålningar i Sverige*. Helsingborg, Forum.

Jenness, D. 1934 Indian Vikings of the Northwest Coast. *Canadian Geographical Journal*, 8 (5), 235–46.

Jiménez Ávila, J. 2021 El contexto arqueológico de la escritura paleohispánica del Suroeste peninsular. *Palaeohispanica. Revista Sobre Lenguas Y Culturas De La Hispania Antigua* 21, 149–188.

Jordán Cólera, C. 2006 [K.3.3]: Crónica de un teicidio anunciado. *Estudios de lenguas y epigrafía antiguas* 7, 37–72.

Kalb, P. 1995 O povoado da Nossa Senhora da Guia, Baiões. In *A Idade do Bronze em Portugal. Discursos de Poder* 68, 68. Lisbon, Museu Nacional de Arqueologia.

Karl, R. 2003 Iron Age chariots and medieval texts: A step too far in 'breaking down boundaries'? *e-Keltoi* 5, 1–29.

Kaul, F. 2017 The xenia concept of guest-friendship: Providing an elucidatory model for Bronze Age communication. In *North Meets South. Theoretical Aspects on the Northern and Southern Rock Art*, eds P. Skoglund, J. Ling & U. Bertilsson, 172–198. Oxford, Swedish Rock Art Series 6.

Kaul, F. 2022 Middle Bronze Age long-distance exchange: amber, early glass and guest friendship, Xenia. In *Trade before Civilization: Long distance exchange and the rise of social complexity*, eds J. Ling, R. Chacon & K. Kristiansen, 109–141. Cambridge: Cambridge University Press. doi:10.1017/9781009086547.008

Klejn, L. S., Haak, W., Lazaridis, I., Patterson, N., Reich, D., Kristiansen, K., Sjögren, K.-G. et al. 2018 Discussion: Are the origins of Indo-European Languages explained by the migration of the Yamnaya Culture to the west? *European Journal of Archaeology* 21 (1), 3–17.

Koch, J. T. Karl, R., Minard, A. & Ó Faoláin, S. 2007 *An Atlas for Celtic Studies. Archaeology and Names in Ancient Europe and Early Medieval Ireland, Britain, and Brittany*. Oxford, Celtic Studies Publications 12.

Koch, J. T. 2013a Out of the flow and ebb of the European Bronze Age: Heroes, Tartessos, and Celtic. In *Celtic from the West 2: Rethinking the Bronze Age and the arrival of Indo-European in Atlantic Europe*, eds J. T. Koch & B. Cunliffe, 101–146. Oxford, Celtic Studies Publications 16.

Koch, J. T. 2013b *Tartessian: Celtic in the south-west at the dawn of history* (2nd edn). Aberystwyth, Celtic Studies Publications 13.

Koch, J. T. 2014 Once again, Herodotus, the Κελτοί, the source of the Danube, and the Pillars of Hercules. In *Celtic Art in Europe: Making connections. Essays in honour of Vincent Megaw on his 80th birthday*, eds C. Gosden, S. Crawford & K. Ulmschneider, 6–18. Oxford, Oxbow Books.

Koch, J. T. 2016 Phoenicians in the West and break-up of the Atlantic Bronze Age. In *Celtic from the West 3. Atlantic Europe in the Metal Ages. Questions of shared language*, eds J. T. Koch, B. Cunliffe, C. D. Gibson & K. Cleary, 431–476. Oxford, Celtic Studies Publications 19.

Koch, J. T. 2019a *Common Ground and Progress on the Celtic of the South-western (SW) Inscriptions*. Aberystwyth, Centre for Advanced Welsh and Celtic Studies. e-book. https://www.wales.ac.uk/Resources/Documents/Centre/2019/Koch-Celtic-of-the-SW-inscriptions-2019.pdf

Koch, J. T. 2019b Rock art and Celto-Germanic vocabulary: Shared iconography and words as reflections of Bronze Age contact. *Adoranten* 2018, 80–95.

Koch J. T. 2020 *Celto-Germanic: Later prehistory and Post-Proto-Indo-European vocabulary in the north and west*. Aberystwyth, Centre for Advanced Welsh and Celtic Studies. https://wales.ac.uk/Resources/Documents/Centre/2020/Celto-Germanic2020.pdf

Koch, J. T. & Fernández Palacios, F. 2019 A case of identity theft? Archaeogenetics, Beaker People, and Celtic origins. In *Exploring Celtic Origins: New ways forward in archaeology, linguistics, and genetics*, Celtic Studies Publications 22, eds. B. Cunliffe & J. T. Koch, 38–79. Oxford, Oxbow Books.

Kradin, N. N. 2015 Nomadic empires in inner Asia. In *Complexity of Interaction Along the Eurasian Steppe Zone in the First Millennium CE*, ed. J. Bemmann, 11–48. Bonn, Rheinische Friedrich-Wilhelms-Universität Bonn.

Kristiansen, K. 1998 *Europe Before History*. Cambridge, Cambridge University Press.

Kristiansen, K. 2002 The tale of the sword – swords and swordfighters in Bronze Age Europe. *Oxford Journal of Archaeology* 21 (4), 319–332.

Kristiansen, K. 2010 Decentralized complexity: The case of Bronze Age Northern Europe. In *Pathways to Power: New perspectives on the emergence of social inequality*, eds T. D. Price & G. M. Feinman, 169–192. New York & Cham, Springer.

Kristiansen, K. 2018a Theorizing trade and civilization. In *Trade and Civilisation: Economic networks and cultural ties, from prehistory to the early modern era*, eds K. Kristiansen, T. Lindkvist & J. Myrdal, 1–24. Cambridge, Cambridge University Press.

Kristiansen, K. 2018b Warfare and the political economy: Europe 1500–1100 BC. In *Warfare in Bronze Age Society*, eds C. Horn & K. Kristiansen, 23–46. Cambridge, Cambridge University Press.

Kristiansen, K. 2022 Bronze Age globalisation in numbers: Volumes of trade and its organisation. In *Baltic in the Bronze Age. Regional Patterns, Interactions and Boundaries*, eds D. Hofmann, F. Nikulka, & R. Schuhmann, 1–20. Leiden, Sidestone.

Kristiansen, K. & Earle, T. 2014 Neolithic versus Bronze Age social formations: A political economy approach. In *Paradigm Found: Archaeological theory – present, past and future. Essays in honour of Evžen Neustupný*, eds K. Kristiansen, L. Šmejda & J. Turek, 236–249. Oxford, Oxbow Books.

Kristiansen, K. & Earle, T. 2022 Modelling modes of production: European 3rd and 2nd millennium BC economies. In *Ancient Economies in Comparative Perspective: Material life, institutions and economic thought*, eds M. Frangipane, M. Poettinger & B. Schefold, 131–163. New York & Cham, Springer.

Kristiansen, K. & Larsson, T. 2005 *The Rise of the Bronze Age: Travels, transmissions, and transformations*. Cambridge, Cambridge University Press.

Kristiansen, K. & Suchowska-Ducke, P. 2015 Connected histories: The dynamics of Bronze Age interaction and trade 1500–1100 BC. *Proceedings of the Prehistoric Society* 81, 361–392.

Kroonen, G. 2013 *Etymological Dictionary of Proto-Germanic*. Leiden, Indo-European Etymological Dictionary Series 11.

Lazaridis, I. 2018 The evolutionary history of human populations in Europe. *Current Opinion in Genetics & Development* 53, 21–27. https://doi.org/10.1016/j.gde.2018.06.007

Lazaridis, I., Alpaslan-Roodenberg, S., Acar, A., Açıkkol, A., Agelarakis, A., Aghikyan, L., Akyüz, U. et al. 2022 The genetic history of the Southern Arc: A bridge between West Asia and Europe. *Science* 377 (6609). https://doi.org/10.1126/science.abm4247

LEIA = Vendryès, J. 1959 *Lexique étymologique de l'irlandais ancien*. Dublin, Dublin Institute for Advanced Studies.

Linderholm, A., Kılınç, G. M., Szczepanek, A., Włodarczak, P., Jarosz, P., Belka, Z., Dopieralska, J. et al. 2020 Corded Ware cultural complexity uncovered using genomic and isotopic analysis from south-eastern Poland. *Scientific Reports* (2020) 10(1), 6885. doi: 10.1038/s41598-020-63138-w

Ling, J. 2012 *Rock Art and Seascapes in Uppland*. Oxford, Swedish Rock Art Series 1.

Ling, J. 2014 *Elevated Rock-Art. Towards a Maritime Understanding of Rock Art in Northern Bohuslän, Sweden*. Oxford, Swedish Rock Art Series 2.

Ling, J. & Bertilsson, U. 2015 Biography of the Fossum panel. *Adoranten* 2016, 58–72.

Ling, J. & Cornell, P. 2017 Violence, warriors, and rock art in Bronze Age Scandinavia. In *Feast, Famine or Fighting? Multiple Pathways to Social Complexity*, eds R. J. Chacon & R. G. Mendoza, 15–33. New York & Cham, Springer.

Ling, J. & Koch, J. T. 2018 A sea beyond Europe to the north and west. In *Giving the Past a Future. Essays in Archaeology and Rock Art Studies in Honour of Dr. Phil. h.c. Gerhard Milstreu*, eds J. Dodd & E. Meijer, 96–111. Oxford, Archaeopress.

Ling, J. & Toreld, A. 2018 Maritime warfare in Scandinavian rock art. In *Warfare in Bronze Age society*, eds C. Horn & K. Kristiansen, 61–80. Cambridge, Cambridge University Press.

Ling, J. & Uhnér, C. 2014 Rock art and metal trade. *Adoranten* 2014, 23–43.

Ling, J., Chacon, R. & Chacon, Y. 2021 Rock art and nautical routes to social complexity: Comparing Haida and Scandinavian Bronze Age societies. *Adoranten* 2020, 5–23.

Ling, J., Chacon, R. & Chacon, Y. 2022a Bronze Age Long-distance exchange, secret societies, rock art, and the supra regional interaction hypothesis. In *Trade before Civilization: Long distance exchange and the rise of social complexity*, eds J. Ling, R. Chacon & K. Kristiansen, 53–74. Cambridge, Cambridge University Press.

Ling, J., Chacon, R. & Kristiansen, K. 2022b New perspectives on long-distance trade and social complexity. In *Trade Before Civilization: Long distance exchange and the rise of social complexity*, eds J. Ling, R. Chacon & K. Kristiansen, 1–20. Cambridge, Cambridge University Press.

Ling, J., Cornell, P. & Kristiansen, K. 2017 Bronze economy and mode of production: The role of comparative advantages in temperate Europe during the Bronze Age. In *Modes of Production and Archaeology*, eds R. M. Rosenswig & J. J. Cunningham, 205–230. Gainesville FL, University Press of Florida.

Ling, J., Earle, T. & Kristiansen, K. 2018 Maritime mode of production: Raiding and trading in seafaring chiefdoms. *Current Anthropology* 59 (5), 488–524.

Ling, J., Stos-Gale, Z., Grandin, L., Billström, K., Hjärthner-Holdar, E. & Persson, P.-O. 2014 Moving metals II: Provenancing Scandinavian Bronze Age artefacts by lead isotope and elemental analyses. *Journal of Archaeological Science* 41, 106–132. https://doi.org/10.1016/j.jas.2013.07.018

Ling, J., Hjärthner-Holdar, E., Grandin, L., Stos-Gale, Z., Kristiansen, K., Melheim, A. L., Artioili, G., Angelini, I., Krause, R. & Canovaro, C. 2019 Moving metals IV: Swords, metal sources and trade networks in Bronze Age Europe. *Journal of Archaeological Science: Reports* 26, 101837. https://doi.org/10.1016/j.jasrep.2019.05.002

Linge, T. E. 2005 Kammeranlegget i Mjeltehaugen: Et rekonstruksjonsforslag. *Mellan sten och järn*, ed. J. Goldhahn, 537–59. Gothenburg, Intellecta.

Littauer, M. A. 1972 The military use of the chariot in the Aegean in the late Bronze Age. *American Journal of Archaeology* 76, 145–157.

López-Sáez, J. A., Blanco-González, A., López-Merino, L., Blanca Ruiz-Zapata, M., Dorado-Valiño, M., Pérez-Díaz, S., Valdeolmillos, A. & Burjachs, F. 2009 Landscape and climatic changes during the end of the late prehistory in the Amblés Valley (Ávila, central Spain), from 1200 to 400 cal BC. *Quaternary International* 1 (200), 90–101.

López-Sáez, J. A., Abel-Schaad, D., Pérez-Díaz, S., Blanco-González, A., Alba-Sánchez, F., Dorado, M., Ruiz-Zapata, B., Gil-García, M. J., Gómez-González, C. & Franco-Múgica, F. 2014 Vegetation history, climate and human impact in the Spanish Central System over the last 9000 years. *Quaternary International* 353, 98–122.

López-Sáez, J. A., Pérez-Díaz, S., Rodríguez-Ramírez, A., Blanco-González, A., Villarías-Robles, J., Luelmo-Lautenschlaeger, R., Jiménez-Moreno, G. *et al.* 2018 Mid–late Holocene environmental and cultural dynamics at the south-west tip of Europe (Doñana National Park, SW Iberia, Spain). *Journal of Archaeological Science: Reports* 22, 58–78. https://doi.org/10.1016/j.jasrep.2018.09.014

Lord, A. B. 1960 *The Singer of Tales*. Cambridge MA, Harvard University Press

Lull, V., Micó, R., Rihuete, C. & Risch, R. 2013 Political collapse and social change at the end of El Argar. In *1600 Cultural Change in the Shadow of the Thera-Eruption?*, eds H. Meller, F. Bertemes, H.-R. Bork & R. Risch, 283–302. Halle, Tagungen des Landesmuseums für Vorgeschichte Halle 9.

Marcigny, C. & Peake, R. 2021 My home is my castle! Field systems and farms: Rhythm and land appropriation during the Bronze Age in north-west France (2300–800 BCE). In *Europe's Early Fieldscapes. Themes in Contemporary Archaeology*, eds S. Arnoldussen, R. Johnston, & M. Løvschal, 131–141. New York & Cham, Springer. https://doi.org/10.1007/978-3-030-71652-3_10

MacWhite, E. 1951 *Estudios sobre las relaciones atlánticas de la Península Hispánica en la Edad del Bronce*, Madrid, Publicaciones del Seminario de Historia primitiva del hombre.

Mallory, J. P. 1989 *In Search of the Indo-Europeans: Language, archaeology and myth*. London, Thames & Hudson.

Mallory, J. P. 1998 The Old Irish chariot. In *Mír Curad. Studies in Honor of Calvert Watkins*, ed. J. Jasanoff, H. C. Melchert & L. Oliver, 451–464. Innsbruck, Institut für Sprachwissenschaft der Universität Innsbruck.

Mallory, J. P. & Adams, D. Q. 2006 *The Oxford Introduction to Proto-Indo-European and the Proto-Indo-European World*. Oxford, Oxford University Press.

Malmström, H., Günther, T., Svensson, E. M., Juras, A., Fraser, M., Munters, A. R., Pospieszny, Ł. et al. 2019 The genomic ancestry of the Scandinavian Battle Axe Culture people and their relation to the broader Corded Ware horizon. *Proceedings of the Royal Society B* 286, 20191528. http://dx.doi.org/10.1098/rspb.2019.1528

Mandt, G. 1991 Vestnorske ristninger i tid og rom: Kronologiske, korologiske og kontekstuelle studier. Unpublished PhD, University of Bergen.

Martínez-Cortizas, A., Costa-Casais, M. & López-Sáez, J. A. 2009 Environmental change in NW Iberia between 7000 and 500 cal BC. *Quaternary International* 200 (1–2), 77–89. https://doi.org/10.1016/j.quaint.2008.07.012

Martínez Cortizas, A., Pontevedra-Pombal, X., Nóvoa-Muñoz, J. C. & García-Rodeja, E. 1997 Four thousand years of atmospheric Pb, Cd and Zn deposition recorded by the ombrotrophic peat bog of Penido Vello (northwest Spain). *Water, Air & Soil Pollution* 100, 387–403. https://doi.org/10.1023/A:1018312223189

Martínez Cortizas, A., García-Rodeja, E., Pontevedra Pombal, X., Nóvoa Muñoz, J. C., Weiss, D. & Cheburkin, A. 2002 Atmospheric Pb deposition in Spain during the last 4600 years recorded by two ombrotrophic peat bogs and implications for the use of peat as archive. *Science of the Total Environment* 292, 33–44. https://doi.org/10.1016/S0048-9697(02)00031-1

Martínez-Cortizas, A., López-Merino, L., Bindler, R., Mighall, T. & Kylander, M. E. 2016 Early atmospheric metal pollution provides evidence for Chalcolithic/Bronze Age mining and metallurgy in Southwestern Europe. *Science of the Total Environment* 545–546, 398–406. https://doi.org/10.1016/j.scitotenv.2015.12.078

Marx, K. 1953 [1939–1941] *Grundrisse der Kritik der politischen Ökonomie* (facsimile reprint). Berlin, Dietz.

Matasović, R. 2009 *Etymological Dictionary of Proto-Celtic*. Leiden, Indo-European Etymological Dictionary Series 9.

Mazzù, A., Uberti, S., Bodini, I., Paderno, D. & Danesi, A. 2021 Dynamical behaviour of Bronze Age war chariots. *Journal of Archaeological Science Reports* 36, 2–15.

McKinley, J. I., Schuster, J. & Millard, A. 2013 Dead sea connections. A Bronze Age and Iron Age ritual site on the Isle of Thanet. In *Celtic from the West 2. Rethinking the Bronze Age and the Arrival of Indo-European in Atlantic Europe*, eds J. T. Koch & B. Cunliffe, 157–183. Oxford, Celtic Studies Publications 16.

McKinley, J. I., Leivers, M., Schuster, J., Marshall, P., Barclay, A. J. & Stoodley, N. (eds) 2015 *Cliffs End Farm, Isle of Thanet, Kent: A mortuary and ritual site of the Bronze Age, Iron Age and Anglo-Saxon period with evidence for long-distance maritime mobility*. Salisbury, Wessex Archaeology Report 31.

Mederos Martín, A. 1996 Representaciones de liras en las estelas decoradas del Bronce Final de la Península Ibérica. *Cuadernos de Prehistoria y Arqueología. Universidad Autónoma de Madrid* 23, 114–123.

Mederos Martín, A. 2008 Carros micénicos del Heládico Final III en las estelas decoradas del Bronce Final II–III del Suroeste de la Península Ibérica. In *Contacto cultural entre el Mediterráneo y el Atlántico (siglos XII-VIII ANE): La Precolonización a debate*, eds S. Celestino Pérez, N. Rafel & X. L. Armada, 437–463. Rome, Escuela Española de Historia y Arqueología de Roma del CSIC.

Melheim, L., Grandin, L., Persson, P. O., Billström, K., Stos-Gale, Z., Ling, J., Williams, A., Angelini, I., Canovaro, C., Hjärthner-Holdar, E. & Kristiansen, K. 2018 Moving metals III. Possible origins for copper in Bronze Age Denmark based on lead isotopes and geochemistry. *Journal of Archaeological Science* 96, 85–105. https://doi.org/10.1016/j.jas.2018.04.003

Meredith, C. 1998 *An Archaeometallurgical Survey for Ancient Tin Mines and Smelting Sites in Spain and Portugal. Mid-Central Western Iberian Geographical Region 1990-1995*. Oxford, British Archaeological Report S714.

Meredith, C. 2009 La Mina El Cerro de San Cristobal: a Bronze Age tin mine (Extremadura, Spain). *Papers from the Institute of Archaeology* 9, 57–69. doi: https://doi.org/10.5334/pia.122

Meunier, E., Dias, F., Fonte, J., Lima, A., Rodrigues, A., Bottiani, C., Silva, R. J. C., Veiga, J. P., Periera, F. C. & Figueiredo, E. 2023 Later prehistoric tin mining in the Ervedosa mine (Vinhais, Portugal): evidence and context. *Archaeological and Anthropological Sciences* 15, 43. https://doi.org/10.1007/s12520-023-01748-x

Mikkelsen, M. 2020 Slaves in Bronze Age southern Scandinavia?. *Acta Archaeologica* 91 (1), 147–190. https://doi.org/10.1111/j.1600-0390.2020.12225.x

Mikkelsen, M. & Kristiansen, K. 2018 Legaard. In *Bronze Age Settlement and Land-use in Thy, Northwest Denmark*, eds J.-H. Bech, B. V. Eriksen & K. Kristiansen, 505–538. Thisted, Jutland Archaeological Society publications/Museum Thy, Højbjerg.

Millard, A. 2015 Isotopic investigation of residential mobility and diet. In *Cliffs End Farm, Isle of Thanet, Kent: A mortuary and ritual site of the Bronze Age, Iron Age and Anglo-Saxon period with evidence for long-distance maritime mobility*, eds J. I. McKinley, M. Leivers, J. Schuster, P. Marshall, A. J. Barclay & N. Stoodley, 135–146. Wessex Archaeology Reports 31.

Milstreu, G. 2017 Re-cut rock art images (with special emphasis on ship carvings). In *New perspectives on the Bronze Age. Proceedings of the 13th Nordic Bronze Age Symposium held in Gothenburg 9th to 13th June 2015*, eds S. Bergerbrant & A. Wessman, 281–287. Oxford, Archaeopress.

Molloy, B. 2007 *The Cutting Edge. Studies in Ancient and Medieval Combat*. Stroud, Tempus.

Monteagudo, L. 1977 *Die Beile auf der Iberischen Halbinsel*. München, C.H. Beck.

Montero-Ruiz, I. 2017 Minería y circulación del cobre en la Prehistoria Reciente de la Península Ibérica. In *Minería y metalurgia históricas en el sudoeste europeo: nuestras raíces mineras*, eds. O. Puche, M. Ayarzagüena, J. F. López & J. Pous, 13–24. Madrid, SEDPGYM.

Montero-Ruiz, I., García-Vuelta, O. & Armada, X.-L. 2014 Estudio arqueometalúrgico del depósito de hachas de talón de Distriz (Monforte de Lemos, Lugo). *Sautuola* 19, 139–156.

Montero-Ruiz, I. & Murillo-Barroso, M. 2022 The first bronzes of El Argar: An approach to the production and origin of the metal. In *Landscapes as Resource Assemblages in the Bronze Age of Southern Spain*, eds M. Bartelheim, F. Contreras Cortés & R. Hardenberg, 201–220. Tübingen, Ressourcen Kulturen 17.

Montero-Ruiz, I., Hunt, M. & Santos Zalduegui, J. F. 2007 El depósito de la Ría de Huelva: procedencia del metal a través de los resultados de análisis de isótopos. In *El hallazgo leonés de Valdevimbre y los depósitos del Bronce Final Atlántico en la Península Ibérica*, eds J. Celis Sánchez, G. Delibes de Castro, J. Fernández Manzano, & L. Grau Lobo, 194–209. Valladolid, Museo de León, Junta de Castilla y León y Diputación de León.

Montero-Ruiz, I., Murillo-Barroso, M. & Hook, D. 2019 La producción de bronces durante El Argar: frecuencia y criterios de uso. *Boletín del Museo Arqueológico Nacional* 38, 9–26. https://www.man.es/man/estudio/publicaciones/boletin-man/2010-2019/2019-38-01-montero.html

Montelius, O. 1889 Förbindelse mellan Skandinavien och vestra Europa före Kristi födelse. *Svenska fornminnesföreningens tidskrift* 7 (2), 124–155.

Moucha, V. 2005 *Hortfunde der frühen Bronzezeit in Böhmen*. Praha, Archeologický Ústav AV CR.

Müller, J. 1999 Zur Radiokarbondatierung des Jung- und Endneolithikums und der Frühbronzezeit im Mittelelbe-Saale-Gebiet (4100–1500 v. Chr.). *Berichte der Römisch-Germanischen-Kommision* 80, 25–90.

Murillo-Barroso, M. & Martinón-Torres, M. 2012 Amber sources and trade in the prehistory of the Iberian Peninsula. *European Journal of Archaeology* 15, 187–216.

Murillo-Barroso, M., Peñalver, E., Bueno, P., Barroso, R., de Balbín, R. & Martinón-Torres, M. 2018 Amber in prehistoric Iberia: New data and a review. *PLoS ONE* 13, e0202235. https://doi.org/10.1371/journal.pone.0202235

Murillo-Barroso, M., Montero-Ruiz, I., Nieto, J. M., Camalich Massieu, M. D., Martin Socas, D. & Martinón-Torres, M. 2019 Trace elements and lead isotopic composition of copper deposits from the eastern part of the internal zone of the Betic Cordillera (SE Iberia): application to provenance of archaeological materials. *Journal of Iberian Geology* 45, Article 4. https://doi.org/10.1007/s41513-019-00111-1

Murillo-Barroso, M., Martinón-Torres, M., García Sanjuán, L., Wheatley, D., Hunt Ortiz, M. A., Gonzáles, M. F. & Hernández Arnedo, M. J. 2015 New objects in old structures. The Iron Age hoard of the Palacio III megalithic funerary complex (Almadén de la Plata, Seville, Spain). *Journal of Archaeological Science* 57, 322–334. https://doi.org/10.1016/j.jas.2015.03.013

Needham, S. P. 2000 Power pulses across a cultural divide: Cosmologically driven acquisition between Armorica and Wessex. *Proceedings of the Prehistoric Society* 66, 151–207.

Needham, S. P. 2009 Encompassing the sea: Maritories and Bronze Age maritime Interactions. In *Bronze Age Connections: Culture contact in prehistoric Europe*, ed. P. Clark, 12–37. Oxford, Oxbow Books.

Needham, S. P. & Bowman, S. 2005 Flesh hooks, technological complexity and the Atlantic Bronze Age feasting complex. *European Journal of Archaeology* 8 (2), 93–136. https://doi.org/10.1177/1461957105066936

Needham, S. P. & Cowie, T. 2012 The halberd pillar at Ri Cruin cairn, Kilmartin, Argyll. In *Visualising the Neolithic: Abstraction, figuration, performance, representation*, eds A. Cochrane & A. M. Jones, 89–110. Oxford, Neolithic Studies Group Seminar Papers 13.

Neitzel, J. E. & Earle, T. K. 2014 Dual-tier approach to societal evolution and types. *Journal of Anthropological Archaeology* 36, 181–195.

Nessel, B., Brugmann, G., Berger, D., Frank, C., Marahrens, J. & Pernicka, E. 2018 Bronze production and tin provenance – new thoughts about the spread of metallurgical knowledge. In *Metals, Minds and Mobility*, eds X.-L. Armada, M. Murillo-Barroso & M. Charlton, 67–84. Oxford, Oxbow Books.

Nimura, C., Skoglund, P. & Bradley, R. 2020 Navigating inland: Bronze Age watercraft and the lakes of southern Sweden. *European Journal of Archaeology* 23 (2), 186–206.

Nocete, F., Lizcano, R., Peramo, A. & Gómez, E. 2010 Emergence, collapse and continuity of the first political system in the Guadalquivir Basin from the fourth to the second millennium BC: The long-term sequence of Úbeda (Spain). *Journal of Anthropological Archaeology* 29, 219–237.

Nordén, A. 1925 *Östergötlands bronsålder: Med omkr. 500 textbilder och 141 pl*. Linköping. H. Carlsons.

Nørgaard, H. W., Pernicka, E. & Vandkilde, H. 2019 On the trail of Scandinavia's early metallurgy: Provenance, transfer and mixing. *Plos One* 14 (12), e0219574. https://doi.org/10.1371/journal.pone.0219574

Nørgaard, H. W., Pernicka, E. & Vandkilde, H. 2021 Shifting networks and mixing metals: Changing metal trade routes to Scandinavia correlate with Neolithic and Bronze Age transformations. *Plos One* 16 (6), e0252376. https://doi.org/10.1371/journal.pone.0252376

Nyegaard, G. 2018 Bronze Age animal husbandry: The faunal remains from Bjerre Enge. In *Bronze Age Settlement and Land-use in Thy, northwest Denmark*, eds J.-H. Bech, B. V. Eriksen & K. Kristiansen, 469–476. Thisted, Jutland Archaeological Society publications/Museum Thy, Højbjerg.

O'Brien, W. 2022 *Derrycarhoon: A later Bronze Age copper mine in south-west Ireland*. Oxford, British Archaeological Report S3069.

Olalde, I., Brace, S., Allentoft, M., Armit, I., Kristiansen, K., Rohland, N., Mallick, S. et al. 2018 The Beaker phenomenon and the genomic transformation of Northwest Europe. *bioRxiv* 135962. https://doi.org/10.1101/135962.

Olalde, I., Mallick, S., Patterson, N., Rohland, N., Villalba-Mouco, V., Silva, M., Dulias, K. et al. 2019 The genomic history of the Iberian Peninsula over the past 8000 years. *Science* 363, 1230–34. https://doi: 10.1126/science.aav4040

Olander, T. 2019 The Indo-European homeland: Introducing the problem. In *Tracing the Indo-Europeans: New evidence from archaeology and historical linguistics*, eds B. A. Olson, T. Olander & K. Kristiansen, 7–34. Oxford, Oxbow Books.

Osborne, R. 1996 *Greece in the Making, 1200–479 BC*. London, Psychology Press.

Osgood, R. 1998 *Warfare in the Late Bronze Age of North Europe*. Oxford, British Archaeological Report S694.

Otto, T., Thrane, H. & Vandkilde, H. (eds) 2006 *Warfare and Society. Archaeological and Social Anthropological Perspectives*. Aarhus, Aarhus University Press.

OXALID = Oxford Archaeological Lead Isotope Database. http://oxalid.arch.ox.ac.uk

Parcero-Oubiña, C., Armada, X.-L., Nión, S. & González Insua, F. 2020 All together now (or not). In *Change, Resistance and Resilience in the NW Iberian Peninsula in the Bronze Age–Iron Age transition*, eds B. X. Currás & I. Sastre, 151–175. London, Routledge.

Patterson, N., Isakov, M., Booth, T., Büster, L., Fischer, C.-E., Olalde, I., Ringbauer, H. et al. 2022 Large-scale migration into britain during the Middle to Late Bronze Age. *Nature* 601, 588–594. https://doi.org/10.1038/s41586-021-04287-4

Pavón Soldevila, I., Duque Espino, D. M., Sanabria Murillo, D. & Collado Giraldo, H. 2018 La estela de "Cabeza del Buey V/El Palacio" en el poblamiento de la Edad del Bronce de la sierra de Tiros (Badajoz). *SPAL - Revista de Prehistoria y Arqueología* 27 (1), 31–60.

Pérez Díaz, S., Lopez Saez, J. A., Pontevedra-Pombal, X., Souto-Souto, M. & Galop, G. 2016 8000 years of vegetation history in the northern Iberian Peninsula inferred from the palaeoenvironmental study of Zalama ombrotrophic bog (Basque-Cantabrian Mountains, Spain). *Boreas* 45 (4), 658–672. https://hal.science/hal-01450967

Raffield, B., Greenlow, C., Price, N. & Collard, M. 2016 Ingroup identification, identity fusion and the formation of Viking war bands. *World Archaeology* 48 (1), 35–50.

Rassmann, K. 2010 Die frühbronzezeitlichen Stabdolche Ostmitteleuropas: Anmerkungen zu Chronologie, Typologie, Technik und Archäometallurgie. In *Der Griff nach den Sternen. Wie Europas Eliten zu Macht und Reichtum kamen*, eds H. Meller & F. Bertemes, 807–821. Langenweißbach, Beier & Beran.

Rassmann, K. & Görsdorf, J. 1993 *Spätneolithikum und frühe Bronzezeit im Flachland zwischen Elbe und Oder*. Lübstorf, Archäologisches Landesmuseum für Mecklenburg-Vorpommern.

Reich, D. 2018 *Who We Are and How We Got There*. Oxford, Oxford University Press.

Renfrew, A. C. 1987 *Archaeology and Language: The puzzle of Indo-European origins*. Cambridge, Cambridge University Press.

Renfrew, A. C. 2013 Early Celtic in the West: The Indo-European context. In *Celtic from the West 2: Rethinking the Bronze Age and the Arrival of Indo-European in Atlantic Europe*, eds J. T. Koch & B. Cunliffe, 207–217. Oxford, Celtic Studies Publications 16.

Ringe, D. 2017 *A Linguistic History of English. From Proto-Indo-European to Proto-Germanic*. Oxford, Oxford University Press.

Ringe, D., Warnow, T. & Taylor, A. 2002 Indo-European and computational cladistics. *Transactions of the Philological Society* 100 (1), 59–129.

Rivera Jiménez, T., García Sanjuán, L., Díaz-Guardamino, M., Donaire Romero, T., Morales González, J. A., Lozano Rodríguez, J. A., Rogerio Candelera, M. A., Bermejo Meléndez, J. & Aguilera Collado, E. 2021

The Cañaveral de León stela (Huelva, Spain). A monumental sculpture in a landscape of settlements and pathways. *Journal of Archaeological Science: Reports* 40, 103251. 10.1016/j.jasrep.2021.103251

Rivet, A. L. F. & Smith, C. 1979 *The Place-names of Roman Britain*. London, Batsford.

Rodriguez, A., Pavón, I. & Duque Espino, D. M. (eds) 2019 *La explotación tartésica del estaño en San Cristóbal de Logrosán (Caceres, España)*. Oxford, British Archaeological Report S2944.

Rodríguez-Corral, J. & Rodríguez-Rellán, C. 2023 In the land of tin men? Warrior stelae, mobility, and interaction in western Iberia during the late prehistory. *Archaeological and Anthropological Sciences* 15 (11), 172. https://doi.org/10.1007/s12520-023-01870-w.

Rohl, B. 1996 Lead isotope data from the Isotrace Laboratory, Oxford: Archaeometry data base 2, galena from Britain and Ireland. *Archaeometry* 38 (1), 165–180.

Rohl, B. & Needham, S. 1998 *The Circulation of Metal in the British Bronze Age: The application of lead isotope analysis*. London, British Museum Occasional Paper 102.

Rovira, S., Montero-Ruiz, I. & Consuegra, S. 1997. *Las primeras etapas metalúrgicas en la Peninsula Ibérica I Analisis de Materiales*. Madrid, Instituto Universitario Ortega y Gasset.

Ruiz-Gálvez, M. L. 1995 La ría en relación con la metalurgia de otras regiones peninsulares durante el Bronce Final. In *Ritos de Paso y Puntos de Paso. La Ría de Huelva en el mundo del Bronce Final Europeo*, ed. M. Ruiz-Gálvez, 59–67. Madrid, Universidad Complutense de Madrid.

Ruiz-Gálvez, M. L. 1998 *La Europa Atlántica en la Edad del Bronce. Un viaje a las raíces de Europa Occidental*. Barcelona, Crítica.

Ruiz-Gálvez, M. L. & Galán, E. 1991 Las estelas del Suroeste como hitos de vias ganaderas y rutas comerciales. *Trabajos de Prehistoria* 48, 257–273. https://doi.org/10.3989/tp.1991.v48.i0.524

Saez, R., Nocete, F., Gil Ibarguchi, J. I., Rodriguez-Bayona, M., Inacio, N., Quispe, D., Rodriguez, J. & Santos-Zalduegu, J. F. 2021 A lead isotope database for copper mineralisation along the Guadalquivir River Valley and surrounding areas. *Journal of Iberian Geology* 47, 411–427. https://doi.org/10.1007/s41513-020-00151-y

Sahlins, M. D. 1972 *Stone Age Economics*. Piscataway NJ, Aldine.

Sampaio, H. & Bettencourt, A. M. S. 2011 Produção e práticas metalúrgicas da Idade do Bronze no Noroeste português. O caso do Pego, Braga. In *Povoamento e Exploração de Recursos Mineiros na Europa Atlântica Ocidental*, eds C. Martins, A. M. Bettencourt, J. I. F. P. Martins & J. Carvalho, 391–407. Braga, CITCEM/UM, APEQ. https://hdl.handle.net/1822/45899

Sanches, M. J. 2019 Os Primeiros habitantes do 13 territorio bragançano. *Bragança: das origens à revolução liberal de 1820*, ed F. de Sousa, 19–67. Bragança, Municipio de Bragança & CEPESE.

Santos, M. J. 2009 Estelas diademadas: revisión de criterios de clasificación. *Herakleion* 2, 7–40.

Santos Cancelas, A. 2015 La música de las estelas: Liras, identidad y memoria en el Suroeste peninsular del Bronce Final. *Revista de Musicología*, 38 (1), 17–45. https://doi.org/10.2307/24878246

Santos-Estévez, M. 2021 The parade of weapons: Ritual landscapes in late prehistory in the north-west Iberian Peninsula. In *Weapons and Tools in Rock Art: A world perspective*, eds A. M. S. Bettencourt, M. Santos-Estévez & H. A. Sampaio, 103–112. Oxford, Oxbow Books.

Santos-Estévez, M. & Bettencourt, A. M. S. 2017 O conjunto de gravuras rupestres de Santo Adrião (Caminha, Portugal): embarcações, armas, cavalos e ex-votos. In *Arqueología em Portugal/2017 - Estado da Questão*, 1055–1070. Lisboa, Atas do Congresso dos Arqueólogos Portugueses.

Santos Zalduegui, J. F., Garcia de Madinabeitia, S., Gil Ibarguchi, J. I. & Palero, F. 2004 A lead isotope database: The Los Pedroches Alcudia area (Spain); implications for archaeometallurgical connections across south western and south eastern Iberia. *Archaeometry* 46 (4), 625–634.

Schreiner, M. 2007 *Erzlagerstätten im Hrontal, Slowakei. Genese und Prähistorische Nutzung*. Rahden/Westfalen, Marie Leidorf.

Senna-Martínez, J. C. 1994 Subsídios para o estudo do Bronze Pleno na Estremadura Atlántica: (1) A alabarda de tipo 'Atlántico' do hábitat da Baútas (Amadora). *Zephyrus* 46, 161–182.

Senna-Martínez, J. C. 1998 Produção, ostentação e redistribuição: Estrutura Social e Economia Política no Grupo Baiões/Santa Luzia. In *Existe uma Idade do Bronze Atlântico?*, ed. S. O. Jorge, 219–230. Lisbon, Trabalhos de Arqueologia 10.

Senna-Martínez, J. C. 2013 Um rio na(s) rota(s) do estanho: O Tejo entre a Idade do Bronze e a Idade do Ferro. Vila Franca de Xira. *CIRA Arqueologia* 2, 7–18.

Senna-Martínez, J. C. & Luís, E. 2016 Technique and social complexity: Development trajectories of peasant societies with metallurgy during the Bronze Age of western Iberia. In *Social Complexity in a Long Term Perspective*, ed. J. Soares, 115–130. Setúbal, Setúbal Arqueológica 16.

Senna-Martínez, J. C., Luís, E., Araújo, M. F., Silva, R., Figueiredo, E. & Valério, P. 2011 First bronzes of north-west Iberia: The data from Fraga dos Corvos Habitat site. In *Povoamento e Exploração dos Recursos Mineiros na Europa Atlântica Ocidental*, coord. C. M. B. Martins, A. M. S. Bettencourt, J. I. F. P. Martins & J. Carvalho, 377–390. Braga, CITEM, APEQ.

Silva, A. C. F. 2011 *Ordo Zoelarum. Arqueologia e identidade do Nordeste de Portugal*. Bragança, Museu do Abade de Baçal.

Sims-Williams, P. P. 2020 An alternative to 'Celtic from the East' and 'Celtic from the West'. *Cambridge Archaeological Journal* 30 (3), 511–529. https://doi:10.1017/S0959774320000098

Skoglund, P. 2016 *Rock Art Through Time: Scanian rock carvings in the Bronze Age and earliest Iron Age*. Oxford, Swedish Rock Art Series 5.

Soares, A. M. M. 2013 O sistema de povoamento do Bronze Final no Baixo Alentejo: Bacia do Guadiana. *Estudos Arqueológicos de Oeiras* 20, 273–302.

Soares, A. M. M., Baptista, L., Mataloto, R., Melo, L., Silva, A. M., Soares, R. M., & Valério, P. 2021 The Bronze Age of Southwestern Iberian Peninsula: endogenous evolution versus migration stimuli. *Revista portuguesa de arqueologia* 24 (1), 59–82.

Sperber, L. 1987 *Untersuchungen zur Chronologie der Urnenfelderkultur im nördlichen Alpenvorland von der Schweiz bis Oberösterreich*. Bonn, Antiquitas. Reihe 3, Abhandlungen zur Vor- und Frühgeschichte, zur klassischen und provinzial-römischen Archäologie und zur Geschichte des Altertums 29.

Sprockhoff, E. 1954 Nordische Bronzezeit und frühes Griechentum. *Jahrbuch des Römisch-Germanischen Zentralmuseums Mainz* 1, 28–110.

Stevenson, A. C. & Harrison, R. 1992 Ancient forests in Spain: A model for land-use and dry forest management in south-west Spain from 4000 BC to 1900 BC. *Proceedings of the Prehistoric Society* 58, 227–247. https://doi.org/10.1017/S0079497X00004175

Stifter, D. 2009 The Old-Irish chariot and its technology: A case of creative transmission in medieval Irish literature. In *Kelten am Rhein: Akten des dreizehnten Internationalen Keltologiekongresses/Proceedings of the 13th International congress of Celtic studies, 23. bis 27. Juli 2007 in Bonn*, ed. S. Zimmer, 279–289. Mainz am Rhein, Beihefte der Bonner Jahrbücher 58 (2).

Stos-Gale, Z. A. 2001 The development of Spanish metallurgy and copper circulation inprehistoric Southern Spain. In *III Congreso Nacional de Arqueometría*, eds B. Gómez Tubío, M. A. Respaldiza Galisteo & M. L. Pardo Rodríguez, 445–456. Seville, Universidad de Sevilla.

Stos-Gale, S., Hunt Ortiz, M. & Gale, N. 1999 Análisis elemental y de isótopos de plomo de objetos metálicos de los sondeos de Gatas. In *Proyecto Gatas 2. La dinámica arqueoecológica de la ocupación prehistórica*, eds P. Castro, R. Chapman, S. Gili, V. Lull, R. Micó, C. Rihuete, R. Risch & M. E. Sanahuja, 347–361. Seville, Monografias Arquelógicas.

Stos-Gale, Z. A., Gale, N. H., Houghton, J. & Speakman, R. 1995 Lead isotope data from the Isotrace Laboratory, Oxford: Archaeometry data base 1, ores from the western Mediterranean. *Archaeometry* 37 (2), 407–415.

Strömberg, M. 1982 *Ingelstorp: Zur Siedlungsentwicklung eines südschwedischen Dorfes*. Bonn, Acta Archaeologica Lundensia, Series in quarto 14.

Swift, L. 2015 Lyric visions of epic combat: the spectacle of war in archaic personal song. In *War as Spectacle: Ancient and modern perspectives on the display of armed conflict*, eds A. Bakogianni & V. Hope, 93–109. London, Bloomsbury Academic.

Talbert, R. J. A. (ed.) 2000 *Barrington Atlas of the Greek and Roman World*. Princeton NJ, Princeton University Press.

Tereso, J. P., Vilaça, R., Osório, M., da Fonte, L. & Seabra, L. 2020 Destroyed by fire, preserved through time: crops and wood from a Late Bronze Age/Early Iron Age structure at Vila do Touro (Sabugal, Portugal). *Complutum* 31 (2), 255–278.

Tereso, J. P., Bettencourt, A. M. S., Ramil-Rego, P., Teira-Brión, A., López-Dóriga, I., Lima, A. & Almeida, R. 2016 Agriculture in NW Iberia during the Bronze Age: A review of archaeobotanical data. *Journal of Archaeological Science: Reports* 10, 44–58.

Tornos, F., Casquet, C. & Relvas, J. M. R. S. 2005 Transpressional tectonics, lower crust decoupling and intrusion of deep mafic sills: A model for the unusual metallogenesis of SW Iberia. *Ore Geology Reviews* 27, 133–163.

Tornos, F., Inverno, C. M. C., Casquet, C., Mateus, A., Ortiz, G. & Oliveira, V. 2004 The metallogenetic evolution of the Ossa-Morena Zone. *Journal of Iberian Geology* 30, 143–181.

Tornos, R. & Chiarada, M. 2004 Plumbotectonic evolution of the Ossa Morena Zone, Iberian Peninsula: Tracing the influence of mantle–crust interaction in ore-forming processes. *Economic Geology* 99, 965–985.

Torres Ortíz, M. 1999 *Sociedad y Mundo Funerario en Tartessos*. Madrid, Real Academia de la Historia.

Treherne, P. 1995 The warrior's beauty: the masculine body and self-identity in Bronze-Age Europe. *Journal of European Archaeology* 3 (1), 105–144. https://doi.org/10.1179/096576695800688269

Uckelmann, M. 2012 *Die Schilde der Bronzezeit in Nord-, West- und Zentraleuropa*. Stuttgart, Prähistorische Bronzefunde III, 4.

Uckelmann, M. 2014 A Bronze Age ornament network: Tracing the Herzsprung symbol across Europe. In *Knowledge Networks and Craft Traditions in the Ancient World: Material Crossovers*, eds K. Rebay-Salisbury, A. Brysbaert & L. Foxhall, 182–197. New York and London: Routledge.

Untermann, J. (with D. S. Wodtko) 1997 *Monumenta Linguarum Hispanicarum IV. Die tartessischen, keltiberischen und lusitanischen Inschriften*. Wiesbaden, Ludwig Reichert.

Valdiosera, C., Günther, T., Vera-Rodríguez, J. C., Ureña, I., Iriarte, E., Rodríguez-Varela, R, Simões, L. G. et al. 2018 Four millennia of Iberian biomolecular prehistory illustrate the impact of prehistoric migrations at the far end of Eurasia. *Proceedings of the National Academy of Sciences* 115 (13), 3428–3433. https://doi.org/10.1073/pnas.1717762115

Valera, R. G., Valera P. G. & Rivildini, A. 2005 Sardinian ore deposits and metals in the Bronze Age. In *Archaeometallurgy in Sardinia*, eds F. Lo Schiavo, A. Giumlia-Mair, U. Sanna & R. Valera, 43–88. Montagnac, Monographies Instrumentum 30.

Valério, P., Soares, A. M., Araújo, M. F., Silva, R., Porfírio, E. & Serra, M. 2013a Estudo de metais e vestígios de produção do povoado fortificado do Bronze Final do Outeiro do Circo (Beja). In *Arqueologia em Portugal 150 anos – Atas do I Congresso da Associação dos Arqueólogos Portugueses, 21 a 24 de Novembro de 2013*, eds J. M. Arnaud, A. Martins & C. Neves, 609–615. Lisbon, Biblioteca Nacional de Portugal.

Valério, P., Soares, A.M.M., Silva, R.J.C., Araújo, M.F., Rebelo, P., Neto, N., Santos, R. & Fontes, T. 2013b Bronze production in Southwestern Iberian Peninsula: the Late Bronze Age metallurgical workshop from Entre Águas 5 (Portugal). *Journal of Archaeological Science* 40, 439–451.

Vandkilde, H. 2006 Warriors and warrior institutions in Copper Age Europe. In *Warfare and Society. Archaeological and Social Anthropological Perspectives*, eds T. Otto, H. Thrane & H. Vandkilde, 355–384. Aarhus, Aarhus University Press.

Vandkilde, H. 2013 Bronze Age voyaging and cosmologies in the making. The helmets from Viksø revisited. In *Counterpoint. Essays in Archaeology and Heritage Studies in Honour of Professor Kristian Kristiansen*, eds S. Bergerbrant & S. Sabatini, 165–177. Oxford, Archaeopress.

Vandkilde, H., Matta, V., Ahlqvist, L. & Nørgaard, H. W. 2021 Anthropomorphised warlike beings with horned helmets: Bronze Age Scandinavia, Sardinia, and Iberia compared. *Praehistorische Zeitschrift* 97 (1), 130–158. https://doi.org/10.1515/pz-2021-2012

Vilaça, R. 1998a Hierarquização e conflito no Bronze Final da Beira Interior. In *Existe uma Idade do Bronze Atlântico?* ed. S. O. Jorge, 203–217. Lisbon, Instituto Português de Arqueologia.

Vilaça, R. 1998b Produção, consumo e circulação de bens na Beira Interior na transição do II para o I milénio a.C. *Estudos Pré-Históricos* 6, 347–374.

Vilaça, R. 2014 Ensaio sobre a região de Beja em torno do ano mil a.C. Entre a a tradição e a inovação. In *Idade do Bronze do Sudoeste: Novas perspetivas sobre uma velha problemática*, eds R. Vilaça & M. Serra, 101–125. Coimbra, University of Coimbra.

Vilaça, R. 2020 O ocidente peninsular de há 3000 anos num cruzamento de escalas. Itinerários das coisas e das pessoas. *Estudos Arqueológicos De Oeiras* 27, 281–316. https://eao.oeiras.pt/index.php/DOC/article/view/355

Vilaça, R. & Cardoso, J. L. 2017 O Tejo português durante o Bronze Final. In *Anejos de AEsPA, LXXX. Territórios comparados: los valles del Guadalquivir, el Guadiana y el Tajo en época tartésica. Reunión Científica, Mérida (Badajoz, España), 3-4 December 2015*, eds S. Celestino Pérez & E. Rodríquez González, 237–281. Mérida, Instituto de Arqueología.

Villa, A. & De Blas, M. A. 2021 Noticia sobre dos cascos de bronce astados y con cimera corniforme procedentes de El Picu les Torres (Cueves, Ribadesella). *Boletín de Humanidades y Ciencias Sociales del RIDEA* 195, 299–323.

Villalba-Mouco, V., Oliart, C., Rihuete-Herrada, C., Childebayeva, A., Rohrlich, A. B., Fregeiro, M. I., Beltran, E. C., *et al.* 2021 Genomic transformation and social organization during the Copper Age–Bronze Age transition in southern Iberia. *Science Advances* 7 (47), eabi7038(2021). https://doi.org/10.1126/sciadv.abi7038

Villar Liébana, F. 2004 The Celtic language of the Iberian Peninsula. In *Studies in Baltic and Indo-European Linguistics in Honor of William R. Schmalstieg*, eds P. Baldi & P. U. Dini, 243–274. Amsterdam, John Benjamins.

Waddington, C. 1998 Cup and ring marks in context. *Cambridge Archaeological Journal* 8 (1), 29–53.

Wang, Q., Strekopytov, S., Roberts, B. W. & Wilkin, N. 2016 Tin ingots from a probable Bronze Age shipwreck off the coast of Salcombe, Devon: Composition and microstructure *Journal of Archaeological Science* 67, 80–92.

Winther Johannsen, J. 2010 The wheeled vehicles of the Bronze Age on Scandinavian rock-carvings. *Acta Archaeologica* 81, 144–247.